THE LITTLE BOOK OF
POLITICS

Penguin
Random
House

DK LONDON
Senior Art Editor Helen Spencer
Project Art Editor Amy Orsborne
Senior Editor Sam Atkinson
Editor Rose Blackett-Ord
US Senior Editor Rebecca Warren
US Editors Kayla Dugger, Kate Johnsen
US Executive Editor Lori Hand
Senior Managing Art Editor Lee Griffiths
Managing Art Editor Karen Self
Managing Editors Gareth Jones, Esther Ripley
Publisher Laura Buller
Art Director Phil Ormerod
Associate Publishing Director Liz Wheeler
Publishing Director Jonathan Metcalf
Illustrations James Graham
Jacket Design Development Manager Sophia MTT
Senior Producer Gemma Sharpe
Pre-Producer Jacqueline Street
Producer Rachel Ng

DK DELHI
Senior Art Editors Ira Sharma, Anjana Nair
Art Editors Sourabh Challariya, Shipra Jain, Nidhi Mehra
Assistant Art Editors Niyati Gosain, Vidit Vashisht, Namita, Gazal Roongta
Design Consultant Shefali Upadhyay
Senior Editors Janashree Singha, Monica Saigal
Editor Tanya Singhal
Assistant Editor Archana Ramachandran
Senior Managing Art Editor Arunesh Talapatra
Managing Editors Soma B. Chowdhury, Pakshalika Jayaprakash
Pre-Production Manager Balwant Singh
Production Manager Pankaj Sharma
DTP Designers Anita Yadav, Nand Kishore Acharya, Arvind Kumar, Rajesh Singh Adhikari, Syed Md Farhan, Dheeraj Arora, Bimlesh Tiwary
Jacket Designer Priyanka Bansal
Picture Researcher Surya Sankash Sarangi

original styling by
studio8 design

produced for DK by
TALLTREE LTD
Managing Editor Rob Colson
Art Direction Ben Ruocco
Senior Editors Richard Gilbert, Camilla Hallinan, Scarlett O'Hara, Sarah Tomley

Content previously published in *The Politics Book*.
This abridged edition first published in the United States in 2020 by DK Publishing, 1450 Broadway, Suite 801, New York, NY 10018

Copyright © 2013, 2020 Dorling Kindersley Limited
DK, a Division of Penguin Random House LLC
20 21 22 23 24   10 9 8 7 6 5 4 3 2 1
001–317633–May/2020

Published in Great Britain
by Dorling Kindersley Limited
A catalog record for this book
is available from the Library of Congress
ISBN 978-1-4654-9426-9
Printed in the United Kingdom

For the curious
www.dk.com

CONTRIBUTORS

PAUL KELLY, CONSULTANT EDITOR

Paul Kelly is a Pro-Director and Professor of Political Theory at the London School of Economics and Political Science. He is the author, editor, and co-editor of 11 books. His main interests are British political thought and contemporary political philosophy.

ROD DACOMBE

Dr. Rod Dacombe is Lecturer in Politics in the Department of Political Economy at King's College, University of London. His research focuses primarily on democratic theory and practice and on the relationship between the voluntary sector and the state.

JOHN FARNDON

John Farndon is the author of many books on the history of science and ideas and on contemporary issues. He also writes widely on science and environmental issues and has been shortlisted four times for the young Science Book prize.

A. S. HODSON

A. S. Hodson is a writer and former contributing editor of BushWatch.com.

JESPER JOHNSØN

Jesper Stenberg Johnsøn is a political scientist advising on governance and anti-corruption reforms in developing countries. He works at the Chr. Michelsen Institute's U4 Anti-Corruption Resource Centre in Bergen, Norway.

NIALL KISHTAINY

Niall Kishtainy teaches at the London School of Economics and specializes in economic history and development. He has worked for the World Bank and the United Nations Economic Commission for Africa.

JAMES MEADWAY

James Meadway is Senior Economist at the New Economics Foundation, an independent British think-tank. He has worked as a policy advisor to the UK Treasury, covering regional development, science, and innovation policy.

ANCA PUSCA

Dr. Anca Pusca is Senior Lecturer in International Studies at Goldsmiths College, University of London. She is the author of *Revolution, Democratic Transition and Disillusionment: The Case of Romania* and *Walter Benjamin: Aesthetics of Change.*

MARCUS WEEKS

Marcus Weeks studied philosophy and worked as a teacher before embarking on a career as an author. He has contributed to many books on the arts and popular sciences.

CONTENTS

THE RISE OF THE MASSES
1848–1910

THE CLASH OF IDEOLOGIES
1910–1945

POSTWAR POLITICS
1945–PRESENT

200 INDEX
207 ACKNOWLEDGMENTS

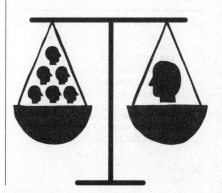

INTRODU

I f everyone could have everything they wanted whenever they wanted, there would be no such thing as politics. Whatever the precise meaning of the complex activity known as politics might be—and, as this book illustrates, it has been understood in many different ways— it is clear that human experience never provides us with everything we want. Instead, we have to compete, struggle, compromise, and sometimes fight for things. In doing so, we develop a language to explain and justify our claims and to challenge, contradict, or answer the claims of others. This might be a language of interests, whether of individuals or groups, or it might be a language of values, such as rights and liberties or fair shares and justice. But central to the activity of politics, from its very beginnings, is the development of political ideas and concepts. These ideas help us make our claims and defend our interests.

But this picture of politics and the place of political ideas is not the whole story. It suggests that politics can be reduced to the question of who gets what, where, when, and how. Political life is undoubtedly in part a necessary response to the challenges of everyday life and the recognition that collective action is often better than individual action. But another tradition of political thinking is associated with the ancient Greek thinker Aristotle, who said that politics was not merely about the struggle to meet material needs in conditions of scarcity. Once complex

societies emerge, different questions arise. Who should rule? What powers should political rulers have, and how do the claims to legitimacy of political rulers compare to other sources of authority, such as that of the family, or the claims of religious authority?

Aristotle said that it is natural for man to live politically, and this is not simply the observation that man is better off in a complex society than abandoned and isolated. It is also the claim that there is something fittingly human about having views on how matters of public concern should be decided. Politics is a noble activity in which men decide the rules they will live by and the goals they will collectively pursue.

Political moralism

Aristotle did not think that all human beings should be allowed to engage in political activity; in his system, women, slaves, and foreigners were explicitly excluded from the right to rule themselves and others. Nevertheless, his basic idea that politics is a unique collective activity that is directed at certain common goals and ends still resonates today. But which ends? Many thinkers and political figures since the ancient world have developed different ideas about the goals that politics can or should achieve. This approach is known as political moralism.

For moralists, political life is a branch of ethics—or moral philosophy—so it is unsurprising that there are many philosophers in the group of moralistic political thinkers. Political moralists argue that politics should be directed toward achieving substantial goals or that political arrangements should be organized to protect certain things. Among these things are political values such as justice, equality, liberty, happiness, fraternity, or national self-determination. At its most radical, moralism produces descriptions of ideal political societies known as Utopias, named after English statesman and philosopher Thomas More's book *Utopia*, published in 1516, which imagined an ideal nation. Utopian political thinking dates back to the ancient Greek philosopher Plato's book the *Republic*, but it is still used by modern thinkers such as Robert Nozick to explore ideas. Some theorists consider Utopian political thinking to be a dangerous undertaking, since it has led in the past to justifications of totalitarian violence. However, at its best, Utopian thinking is part of a process of striving toward a better society, and many of the thinkers discussed in this book use it to suggest values to be pursued or protected.

Political realism

Another major tradition of political thinking rejects the idea that politics exists to deliver a moral or ethical value such as happiness or freedom. Instead, they argue that politics is about power. Power is the means by which ends are achieved, enemies are defeated, and compromises sustained. Without the ability to gain and exercise power, values—however noble they may be—are useless.

The group of thinkers who focus on power as opposed to morality are described as realists. Realists focus their attention on power, conflict, and war, and are often cynical about human motivations. Perhaps the two greatest theorists of power were Italian Niccolò Machiavelli and Englishman Thomas Hobbes, both of whom lived through periods of civil war and disorder, in the 16th and 17th centuries respectively. Machiavelli's view of human nature emphasizes that men are "ungrateful liars" and neither noble nor virtuous. He warns of the dangers of political motives that go beyond concerns with the exercise of power. For Hobbes, the lawless "state of nature" is one of a war of all men against each other. Through a "social contract" with his subjects, a sovereign exercises absolute power to save society from this brutish state. But the concern with power is not unique to early modern Europe. Much 20th-century political thought is concerned with the sources and exercise of power.

Wise counsel

Realism and moralism are grand political visions that try to make sense of the entire political experience and its relationship with other features of the human condition. Yet not all political thinkers have taken such a wide perspective on events. Alongside the political philosophers, there is an equally ancient tradition that is pragmatic and concerned merely with delivering the best possible outcomes. The problems of war and conflict may never be eradicated, and »

arguments about the relationship between political values such as freedom and equality may also never be resolved, but perhaps we can make progress in constitutional design and policy making or in ensuring that government officials are as able as possible. Some of the earliest thinking about politics, such as that of Chinese philosopher Confucius, is associated with the skills and virtues of the wise counselor.

Rise of ideology

One further type of political thinking is often described as ideological. An important strand of ideological thinking emphasizes the ways in which ideas are peculiar to different historical periods. The origins of ideological thinking can be found in the historical philosophies of German philosophers Georg Hegel and Karl Marx. They explain how the ideas of each political epoch differ because the institutions and practices of the societies differ and the significance of ideas changes across history.

Plato and Aristotle thought of democracy as a dangerous and corrupt system, while most people in the modern world see it as the best form of government. Contemporary authoritarian regimes are encouraged to democratize. Similarly, slavery was once thought of as a natural condition that excluded many from any kind of rights, and until the 20th century, most women were not considered citizens.

This raises the question of what causes some ideas to become important, such as equality, and others to fall out of favor, such as slavery or the divine right of kings. Marx accounts for this historical change by arguing that ideas are attached to the interests of social classes such as the workers or the capitalists. These class interests gave rise to the great "isms" of ideological politics, from communism and socialism to conservatism and fascism.

The social classes of Marx are not the only source of ideological politics. Many recent political ideas have also emerged from developments within liberalism, conservatism, socialism, and nationalism.

Ideological political thinking has also been the subject of hostility and criticism. If ideas are merely a reflection of historical processes, critics argue, that must mean that the individuals caught up in those processes are playing an essentially passive role and that rational deliberation and argument have limited value. Ideological struggle is rather like the competition between football teams. Passion, as opposed to reason, matters in supporting one's team, and winning is ultimately all that counts. Many worry that ideological politics results in the worst excesses of realism, in which the ends are seen to justify brutal or unjust means. Ideological politics appears to be a perpetual struggle or war between rival and irreconcilable camps.

Marx's solution to this problem was the revolutionary triumph of the working class and the technological overcoming of scarcity, which would solve the problem of political conflict. In light of the 20th century, this approach to politics seems to many to be

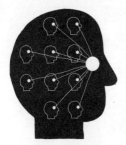  

highly overoptimistic, since revolutionary change has been seen to have replaced one kind of tyranny for another. In this view, Marxism and other ideologies are merely the latest forms of unrealistic Utopian moralism.

A disputed future

According to Georg Hegel, political ideas are an abstraction from the political life of a society, state, culture, or political movement. Making sense of those ideas and the institutions or movements they explain involves examining their history and development. That history is always a story of how we got to where we are now. What we cannot do is look forward to see where history is going.

In Roman mythology, the Owl of Minerva was a symbol of wisdom. For Hegel, the Owl only "takes flight at twilight." By this, he means that understanding can only come retrospectively. Hegel is warning against optimism about developing ideas for where to go next. He is also issuing a subtle warning against his other famous claim that the rise of the modern state is the end of history. It is very easy to see ourselves as the most progressive, enlightened, and rational age ever—after all, we believe in open economies, constitutional government, human rights, and democracy. But as we will see in this book, these are not simple ideas, and they are not shared by all societies and people even today.

The last 80 years of world history have seen the rise of new nation-states as a result of imperial retreat and decolonization.

Federations such as Yugoslavia and Czechoslovakia have fragmented into new states, as has the former USSR. The desire for national sovereignty is also strong in places such as Quebec, Catalonia, Kurdistan, and Kashmir. Yet, while people have struggled for statehood, states have sought complex federations and political union. The last three decades have seen the rise of the European Union, which aspires to closer political integration, as well as the North American Free Trade area and many other organizations for regional cooperation.

Old ideas of state sovereignty have an awkward role in the new political world of pooled sovereignty, economic cooperation, and globalization. Hegel's point seems very pertinent here—we cannot predict how we will appear to those in the future, nor whether what seems like common sense to us will be seen as persuasive by our descendants.

Making sense of the present requires an understanding of the variety of political ideas and theories conceived throughout history. These ideas serve as an explanation of the possibilities of the present, as well as a warning against overconfidence in our own political values, and they remind us that the demands of organizing and governing the collective life of society change in ways that we cannot fully predict. As new possibilities for the exercise of power arise, so will new demands for its control and accountability, and with these will come new political ideas and theories. Politics concerns all of us, so we should all be involved in that debate. ■

ANCIENT AN

POLITICAL

800 BCE–1515 CE

Political theory can trace its beginnings to the civilizations of ancient China and Greece, where, from around 600 BCE, philosophers turned their attention to the way we organize societies. At first, these questions were considered part of moral philosophy or ethics. Philosophers examined how society should be structured not only to ensure the happiness and security of the people, but to enable people to live a "good life."

Ancient political thought

By far the most influential of the Chinese philosophers to emerge was Confucius, who combined moral and political philosophy in his proposals for upholding traditional Chinese moral values in a state led by a virtuous ruler and advised by a class of administrators. In later, less peaceful, times, thinkers such as Han Fei Tzu and the military leader Sun Tzu applied the principles of warfare and discipline to ideas of foreign policy and domestic government. These more authoritarian political philosophies brought stability to the new Chinese Empire.

Like China, ancient Greece was not a single nation, but a collection of separate city-states under various systems of

government. Athens established a form of democracy under a constitution in 594 BCE, and the city became a place where philosophers could speculate on what constituted the ideal state and how it should be governed. Here, Plato advocated rule by an elite of "philosopher kings," while his pupil Aristotle compared the various possible forms of government. Their theories would form the basis for Western political philosophy.

The Indian subcontinent was also composed of various separate states at that time, but an innovative political theorist, Chanakya, helped transform it into a unified empire under the rule of his protégé, Chandragupta Maurya. Chanakya believed in a pragmatic but disciplined approach to political thinking, with the aim of securing economic and material security for the state rather than the moral welfare of the people.

The rise of Rome

Meanwhile, another power was rising in Europe. The Roman Republic had been founded in about 510 BCE, and established a form of representative democracy similar to that of Athens. However, in the 1st century BCE, civil conflict brought the Republic to an end, as Julius Caesar proclaimed himself

D MEDIEVAL THOUGHT

dictator and then emperor. The new Roman Empire was to dominate most of Europe for the next 500 years, and Roman imperial culture—with its emphasis on prosperity and stability—largely replaced the values of scholarship and philosophy associated with the republics of Athens and Rome.

Religious influence

Simultaneously, a new religion was taking root within the empire: Christianity. For the next millennium, political thinking in Europe was led by the Church, and political theory during the Middle Ages was shaped by Christian theology. Early Christian thinkers such as Augustine of Hippo examined questions such as the distinction between divine and human law and the justification for war in terms of Christian doctrine.

In the 7th century, Muhammad established Islam as a religion with an imperialist agenda, and it became a major political as well as religious power. Unlike Christianity, Islam was open to secular political thinking, encouraging wide scholarship and the study of non-Muslim thinkers, and scholars integrated the ideas of Plato and Aristotle into Islamic theology. Cities such as Baghdad became centers of learning, and scholars such as Ibn Khaldun emerged as political theorists.

Difficult questions

Classical texts that Islamic scholars had preserved and translated began to come to the notice of Christian scholars in the 12th century, and a new generation of Christian philosophers became acquainted with classical thinking. Thomas Aquinas tried to integrate the ideas of Aristotle into Christian theology, tackling subjects such as the divine right of kings and reviving debate about secular versus divine law. The authority of the Church in civil affairs was challenged as separate nation-states gained independence and their rulers came into conflict with the papacy.

People were also beginning to question the authority of their monarchs. In England, King John was forced by his barons to concede some of his powers. In Italy, dynastic tyrants were replaced by republics such as Florence, where the Renaissance began. It was in Florence that Niccolò Machiavelli, a potent symbol of Renaissance thought, shocked the world by producing a political philosophy that was entirely pragmatic in its morality. ■

IF YOUR DESIRE IS FOR GOOD, THE PEOPLE WILL BE GOOD

CONFUCIUS (551–479 BCE)

IN CONTEXT

IDEOLOGY
Confucianism

FOCUS
Paternalist

BEFORE
1045 BCE Under the Zhou dynasty of China, political decisions are justified by the Mandate of Heaven.

8th century BCE The Spring and Autumn period begins, and the "Hundred Schools of Thought" emerge.

AFTER
5th century BCE Mozi proposes an alternative to the potential nepotism and cronyism of Confucianism.

4th century BCE The philosopher Mencius popularizes Confucian ideas.

3rd century BCE The more authoritarian principles of Legalism come to dominate the system of government.

A leader should be a *junzi*, a **"superior man."**

Less than perfect people **can be changed** by an example of sincere goodness.

↓

The *junzi* possesses the qualities of **virtue**, **faithfulness**, and **sincerity**, which he shows in rituals and ceremonies.

↓

The *junzi* therefore sets **a good example** for his people.

↓

If a leader's desire is for good, the people will be good.

Kong Fuzi ("Master Kong"), who later became known in the West by the Latinized name of Confucius, lived during a turning point in China's political history. He lived at the end of China's Spring and Autumn period—around 300 years of prosperity and stability during which there was a flowering of art; literature; and, in particular, philosophy. This gave rise to the so-called Hundred Schools of Thought, in which a wide range of ideas was freely discussed. In the process, a new class of thinkers and scholars emerged, most of them based in the courts of noble families as valued advisors.

The influence of these scholars' new ideas inspired a shake-up of the structure of Chinese society. The scholars were

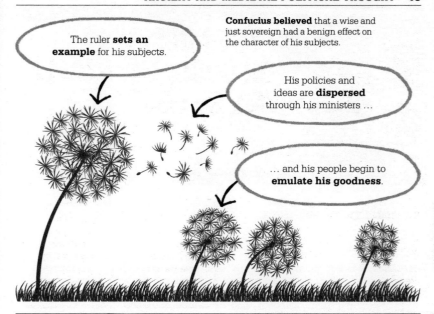

The ruler **sets an example** for his subjects.

Confucius believed that a wise and just sovereign had a benign effect on the character of his subjects.

His policies and ideas are **dispersed** through his ministers ...

... and his people begin to **emulate his goodness**.

appointed on merit rather than due to family connections, and this new meritocratic class of scholars was a challenge to the hereditary rulers, who had previously governed with what they believed was a mandate from Heaven. This caused a series of conflicts as various rulers vied for control over China. During this era, which became known as the Warring States period, it became increasingly clear that a strong system of government was necessary.

The superior man

Like most educated, middle-class young men, Confucius pursued a career as an administrator, and it was in this role that he developed his ideas about the organization of government. Seeing firsthand the relationships between the ruler and his ministers and subjects and keenly aware of the fragility of the political situation of the time, he set about formulating a framework that would enable rulers to govern justly based on his own system of moral philosophy.

Confucius's moral standpoint was firmly rooted in Chinese convention and had at its heart the traditional virtues of loyalty,

duty, and respect. These values were personified in the *junzi*: the "gentleman" or "superior man," whose virtue would act as an example to others. Every member of society would be encouraged to aspire to the *junzi*'s virtues. In Confucius's view, human nature is not perfect, but it is capable of being changed by the example of sincere virtue. Similarly, society can be transformed by the example of fair and benevolent government.

The notion of reciprocity—the idea that just and generous treatment will be met with a just and generous response— underpins Confucius's moral philosophy, and it is also a cornerstone of his political thinking. For a society to be good, its ruler must be the embodiment of the virtues he wishes to see in his subjects; in turn, the people will be inspired through loyalty and respect to emulate those virtues. In the collection of his teachings and sayings known as the *Analects*, Confucius advises, "If your desire is for good, the people will be good. The moral character of the ruler is the wind; the moral character of those beneath him is the grass. When the wind blows, the grass bends." In order for this »

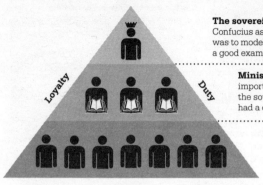

The sovereign was regarded by Confucius as inherently superior. His task was to model perfect behavior, setting a good example for those below him.

Ministers and advisors played an important role as "middle men" between the sovereign and his subjects. They had a duty of loyalty to both parties.

The people, given a good example to follow and a clear idea of what was expected of them, would behave correctly, according to Confucius.

idea to work effectively, however, a new structure for society had to be established, creating a hierarchy that took account of the new meritocratic administrative class while respecting the traditional rule of the noble families. In his proposal for how this might be achieved, Confucius again relied a great deal on traditional values, modeling society on relationships within the family. For Confucius, the benevolence of the sovereign and the loyalty of his subject mirror the loving father and obedient son relationship (a relationship considered by the Chinese to be of the utmost importance).

Confucius considers that there are five "constant relationships": sovereign/subject, father/son, husband/wife, elder brother/younger brother, and friend/friend. In these relationships, he emphasizes not only the rank of each person according to generation, age, and gender, but the fact that there are duties on both sides and that the responsibility of the superior to the inferior in any relationship is just as important as that of the junior to the senior. Extending these relationships to the wider society, their reciprocal rights and responsibilities give society its cohesion, creating an atmosphere of loyalty and respect from each social stratum toward the next.

Justifying hereditary rule
At the top of Confucius's hierarchy was the sovereign, who would unquestionably have inherited this status, and in this respect Confucius shows the conservative nature

of his political thinking. Just as the family provided a model for the relationships within society, the traditional respect shown to parents (especially fathers) extended also to ancestors, and this justified the hereditary principle. Just as a father was considered the head of the family, the state should naturally be ruled over by a paterfamilias figure—the sovereign.

Nevertheless, the sovereign's position was not unassailable in Confucius's thinking, and an unjust or unwise ruler deserved to be opposed or even removed. However, it was in the next layer of society that Confucius was at his most innovative, advocating a class of scholars to act as ministers, advisors, and administrators to the ruler. Their position between the sovereign and his subjects was crucial, because they had a duty of loyalty both to their ruler and the people. They carried a high degree of responsibility, so it was essential that they be recruited from the most able and educated candidates and that anybody serving in public office should be of the highest moral character—

 Good government consists in the ruler being a ruler, the minister being a minister, the father being a father, and the son being a son.
Confucius

a *junzi*. These ministers were to be appointed by the sovereign in Confucius's system, so much depended upon the sovereign's own good character. Confucius said, "The administration of government lies in getting proper men. Such men are to be gotten by means of the ruler's own character. That character is to be cultivated by his treading in the ways of duty. And the treading of those ways of duty is to be cultivated by the cherishing of benevolence."

The role of these public servants was mainly advisory, and ministers were not only expected to be well-versed in the administration and structure of Chinese society, but also to have a thorough knowledge of history, politics, and diplomacy. This was necessary to advise the ruler on matters such as alliances and wars with neighboring states. However, this new class of civil servants also served an equally important function in preventing the ruler from becoming despotic, because they showed loyalty to their superior, but also benevolence to their inferiors. Like their ruler, they, too, had to lead by example, inspiring both the sovereign and his subjects by their virtue.

The importance of ritual

Many parts of Confucius's writings read like a handbook of etiquette and protocol, detailing the proper conduct for the *junzi* in various situations, but he also stressed that this should not merely be empty show. The rituals he outlined were not mere social niceties, but served a much deeper purpose, and it was important that the participants behaved with sincerity for the rituals to have any meaning. Public servants not only had to fulfill their duties virtuously, they also had to be seen to be acting virtuously. For this reason, Confucius laid great emphasis on ceremonies and rituals. These also worked to underline the positions of the various members within a society, and Confucius's approval of this illustrates his tendency to conservatism. »

Actors performing a Confucian ritual in Shandong Province, China, convey the importance of restraint and respect to modern visitors unversed in their highly formalized tradition.

Confucius

Despite his importance in Chinese history, little is known of Confucius's life. He is traditionally believed to have been born in 551 BCE, in Qufu in the state of Lu, China. His name was originally Kong Qiu (he earned the honorific title "Kong Fuzi" much later), and his family was both respected and comfortably well off. Nevertheless, as a young man, he worked as a servant after his father died in order to support his family and studied in his spare time to join the civil service. He became an administrator in the Zhou court, where he developed his ideas of how a state should be governed. But his advice was ignored, and he resigned from the position. He spent the rest of his life traveling throughout the Chinese Empire, teaching his philosophy and theories of government. He eventually returned to Qufu, where he died in 479 BCE.

Key works

Analects
Doctrine of the Mean
The Great Learning
(All were assembled during the 12th century by Chinese scholars.)

The Chinese emperor presides over the civil service examinations in this Song dynasty painting. The exams were introduced during Confucius's lifetime and were based on his ideas.

The ceremonies and rituals allowed people to manifest their devotion to those above them in the hierarchy and their consideration toward those below them. According to Confucius, these rituals were to permeate the whole of society, from formal royal and state ceremonies right down to everyday social interactions, with participants meticulously observing their respective roles. Only when virtue was sincerely and honestly manifested in this way could the idea of leading by example succeed. For this reason, Confucius held sincerity and honesty to be the most important of virtues, second only to loyalty.

Many of these rituals and ceremonies had their basis in religious rites, but this aspect was not important to Confucius. His moral philosophy was not founded on religion, and the political system he derived from it simply acknowledged that there was a place for religion in society. In fact, he seldom referred to the gods in his writings except in terms of a hope that society could be organized and governed in accordance with the Mandate of Heaven, which would help unify the states vying for power. Although he firmly believed in rule by a hereditary sovereign, he did not feel the need to justify it as a divine right.

This implicit dismissal of the divine right, combined with a class system based on merit rather than inheritance, showed Confucius at his most radical. While he advocated a hierarchy reinforced by strict rules of etiquette and protocol so that everybody was very aware of their place in society, this did not mean there should be no social mobility. Those with ability (and good character) could rise through the ranks to the highest levels of government, whatever their family background, and those in positions of power could be removed from office if they failed to show the necessary qualities, no matter how noble the family they were born into. This principle extended even to the sovereign himself. Confucius saw the assassination of a despotic ruler as the necessary removal of a tyrant rather than the murder of a legitimate ruler. He argued that the flexibility of this hierarchy engendered more real respect for it, and that this in turn engendered political consent—a necessary basis for strong and stable government.

Crime and punishment

The principles of Confucius's moral philosophy also extended into the fields of law and punishment. Previously, the legal system had been based on the codes of conduct prescribed by religion, but he advocated a more humanistic approach to replace the divinely ordained laws. As with his social structure, he proposed a system based on reciprocity: if you are treated with respect, you will act with respect. His version of the Golden Rule ("do as you would be done by") was in the negative—"what you do not desire for yourself, do not do to others"—moving the emphasis from specific crimes to avoidance of bad behavior. Once again, this could best be achieved by example because, in his words, "When you meet someone better than yourself, turn your thoughts to becoming his equal. When you meet someone not as good as you are, look within and examine your own self."

Rather than imposing rigid laws and stern punishments, Confucius felt that the best way to deal with crime lay in instilling a sense of shame for bad behavior. Although people may avoid committing crime if guided by laws and subdued by punishment, they do not learn a real sense of right and wrong, while if they are guided by example and subdued by respect, they develop a sense of shame for any misdemeanors and learn to become truly good.

He who governs by means of his virtue is ... like the Pole Star: it remains in its place while all the lesser stars do homage to it.
Confucius

Unpopular ideas

Confucius's moral and political philosophy combined ideas about the innate goodness and sociability of human nature with the rigid, formal structure of traditional Chinese society. Unsurprisingly, given his position as a court administrator, he found an important place for the new meritocratic class of scholars. However, his ideas were met with suspicion and were not adopted during his lifetime. Members of the royal and noble ruling families were unhappy with his implied dismissal of their divine right to rule and felt threatened by the power he proposed for their ministers and advisors. The administrators might have enjoyed more control to rein in potentially despotic rulers, but they doubted the idea that the people could be governed by example and were unwilling to give up their right to exercise power through laws and punishment.

Later political and philosophical thinkers also had their criticisms of Confucianism. Mozi, a Chinese philosopher born shortly after Confucius's death, agreed with his

Religious functions were absorbed into Confucianism when it became the official philosophy of China. Confucian temples such as this one in Nanjing sprang up throughout the country.

more modern ideas of meritocracy and leading by example but felt that his emphasis on family relationships would lead to nepotism and cronyism. Around the same time, military thinkers such as Sun Tzu had little time for the moral philosophy underlying Confucius's political theory and instead took a more practical approach to matters of government, advocating an authoritarian and even ruthless system to ensure the defense of the state. Nevertheless, elements of Confucianism were gradually incorporated into Chinese society in the two centuries following his death. Championed by Mencius (372–289 BCE), they gained some popularity in the 4th century BCE.

The state philosophy

Confucianism may have been adequate to govern in peacetime, but it was felt by many not to be robust enough for the ensuing Warring States period and the struggle to form a unified Chinese Empire. During this period, a pragmatic and authoritarian system of government known as Legalism supplanted Confucius's ideas and continued as the emperor asserted his authority over the new empire. By the 2nd century BCE, however, peace had returned to China, and Confucianism was adopted as the official philosophy of the state under the Han dynasty. It continued to dominate the structure of Chinese society from then on, particularly in the practice of recruiting the most able scholars to the administrative class. The civil service exams introduced in 605 CE were based on classic Confucian texts, and this practice continued into the 20th century and the formation of the Chinese Republic.

Confucianism has not entirely disappeared under China's communist regime, and it had a subtle influence on the structure of society right up to the Cultural Revolution. Today, elements of Confucian thinking, such as those that deal with societal relationships and the notion of filial loyalty, are still deeply ingrained in the Chinese way of life. Confucian ideas are once again being taken seriously as the country shifts from Maoist communism to a Chinese version of a mixed economy. ∎

THE ART OF WAR IS OF VITAL IMPORTANCE TO THE STATE

SUN TZU (c.544–c.496 BCE)

IN CONTEXT

IDEOLOGY
Realism

FOCUS
Diplomacy and war

BEFORE
8th century BCE A "golden age" of Chinese philosophy begins, which produces the so-called Hundred Schools of Thought.

6th century BCE Confucius proposes a framework for civil society based on traditional values.

AFTER
4th century BCE Chanakya's advice to Chandragupta Maurya helps establish the Mauryan Empire in India.

1532 Niccolò Machiavelli's *The Prince* is published 5 years after his death.

1937 Mao Zedong writes *On Guerrilla Warfare*.

In the late 6th century BCE, China was reaching the end of an era of peaceful prosperity—the so-called Spring and Autumn period—in which philosophers had flourished. Much of the thinking had focused on moral philosophy or ethics, and the political philosophy that followed from this concentrated on the morally correct way that the state should organize its internal affairs. The culmination of this came with Confucius's integration of traditional virtues into a hierarchy led by a sovereign and administered by a bureaucracy of scholars.

Toward the end of the Spring and Autumn period, however, the political stability of the various states of China became fragile, and tensions between them increased as the population grew. Rulers of the states not only had to manage their internal affairs, but also defend themselves against attack from neighboring states.

Military strategy

In this atmosphere, military advisors became as important as the civil bureaucrats, and military strategy began to inform political thinking. The most influential work on the subject was *The Art of War*, believed to have been written by Sun Tzu, a general in the army of the king of Wu. The opening passage reads, "The art of war is of vital importance to the state. It is a matter of life and death, a road either to safety or to ruin. Hence it is a subject of inquiry which can on no account be neglected." This marked a distinct break from the political philosophy of the time, and Sun Tzu's work was perhaps the first explicit statement that war and military intelligence are critical elements of the business of the state.

The Art of War deals with the practicalities of protecting and maintaining the prosperity of the state. Where previous thinkers had concentrated on the structure of civil society, this treatise focuses on

A terra-cotta army was built to line the tomb of Emperor Qin Shi Huang, showing the importance of the military to him. Qin lived 200 years after Sun Tzu but would have read his works closely.

international politics, discussing public administration only in connection with the business of planning and waging wars or the economics of maintaining military and intelligence services.

Sun Tzu's detailed description of the art of war has been seen as providing a framework for political organization of any sort. He gives a list of the "principles of war" that are to be considered when planning a campaign. In addition to practical matters such as weather and terrain, the list includes the moral influence of the ruler, the ability and qualities of the general, and the organization and discipline of the men. Implicit in these principles of war is a hierarchical structure with a sovereign at its head taking advice from and giving commands to his generals, who lead and organize their troops.

For Sun Tzu, the role of the sovereign is to provide moral leadership. The people must be convinced that their cause is just before they will give their support, and a ruler should lead by example; this was an idea that Sun Tzu shared with Confucius. Like the bureaucrat of civil society, the general acts as both advisor to the ruler and administrator of his commands.

Unsurprisingly, Sun Tzu places great emphasis on the qualities of the general, describing him as the "bulwark of the state." His training and experience inform the counsel he gives the sovereign, effectively determining policy, but are also vital to the organization of the army. At the head of the chain of command, he controls the logistics and especially the training and discipline of the men. *The Art of War* recommends that discipline be rigorously enforced with harsh penalties for disobedience but that this should be tempered by a consistent application of rewards and punishments.

Knowing when to fight

While this description of a military hierarchy mirrored the structure of Chinese society, *The Art of War* was much more innovative in its recommendations for international politics. Like many generals before and since, Sun Tzu believed that the purpose »

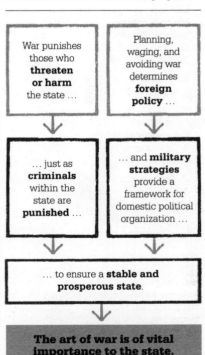

War punishes those who **threaten or harm** the state …

Planning, waging, and avoiding war determines **foreign policy** …

… just as **criminals** within the state are **punished** …

… and **military strategies** provide a framework for domestic political organization …

… to ensure a **stable and prosperous state**.

The art of war is of vital importance to the state.

The Five Fundamentals of Warfare

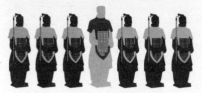

The *Dao*, or **the Way**, allows all soldiers to be of one mind with their rulers.

Generals must be aware of **Heaven**, which is Yin and Yang, and the cycle of the seasons.

A strategist must take into account the **Earth**: high and low, near and distant, open and confined.

Command is shown by wisdom, integrity, compassion, and courage.

Organization and the proper chain of command instill **Discipline**.

> If you know both yourself and your enemy, you can win a hundred battles without jeopardy.
> **Sun Tzu**

of the military was to protect the state and ensure its welfare and that war should always be a last resort. A good general should know when to fight and when not to fight, remembering that an enemy's resistance can often be broken without armed conflict. A general should first try to thwart the enemy's plans; failing that, he should defend against attack; only failing that should he launch an offensive.

To avoid the necessity for war, Sun Tzu advocated maintaining a strong defense and forming alliances with neighboring states. Because a war is harmful to both sides, it often makes sense to come to a peaceful settlement. Prolonged campaigns, especially tactics such as laying siege to an enemy's city, are such a drain on resources that their cost often outweighs the benefits of victory. The sacrifices that have to be made by the people put a strain on their loyalty to the moral justness of the cause.

Military intelligence

The key to stable international relationships, argues Sun Tzu, is intelligence, which was then the responsibility of the military. Spies provide vital information on a potential enemy's intentions and capabilities, allowing the generals who command the spies to advise the ruler on the likelihood of victory in the event of conflict. Along the same lines, Sun Tzu goes on to explain that the next most important element in this information warfare is deception. By feeding misinformation to the enemy about defenses, for example, war can often be averted. He also advised against what he saw as the folly of attempting to destroy an enemy in battle: this decreased the rewards that could be

The Great Wall of China, begun in the 7th century BCE, acted to fence off newly conquered territories. For Sun Tzu, such defensive measures were as important as attacking force.

gained from the victory—both the goodwill of any defeated soldiers and the wealth of any territory gained.

Underlying the very practical advice in *The Art of War* is a traditional cultural foundation based on moral values of justice, appropriateness, and moderation. It states that military tactics, international politics, and war exist to uphold these values and should be conducted in accordance with them. The state exercises its military capability to punish those that harm or threaten it from outside, just as it uses the law to punish criminals within it.

When done in a morally justifiable way, the state is rewarded by happier people and the acquisition of territory and wealth. *The Art of War* became an influential text among the rulers, generals, and ministers of the various states in the struggle for a unified Chinese Empire. It was later an important influence on the tactics of revolutionaries, including Mao Zedong and Ho Chi Minh. It is now required reading at many military academies and is often included as a text in courses on politics, business, and economics. ∎

Sun Tzu

Traditionally believed to be the author of the legendary treatise *The Art of War*, Sun Wu (later known as Sun Tzu, "the Master Sun") was probably born in the state of Qi or Wu in China in around 544 BCE. Nothing is known of his early life, but he rose to fame as a general serving the state of Wu in many successful campaigns against the neighboring state of Chu.

He became an indispensable advisor (equivalent to a contracted military consultant today) to King Helü of Wu on matters of military strategy, writing his famous treatise to be used as a handbook by the ruler.

A concise book made up of 13 short chapters, it was widely read after his death in c.496 BCE, both by state leaders fighting for control of the Chinese Empire and military thinkers in Japan and Korea. It was first translated into a European language, French, in 1782, and may have influenced Napoleon.

Key work

6th century BCE
The Art of War

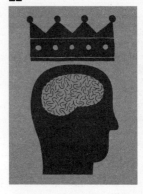

UNTIL PHILOSOPHERS ARE KINGS, CITIES WILL NEVER HAVE REST FROM THEIR EVILS

PLATO (427–347 BCE)

IN CONTEXT

IDEOLOGY
Rationalism

FOCUS
Philosopher kings

BEFORE
594 BCE The Athenian lawmaker Solon lays down laws that act as the foundation for Greek democracy.

c.450 BCE Greek philosopher Protagoras says that political justice is an imposition of human ideas, not a reflection of natural justice.

AFTER
335–323 BCE Aristotle suggests that polity (constitutional government) is the most practical of the better ways to run a state.

54–51 BCE Cicero writes *De republica*, advocating a more democratic form of government than suggested by Plato's *Republic*.

The **role of rulers** is to ensure the people follow the **"good life."**

↓

Knowing what the "good life" is requires **intellectual ability** and knowledge of **ethics and morality**.

↓

Only philosophers have this **ability and knowledge**.

↓

Political power should only be given to **philosophers**.

↓

Until philosophers are kings, cities will never have rest from their evils.

At the end of the 6th century BCE, a cultural golden age began in Greece that was to last for 200 years. Now referred to as the Classical period, it saw the blooming of literature, architecture, science, and, above all, philosophy, all of which profoundly influenced the development of Western civilization.

At the very beginning of the Classical period, the people of the city-state of Athens overthrew their tyrannical leader and instituted a form of democracy. Under this system, government officials were chosen by a lottery from among the citizens, and decisions were made by a democratic assembly. All the citizens could speak and vote at the assembly—

they did not elect representatives to do this on their behalf. It should be noted, however, that the "citizens" were a minority of the population; they were free men aged over 30 whose parents were Athenians. Women, slaves, children, younger men, and foreigners or first-generation settlers were excluded from the democratic process.

This political environment quickly made Athens a major cultural center, attracting some of the foremost thinkers of the time. One of the greatest of these was an Athenian named Socrates, whose philosophical questioning of the generally accepted notions of justice and virtue gained him a following of young disciples. Unfortunately, it also attracted unwanted attention from the authorities, who persuaded the democratic assembly to issue Socrates with a death sentence, on charges of corrupting the young. One of Socrates' young followers was Plato, who shared his teacher's inquisitive nature and skeptical attitude. Plato was to become disillusioned with the Athenian system after what he saw as its unfair treatment of his teacher.

Plato went on to become as influential a philosopher as Socrates, and toward the end of his career, he turned his considerable intellect to the business of politics, most famously in the *Republic*. Unsurprisingly, given that he had seen Socrates condemned and was himself from a noble family, Plato had little sympathy for democracy. But neither did he find much to commend in any other existing form of government, all of which he believed led the state into "evils."

The good life

To understand what Plato meant by "evils" in this context, it is important to bear in mind the concept of *eudaimonia*, the "good life," which for ancient Greeks was a vital aim. "Living well" was not a question of achieving material well-being, honor, or mere pleasure, but rather living according to fundamental virtues such as wisdom, piety, and, above all, justice. The purpose of the state, Plato believed, was to promote these virtues so that its citizens could lead this good life. Issues such as protection of property, liberty, and stability were only important insofar as they created

Socrates chose to drink poison rather than renounce his views. The trial and conviction of Socrates caused Plato to doubt the virtues of the democratic political system of Athens.

conditions that allowed citizens to live well. In his opinion, however, no political system had yet existed that fulfilled this objective—and the defects within them encouraged what he saw as "evils," or the opposite of these virtues.

The reason for this, Plato maintained, is that rulers—whether in a monarchy, oligarchy (rule of the few), or democracy— tend to rule in their own interests rather than for the good of the state and its people. Plato explains that this is due to a general ignorance of the virtues that constitute the good life, which in turn leads people to desire the wrong things, especially the transitory pleasures of honor and wealth. These prizes come with political power, and the problem is intensified in the political arena. The desire to rule, for what Plato saw as the wrong reasons, leads to conflict among citizens. With everyone seeking increased power, this ultimately undermines the stability and unity of the state. Whoever emerges victorious from the power struggle deprives his opponents of the power to achieve their desires, which leads to injustice—an evil that is exactly contrary to the cornerstone of Plato's notion of the good life.

In contrast, Plato argued, there is a class of people who understand the meaning of the good life: philosophers. They alone recognize the worth of virtues above the pleasures of honor and money, and they have devoted their lives to the pursuit of the good life. Because of this, they do not »

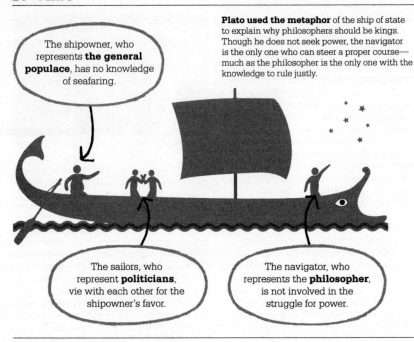

The shipowner, who represents **the general populace**, has no knowledge of seafaring.

Plato used the metaphor of the ship of state to explain why philosophers should be kings. Though he does not seek power, the navigator is the only one who can steer a proper course—much as the philosopher is the only one with the knowledge to rule justly.

The sailors, who represent **politicians**, vie with each other for the shipowner's favor.

The navigator, who represents the **philosopher**, is not involved in the struggle for power.

lust after fame and fortune, so they have no desire for political power—paradoxically, this is what qualifies them as ideal rulers. At face value, Plato's argument would seem to be simply that "philosophers know best" and (coming from a philosopher) might appear to contradict his assertion that they have no desire to rule. But behind it, he gives a much richer and more subtle reasoning.

Ideal Forms

From Socrates, Plato had learned that virtue is not innate, but dependent on knowledge and wisdom, and in order to lead a virtuous life, it is necessary first to understand the essential nature of virtue. Plato developed his mentor's ideas, showing that while we might recognize individual instances of qualities such as justice, goodness, or beauty, this does not allow us to understand what gives them their essential nature. We might imitate them—acting in a way that we think is just, for example—but this is mere mimicry rather than truly behaving according to those virtues.

In his Theory of Forms, Plato suggested the existence of ideal archetypes of these virtues (and of everything that exists) that consist of the essence of their true nature. This means that what we see as instances of these virtues are only examples of these Forms and may show only a part of their nature. They are like inadequate reflections or shadows of the real Forms.

These ideal Forms—or Ideas, as Plato called them—exist in a realm outside the world we live in, accessible only via philosophical reasoning and inquiry. It is this that makes philosophers uniquely qualified to define what constitutes the good life and of leading a truly virtuous life rather than simply imitating individual examples of virtue. Plato had already demonstrated that to be good, the state has to be ruled by the virtuous; while others value money or honor above all, only philosophers value knowledge and wisdom, and therefore virtue. It follows then that only the interests of philosophers benefit the state, and therefore "philosophers must become kings." Plato goes as far as to suggest that they should be compelled to take positions of power in order to avoid the conflict and injustice inherent in other forms of government.

Educating kings

Plato recognizes that this is a utopian stance and goes on to say, "... or those now called kings must genuinely and adequately philosophize," suggesting the education of a potential ruling class as a more practical proposition. In his later dialogues, *Statesman* and *Laws*, he describes a model for a state in which this can be achieved, teaching the philosophical skills necessary to understanding the good life in the same way as any other skills that can be of use to society. However, he points out that not every citizen has the aptitude and intellectual ability to learn these skills. He suggests that where this education is appropriate—for a small, intellectual elite— it should be enforced rather than offered. Those chosen for power because of their "natural talents" should be separated from their families and reared in communes so that their loyalties are to the state.

Plato's political writings were influential in the ancient world, in particular in the Roman Empire, and echoed the notions of virtue and education in the political philosophy of Chinese scholars such as Confucius and Mozi. It is even possible

 Democracy ... is full of variety and disorder, dispensing a sort of equality to equals and unequals alike.
Plato

that they influenced Chanakya in India when he wrote his treatise on training potential rulers. In medieval times, Plato's influence spread to the Islamic Empire and to Christian Europe, where Augustine incorporated them into the teachings of the Church. Later, Plato's ideas were overshadowed by those of Aristotle, whose advocacy of democracy worked better with the political philosophers of the Renaissance.

Plato's political notions have been seen as unacceptably authoritarian and elitist by later thinkers, and they fell out of favor with many in the modern world while it struggled to establish democracy. He has been criticized as advocating a totalitarian, or at best paternalistic, system of government run by an elite that claims to know what is best for everyone else. Recently, however, his central notion of a political elite of "philosopher kings" has been reappraised by political thinkers. ∎

Plato

Born around 427 BCE, Plato was originally called Aristocles, later acquiring the nickname Plato (meaning "broad")

because of his muscular physique. From a noble Athenian family, he was probably expected to follow a career in politics, but instead became a disciple of the philosopher Socrates and was present when his mentor chose to die rather than renounce his views.

Plato traveled widely around the Mediterranean before returning to Athens, where he established a school of philosophy, the Academy, which numbered among its students the young Aristotle. While teaching, he wrote a

number of books in the form of dialogues, generally featuring his teacher Socrates, exploring ideas of philosophy and politics. He is believed to have carried on teaching and writing well into his later years, and died at about the age of 80 in 348/347 BCE.

Key works

c.399–387 BCE *Crito*
c.380–360 BCE *Republic*
c.355–347 BCE *Statesman*, *Laws*

MAN IS BY NATURE A POLITICAL ANIMAL
ARISTOTLE (384–322 BCE)

IN CONTEXT

IDEOLOGY
Democracy

FOCUS
Political virtue

BEFORE
431 BCE Athenian statesman Pericles states that democracy provides equal justice for all.

c.380–360 BCE In the *Republic*, Plato advocates rule by "philosopher kings," who possess wisdom.

AFTER
13th century Thomas Aquinas incorporates Aristotle's ideas into Christian doctrine.

c.1300 Giles of Rome stresses the importance of the rule of law to living in a civil society.

1651 Thomas Hobbes proposes a social contract to prevent man from living in a "brutish" state of nature.

Ancient Greece was not a unified nation-state as we would recognize one today, but a collection of independent regional states with cities at their center. Each city-state, or *polis*, had its own constitutional organization: some, such as Macedon, were ruled by a monarch, while others—most notably Athens—had a form of democracy in which at least some of the citizens could participate in their government.

Aristotle, who was brought up in Macedon and studied in Athens, was well acquainted with the concept of the *polis* and its various interpretations, and his analytical mind made him well qualified to examine the merits of the city-state. He also spent some time in Ionia classifying animals and plants according to their characteristics. He was later to apply these skills of categorization to ethics and politics, which he saw as both natural and practical sciences. Unlike his mentor Plato, Aristotle believed that knowledge was acquired through observation rather than intellectual reasoning and that the science of politics should be based on empirical data, organized in the same way as the taxonomy of the natural world.

Naturally social
Aristotle observed that humans have a natural tendency to form social units: individuals come together to form households, households to form villages, and villages to form cities. Just as some animals, such as bees or cattle, are distinguished by their disposition to live in colonies or herds, humans are by nature social. Just as he might define a wolf by saying it is by nature a pack animal, Aristotle says that "Man is by nature a political animal." By this, Aristotle means simply that Man is an animal whose nature it is to live socially in a *polis*; he is not implying a natural tendency toward political activity in the modern sense of the word.

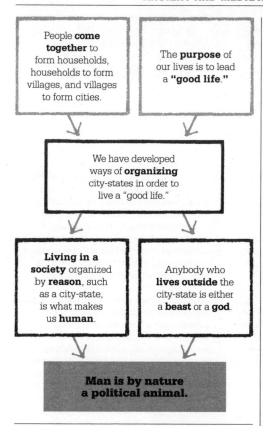

People **come together** to form households, households to form villages, and villages to form cities.

The **purpose** of our lives is to lead a **"good life."**

We have developed ways of **organizing** city-states in order to live a "good life."

Living in a society organized by **reason**, such as a city-state, is what makes us **human**.

Anybody who **lives outside** the city-state is either a **beast** or a **god**.

Man is by nature a political animal.

Aristotle

The son of a physician to the royal family of Macedon, Aristotle was born in Stagira, Chalcidice, in the northeast of modern Greece. He was sent to Athens at 17 to study with Plato at the Academy and remained there until Plato's death 20 years later. Surprisingly, Aristotle was not appointed Plato's successor to lead the Academy. He moved to Ionia, where he made a study of wildlife, until he was invited by Philip of Macedon to be tutor to the young Alexander the Great.

Aristotle returned to Athens in 335 BCE to establish a rival school to the Academy, at the Lyceum. While teaching there, he formalized his ideas on the sciences, philosophy, and politics, compiling a large volume of writings, of which few have survived. After the death of Alexander in 323 BCE, anti- Macedonian feeling in Athens prompted him to leave the city for Euboea, where he died the following year.

Key works

c.350 BCE
Nicomachean Ethics
Politics
Rhetoric

The idea that we have a tendency to live in large civil communities might seem relatively unenlightening today, but it is important to recognize that Aristotle is explicitly stating that the *polis* is just as much a creation of nature as an ants' nest. For him, it is inconceivable that humans can live in any other way. This contrasts markedly with ideas of civil society as an artificial construct that has taken us out of an uncivilized "state of nature"—something Aristotle would not have understood. Anyone living outside a *polis*, he believed, was not human—he must be either superior to men (that is, a god) or inferior to them (that is, a beast).

The good life
This idea of the *polis* as a natural phenomenon rather than a man-made one underpins Aristotle's ideas about ethics and the politics of the city-state. From his study of the natural world, he gained a notion »

that everything that exists has an aim or a purpose, and he decided that for humans, this is to lead a "good life." Aristotle takes this to mean the pursuit of virtues, such as justice, goodness, and beauty. The purpose of the *polis*, then, is to enable us to live according to these virtues. The ancient Greeks saw the structure of the state—which enables people to live together and protects the property and liberty of its citizens—as a means to the end of virtue.

Aristotle identified various "species" and "subspecies" within the *polis*. He found that what distinguishes man from the other animals is his innate powers of reason and the faculty of speech, which give him a unique ability to form social groups and set up communities and partnerships. Within the community of a *polis*, the citizens develop an organization that ensures the security, economic stability, and justice of the state not by imposing any form of social contract, but because it is in their nature to do so. For Aristotle, the different ways of organizing the life of the *polis* exist not so that people can live together (since they do this by their very nature), but so that they can live well. How well they succeed in achieving this goal, he observes, depends on the type of government they choose.

Species of rule

An inveterate classifier of data, Aristotle devised a comprehensive taxonomy of the natural world, and in his later works, especially *Politics*, he set about applying the same methodical skills to systems of government. While Plato had reasoned theoretically about the ideal form of government, Aristotle chose to examine existing regimes to analyze their strengths and weaknesses. To do this, he asked two simple questions: who rules, and on whose behalf do they rule?

In answer to the first question, Aristotle observes that there are basically three types of rule: by a single person, by a select few, or by many. And in answer to the second question, the rule could be either on behalf of the population as a whole, which he considered true or good government, or in the self-interest of the ruler or ruling class, a defective form of government. In all, he identified six "species" of rule, which came in pairs. Monarchy is rule by an individual on behalf of all; rule by an individual in his own interests, or tyranny, is corrupted monarchy. Rule by aristocracy (which to the Greeks meant rule by the best rather than rule by hereditary noble families) is rule by a few for the good of all; rule by a self-interested few, or oligarchy, is its corrupted form. Finally, polity is rule by the many for the benefit of all. Aristotle saw democracy as the corrupted form of this last form of rule, as in practice it entails ruling on behalf of the many rather than every single individual.

Aristotle argues that the self-interest inherent in the defective forms of government leads to

In ancient Athens, citizens debated political affairs at a stone dais called the Pnyx. To Aristotle, the active participation of citizens in government was essential for a healthy society.

Aristotle's Six Species of Government

	Rule By A Single Person	Rule By A Select Few	Rule By The Many
True Government	Monarchy	Aristocracy	Polity
Corrupt Government	Tyranny	Oligarchy	Democracy

inequality and injustice. This translates into instability, which threatens the role of the state and its ability to encourage virtuous living. In practice, however, the city-states he studied did not all fall neatly into just one category, but exhibited characteristics from the various types.

Although Aristotle had a tendency to view the *polis* as a single "organism," of which the citizens are merely a part, he also examined the role of the individual within the city-state. Again, he stresses Man's natural inclination toward social interaction and defines the citizen as one who shares in the structure of the civil community, not merely by electing representatives, but through active participation. When this participation is within a "good" form of government (monarchy, aristocracy, or polity), it fosters the ability of the citizen to lead a virtuous

life. Under a "defective" regime (tyranny, oligarchy, or democracy), the citizen becomes involved with the self-interested pursuits of the ruler or ruling class—the tyrant's pursuit of power, the oligarchs' thirst for wealth, or the democrats' search for freedom. Of all the possible regimes, Aristotle concludes, polity provides the best opportunity to lead a good life.

Although Aristotle categorizes democracy as a "defective" form of regime, he argues that it is only second best to polity and better than the "good" aristocracy or monarchy. While the individual citizen may not have the wisdom and virtue of a good ruler, collectively "the many" may prove to be better rulers than "the one."

The detailed description and analysis of the Classical Greek *polis* seems on the face of it to have little relevance to the nation-states that followed, but Aristotle's ideas had a growing influence on European political thought throughout the Middle Ages. Despite being criticized for his often authoritarian standpoint (and his defense of slavery and the inferior status of women), his arguments in favor of constitutional government anticipate ideas that emerged in the Enlightenment. ∎

> 66 The basis of a democratic state is liberty.
> **Aristotle** 99

A SINGLE WHEEL DOES NOT MOVE
CHANAKYA (c.350–c.275 BCE)

IN CONTEXT

IDEOLOGY
Realism

FOCUS
Utilitarian

BEFORE
6th century BCE The Chinese general Sun Tzu writes his treatise *The Art of War*, bringing an analytical approach to statecraft.

424 BCE Mahapadma Nanda establishes the Nanda dynasty in India and relies on his generals for tactical advice.

AFTER
c.65 BCE The Mauryan Empire, which Chanakya helped to found, reaches its height and rules over all but the southern tip of the Indian subcontinent.

1904 Texts of Chanakya's treatises are rediscovered and, in 1915, are translated into English.

D uring the 5th and 4th centuries BCE, the Nanda dynasty slowly gained control over the northern half of the Indian subcontinent, defeating its rivals one by one and holding off the threat of invasion by the Greeks and Persians from the west. The rulers of this expanding empire relied on generals for tactical advice in battle, but they also began to recognize the value of ministers to advise on matters of policy and government. Scholars, especially those from Takshashila, a university established c.600 BCE in Rawalpindi (now part of Pakistan), frequently became these ministers. Many important thinkers developed their ideas at Takshashila, but perhaps the most significant was Chanakya (also known as Kautilya and Vishnugupta). He wrote a treatise on statecraft titled *Arthashastra*, meaning "the science of material gain" or "the art of polity." *Arthashastra* combined the accumulated wisdom of the art of politics with Chanakya's own ideas and was remarkable in its dispassionate, and at times ruthless, analysis of the business of politics.

Advising the sovereign

Although sections of the treatise dealt with the moral qualities desirable in the leader of a state, the emphasis was on the practical, describing in direct terms how power could be gained and maintained. For the first time in India, it explicitly described a civil structure in which ministers and advisors played a key role in the running of the state.

A commitment to the prosperity of the state lies at the heart of Chanakya's political thought, and he makes repeated references to the welfare of the people as the ultimate goal of government. This, he believed, was the responsibility of a sovereign who would ensure his people's well-being and security

The lion capital of Ashoka stood on top of a pillar in Sarnath at the center of the Mauryan Empire. Chanakya helped to found this powerful empire, which came to rule nearly all of India.

by administering order and justice and leading his country to victory over rival states. The power to carry out his duties to his country and its people is dependent on several different factors, which Chanakya describes in *Arthashastra*: the personal qualities of the ruler, the abilities of his advisors, his territory and towns, his wealth, his army, and his allies.

The sovereign, as head of state, has the central role in this system of government. Chanakya emphasizes the importance of finding a ruler with the appropriate qualities, but then goes on to say that personal qualities of leadership are not sufficient on their own: the sovereign must also be trained for the job. He must learn the various skills of statecraft, such as military tactics and strategy, law, administration, and the arts of diplomacy and politics. But in addition, he should be taught the skills of self-discipline and ethics in order to develop the moral authority necessary to command the loyalty and obedience of his people. Before taking office, the sovereign needs assistance from experienced and knowledgable teachers.

Once instated, a wise sovereign does not rely solely on his own wisdom, but can turn to trusted ministers and advisors for counsel. In Chanakya's view, such individuals are as important as the sovereign in governing the state. In *Arthashastra*, Chanakya states: "Governance is possible only with assistance—a single wheel does not move." This is a warning to the sovereign

not to be autocratic, but to arrive at decisions of state after consulting his ministers.

The appointment of ministers with the necessary qualifications is therefore just as important as the people's choice of leader. The ministers can provide a range of knowledge and skills. They must be utterly trustworthy, not only so that the sovereign can rely on their advice, but also to ensure that decisions are made in the interests of the state and its people—if necessary, preventing a corrupt ruler from acting in his own interests.

The end justifies the means

It was this recognition of the realities of human nature that distinguished Chanakya from other Indian political philosophers »

A ruler is responsible for the **welfare, security, and discipline** of his people.

He needs to have a wide range of **knowledge, skills, and personal qualities**.

He must be **trained** in self-discipline and statecraft before taking office.

While in office, he must be **advised** by able and experienced ministers.

Governance is possible only with assistance. A single wheel does not move.

of the time. *Arthashastra* is not a work of moral philosophy, but a practical guide to governance, and in ensuring the welfare and security of the state, it often advocates using whatever means are necessary. Although *Arthashastra* advocates a regime of learning and self-discipline for an ideal ruler and mentions certain moral qualities, it doesn't flinch from describing how to use underhanded methods to gain and maintain power. Chanakya was a shrewd observer of human weaknesses as well as strengths, and he was not above exploiting these to increase the sovereign's power and undermine that of the sovereign's enemies.

This is particularly noticeable in his advice on defending and acquiring territory. Here, he recommends that the ruler and his ministers should carefully assess the strength of their enemies before deciding on a strategy to undermine them. They can then choose from a number of different tactics ranging from conciliation, encouraging dissent in the enemy's ranks, and forming alliances of convenience with other rulers, to the simple use of military force. In deploying these tactics, the ruler should be ruthless, using trickery, bribery, and any other inducements deemed necessary. Although this seems contradictory to the moral authority Chanakya advocates in a leader, he

66 All things begin with counsel.
Chanakya 99

stipulates that after victory has been achieved, the ruler should "substitute his virtues for the defeated enemy's vices, and where the enemy was good, he shall be twice as good."

Intelligence and espionage

Arthashastra reminds rulers that military advisors are also needed, and the gathering of information is important for decision-making. A network of spies is vital in assessing the threat posed by neighboring states or to judge the feasibility of acquiring territory. But Chanakya goes further, suggesting that espionage within the state is also a necessary evil in order to ensure social stability. At home and in international relations, morality is of secondary importance to the protection of the state. The state's welfare is used as justification for clandestine operations, including political assassination, should this be necessary, aimed at reducing the threat of opposition.

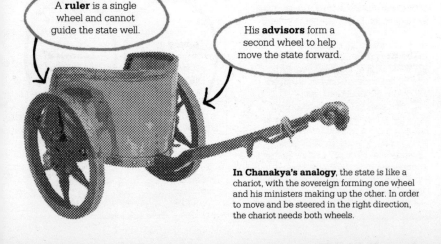

A **ruler** is a single wheel and cannot guide the state well.

His **advisors** form a second wheel to help move the state forward.

In Chanakya's analogy, the state is like a chariot, with the sovereign forming one wheel and his ministers making up the other. In order to move and be steered in the right direction, the chariot needs both wheels.

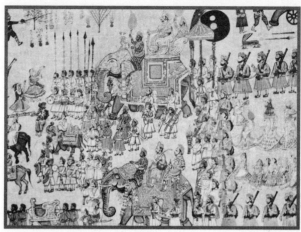

Elephants played a big role in Indian warfare, often terrifying enemies so much that they would withdraw rather than fight. Chanakya developed new strategies for warfare with elephants.

Chandragupta Maurya, who successfully defeated King Nanda to establish the Mauryan Empire in around 321 BCE. This became the first empire to cover the majority of the Indian subcontinent, and Maurya also successfully held off the threat from Greek invaders led by Alexander the Great. Chanakya's ideas were to influence government and policy-making for several centuries, until India eventually succumbed to Islamic and Mughal rule in the Middle Ages.

The text of *Arthashastra* was rediscovered in the early 20th century, and regained some of its importance in Indian political thinking, gaining iconic status after India won independence from Great Britain in 1948. Despite its central place in Indian political history, it was little known in the West, and it is only recently that Chanakya has been recognized outside India as a significant political thinker. ■

This amoral approach to taking and holding onto power, and the advocacy of a strict enforcement of law and order, can be seen either as shrewd political awareness or as ruthlessness. It has earned *Arthashastra* comparison with Machiavelli's *The Prince*, written around 2,000 years later. However, the central doctrine of rule by a sovereign and ministers has more in common with Confucius and Mozi or Plato and Aristotle, whose ideas Chanakya may have come across as a student in Takshashila.

A proven philosophy

The advice contained in the pages of *Arthashastra* soon proved its usefulness when adopted by Chanakya's protégé

Chanakya

The birthplace of Indian scholar Chanakya is not certain. It is known that he studied and taught in Takshashila (modern Taxila, Pakistan). Leaving Takshashila to become involved in government, he traveled to Pataliputra, where he became an advisor to King Dhana Nanda.

There are many conflicting accounts of what happened next, but all agree that he left the Nanda court after a dispute and in revenge groomed the young Chandragupta Maurya to be Nanda's rival. Chandragupta overthrew Dhana Nanda and founded the Mauryan Empire, which governed all of modern India except the very south. Chanakya

became chief advisor to Chandragupta but is said to have starved himself to death after being falsely accused by Chandragupta's son, Bindusara, of poisoning his mother.

Key works

4th century BCE
Arthashastra
Neetishastra

IF JUSTICE BE TAKEN AWAY, WHAT ARE GOVERNMENTS BUT GREAT BANDS OF ROBBERS?
AUGUSTINE OF HIPPO (354–430 CE)

IN CONTEXT

IDEOLOGY
Christianity

FOCUS
Just government

BEFORE
4th century BCE In the *Republic* and *Laws*, Plato stresses the importance of justice in an ideal state.

1st century BCE Cicero opposes the overthrow of the Roman Republic and its replacement with an emperor.

306 CE Constantine I becomes the first Christian emperor of the Roman Empire.

AFTER
13th century Thomas Aquinas uses Augustine's arguments to define a just war.

14th century Ibn Khaldun says that government's role is to prevent injustice.

c.1600 Francisco Suárez and the School of Salamanca create a philosophy of natural law.

States have a ruler or government and laws governing **conduct and the economy**.

Robbers band together under a leader and have rules for **discipline and dividing** their booty.

States led by unjust rulers wage war on their neighbors **to seize territory and resources**.

Each band has its **own territory** and **steals** from neighboring territories.

If justice be taken away, what are governments but great bands of robbers?

I n 380 CE, Christianity was effectively adopted as the official religion of the Roman Empire, and as the Church's power and influence grew, its relationship with the state became a disputed issue. One of the first political philosophers to address this question was Augustine of Hippo, a scholar and teacher who became a convert to Christianity. In his attempt to integrate classical philosophy into the religion, he was greatly influenced by his study of Plato, which also formed the basis for his political thinking.

As a Roman citizen, Augustine believed in the tradition of a state bound by the rule of law, but as a scholar, he agreed with Aristotle and Plato that the goal of the state was to enable its people to lead the good and virtuous life. For a Christian, this meant living by the divine laws prescribed by the Church. However, Augustine believed that, in practice, few men lived according to divine laws, and the vast majority lived in a state of sin. He distinguished between two kingdoms: the *civitas Dei* (city of God) and the *civitas terrea* (city of Earth). In the latter kingdom, sin predominates. Augustine sees the influence of the Church on the state as the only means to ensure that the laws of the land are made with reference to divine laws, allowing people to live in the *civitas Dei*. The presence of such just laws distinguishes a state from a band of robbers. Robbers and pirates join together under a leader to steal from their neighbors. The robbers may have rules, but they are not just rules. However, Augustine further points out that even in a sinful *civitas terrea*, the authority of the state can ensure order through the rule of law, and that order is something we all have a reason to want.

Just war

Augustine's emphasis on justice, with its roots in Christian doctrine, also applied to the business of war. While he believed all war to be evil and that to attack and plunder other states was unjust, he conceded that a "just war" fought for a just cause, such as defending the state against aggression or to restore peace, did exist. However, it should be embarked upon with regret and only as a last resort.

This conflict between secular and divine law and the attempt to reconcile the two began the power struggle between Church and state that ran through the Middle Ages. ∎

Augustine of Hippo

Aurelius Augustine was born in Thagaste (now Souk-Ahras, Algeria) in Roman North Africa to a pagan father and a Christian mother. He studied Latin literature in Madaurus and rhetoric in Carthage, where he came across the Persian Manichean religion and became interested in philosophy through the works of Cicero. He taught in Thagaste and Carthage until 373, when he moved to Rome and Milan. There, he was inspired by theologian Bishop Ambrose to explore Plato's philosophy and later to become a Christian. He was baptized in 387, and was ordained a priest in Thagaste in 391. He finally settled in Hippo (now Bone, Algeria), establishing a religious community and becoming its bishop in 396. As well as his autobiographical *Confessions*, he wrote a number of works on theology and philosophy. He died during a siege of Hippo by the Vandals in 430.

Key works

387–395 *On Free Will*
397–401 *Confessions*
413–425 *City of God*

Augustine's vision of a state living according to Christian principles was outlined in his work *City of God*, in which he described the relationship between the Roman Empire and God's law.

FIGHTING HAS BEEN ENJOINED UPON YOU WHILE IT IS HATEFUL TO YOU
MUHAMMAD (570–632 CE)

IN CONTEXT

IDEOLOGY
Islam

FOCUS
Just war

BEFORE
6th century BCE In *The Art of War*, Sun Tzu argues that the military is essential to the state.

c.413 Augustine describes a government without justice as no better than a band of robbers.

AFTER
13th century Thomas Aquinas defines the conditions for a just war.

1095 Christians launch the First Crusade to wrest control of Jerusalem and the Holy Land from the Muslims.

1932 In *Towards Understanding Islam*, Abul Ala Maududi insists that Islam embraces all aspects of human life, including politics.

Islam is a **peaceful religion**, and all Muslims wish to live in peace.

↓

But even believers in Islam need to **defend** themselves against invasion …

↓

… and **attack the unbelievers** who threaten their peace and religion.

↓

Fighting has been enjoined upon you while it is hateful to you.

Revered by Muslims as the prophet of the Islamic faith, Muhammad also laid the foundations for an Islamic Empire; he was its political and military leader as much as its spiritual guide. Exiled from Mecca because of his faith, in 622, he traveled to Yathrib (on a journey that became known as the Hijra), where he gained huge numbers of followers and ultimately organized the city into a unified Islamic city-state. The city was renamed Medina ("city of the Prophet"), and it became the world's first Islamic state. Muhammad created a constitution for the state—the Constitution of Medina—which formed the basis of an Islamic political tradition.

The constitution addressed the rights and duties of every group within the community, the rule of law, and the issue of war. It recognized the Jewish community of Medina as separate, and agreed reciprocal obligations with them. Among its edicts, it obliged the whole community—members of all the religions in Medina—to fight as one if the community came under threat. The key aims were peace within the Islamic state of Medina and the construction of a political structure that would help Muhammad gather followers and soldiers for his conquest of the Arabian peninsula.

The authority of the constitution was both spiritual and secular, stating, "Whenever you differ about a matter, it must be referred to God and Muhammad." Because God spoke through Muhammad, his word carried unquestionable authority.

Peaceful but not pacifist

The constitution confirms much of the Islamic holy book known as the Quran, which it predates. However, the Quran is more detailed on religious duties than political practicalities. In the Quran, Islam is described as a peace-loving religion but not a pacifist religion. Muhammad repeatedly stresses that Islam should be defended from unbelievers and implies that this may in some cases mean taking

 Fight in the name of Allah and in the way of Allah. Fight against those who disbelieve in Allah.
Sunni Hadith

Muslim pilgrims pray near the Prophet Muhammad Mosque in the holy city of Medina, Saudi Arabia, where Muhammad established the first Islamic state.

preemptive action. Although violence should be abhorrent to a believer in Islam, it can be a necessary evil to protect and advance the religion, and Muhammad states that it is the moral obligation of all Muslims to defend the faith.

This duty is encapsulated in the Islamic idea of *jihad* (literally "struggle" or "striving"), which was originally directed against neighboring cities that attacked Muhammad's Islamic state. As these were conquered one by one, fighting became a way of spreading the faith and, in political terms, expanding the Islamic Empire.

While the Quran describes jihad as a religious duty, and fighting as hateful but necessary, it also states that there are strict rules governing the conduct of war. The conditions for a "just war" (just cause, right intention, proper authority, and last resort) are very similar to those that evolved in Christian Europe. ∎

Muhammad

Muhammad was born in Mecca in 570, shortly after the death of his father. His mother died when he was 6, and he was left in the care of his grandparents and an uncle, who employed him managing caravans trading with Syria. In his late 30s, he made regular visits to a cave on Mount Hira to pray, and in 610, he is said to have received his first revelation from the angel Gabriel. He began preaching and slowly gained a following but was eventually driven from Mecca with his disciples. Their escape to Medina in 622 is celebrated as the beginning of the Muslim calendar. By the time of his death in 632, nearly all of Arabia was under his rule.

Key works

c.622 *Constitution of Medina*
c.632 The Quran
8th and 9th centuries The *Hadith*

NO FREE MAN SHALL BE IMPRISONED, EXCEPT BY THE LAW OF THE LAND

BARONS OF KING JOHN (EARLY 13TH CENTURY)

IN CONTEXT

IDEOLOGY
Parliamentarism

FOCUS
Liberty

BEFORE
c.509 BCE The monarchy in Rome is overthrown and replaced by a republic.

1st century BCE Cicero argues for a return to the Roman Republic after Julius Caesar takes power from the Senate.

AFTER
1640s The English Civil War and subsequent overthrow of the monarchy establish that a monarch cannot govern without parliamentary consent.

1776 The Declaration of Independence lists "Life, Liberty, and the pursuit of Happiness" as inherent rights.

1948 The United Nations General Assembly adopts the Universal Declaration of Human Rights in Paris.

King John of England became increasingly unpopular during his reign due to his mishandling of the wars with France and his high-handed attitude toward his feudal barons, who provided him with both knights and tax revenue. By 1215, he faced rebellion and was forced to negotiate with his barons when they arrived in London. They presented him with a document detailing their demands—modeled on the Charter of Liberties of 100 years earlier issued by King Henry I—which effectively reduced John's power and protected their own privileges. The "Articles of the Barons" included clauses relating to their property, rights, and duties, but also made the king subject to the law of the land.

Freedom from tyranny

Clause 39, in particular, had profound implications: "No free man shall be seized or imprisoned, or stripped of his rights or possessions, or outlawed or exiled, or deprived of his standing in any other way, nor will we proceed with force against him, or send others to do so, except by the lawful judgment of his equals or by the law of the land." Implicit in the barons' demands was the concept of *habeas corpus*. This requires that a person under arrest be brought before a court and protects individuals from arbitrary abuse of power. For the first time, the freedom

The Houses of Parliament in London, England, has its origin in the insistence of the barons in 1215 that the monarch could not levy additional taxes without the consent of his royal council.

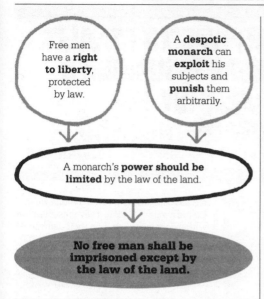

Free men have a **right to liberty**, protected by law.

A **despotic monarch** can **exploit** his subjects and **punish** them arbitrarily.

A monarch's **power should be limited** by the law of the land.

No free man shall be imprisoned except by the law of the land.

Feudal Barons of England

First created by William the Conqueror (1028–1087), the barony was a form of feudal land tenure granted by the king, with certain duties and privileges allocated to the holder. The barons paid taxes to the king in return for their holding of the land, but also had an obligation—the *servitium debitum* ("service owed")—to provide a quota of knights to fight for the king when asked. In return, the barons were granted the privilege of participation in the king's council or parliament—but only when summoned to do so by the king. They did not meet regularly and, because the king's court often moved from place to place, they did not have a regular venue.

Although the barons at the time of King John (pictured above) forced *Magna Carta* on their king, the power of the feudal barony weakened during the 13th century and was rendered all but obsolete during the English Civil War.

Key works

1100 *Charter of Liberties*
1215 *Magna Carta*

of the individual from a tyrannical ruler was explicitly guaranteed. John had no choice but to accept the terms and attach his seal to what later became known as *Magna Carta* (Latin for "Great Charter").

Unfortunately, John's assent was only a token, and much of the document was later ignored or repealed. Nevertheless, the key clauses remained, and the spirit of *Magna Carta* was highly influential in the political development of Britain. The restriction of the power of the monarch in favor of the rights of the "free man"—which at the time meant only the feudal landowners and not the serfs—laid the foundations for an independent parliament. The rebellious De Montfort's Parliament in 1265 was the first such body, featuring elected representatives, knights, and burgesses (borough officials), as well as barons for the first time.

Toward a parliament

In the 17th century, the idea of making the English monarch bound by the law of the land came to a head in the English Civil War, and *Magna Carta* symbolized the cause of the Parliamentarians under Oliver Cromwell. Although at the time it applied only to a minority of already privileged citizens, *Magna Carta* pioneered the idea of laws to protect the liberty of the individual from despotic authority. It also inspired the bills of rights enshrined in many modern constitutions, particularly that of the United States, as well as many declarations of human rights. ∎

FOR WAR TO BE JUST, THERE IS REQUIRED A JUST CAUSE

THOMAS AQUINAS (1225–1274)

IN CONTEXT

IDEOLOGY
Natural law

FOCUS
Just war

BEFORE
44 BCE In *De Officiis*, Cicero argues against war except as a last resort in order to defend the state and restore peace.

5th century Augustine of Hippo argues that the state should promote virtue.

620s Muhammad calls on Muslims to fight in defense of Islam.

AFTER
1625 Hugo Grotius puts the theory of just war into the context of international law in *On the Law of War and Peace*.

1945 The United Nations (UN) Charter prohibits the use of force in international conflict unless authorized by the UN.

The **purpose** of the state is to enable people to live a **good life** …

War can only be fought with the authority of the **sovereign or government**.

⬇ ⬇

… so a state can only deem war necessary when it **promotes good and avoids evil**.

To have authority, a sovereign or government must **rule with justice**.

⬇ ⬇

For war to be just, there is required a just cause.

The Roman Catholic Church held a monopoly over learning for several centuries in medieval Europe. Ever since the adoption of Christianity as the official religion of the Roman Empire by Constantine at the end of the 4th century CE, political thinking had been dominated by Christian teaching. The relationship between state and Church preoccupied philosophers and theologians, most notably Augustine of Hippo, who laid the foundations for the debate by integrating the political analysis of Plato's *Republic* with Christian doctrine. However, as translations of classical Greek texts became available in Europe in the 12th century through contact with Islamic

> Peace is the work of
> justice indirectly, in so
> far as justice removes the
> obstacles to peace; but
> it is the work of charity,
> according to its very notion,
> that causes peace.
> **Thomas Aquinas**

scholars, some European thinkers began to take an interest in other philosophers—in particular, in Aristotle and his Islamic interpreter, the Andalusian polymath Averroes.

A reasoned method

By far the most significant of the Christian thinkers to emerge in the late Middle Ages was the Italian scholar Thomas Aquinas, a member of the newly formed Dominican religious order. An order that valued the tradition of scholasticism, the Dominicans used reasoning and inference as a method of education rather than simply teaching Christian dogma. In this spirit, Aquinas set about reconciling Christian theology with the rational arguments put forward by philosophers such as Plato and Aristotle. As a priest, his concerns were primarily theological, but because the Church was the dominant political power at the time, the distinction between theological and political was not as clear-cut as it is today. In arguing for an integration of the rational and the dogmatic, of philosophy and theology, Aquinas addressed the question of secular power versus divine authority and the conflict between Church and state that was growing in many countries. He also used this method to examine ethical questions, such as when it might be justified to wage war.

Justice, the prime virtue

In his moral philosophy, Aquinas explicitly examines political issues, stressing that reasoning is as important in political thinking as it is in theological argument. As a starting point, he took the works of Augustine of Hippo, who had successfully integrated into his Christian beliefs the classical Greek notion that the purpose of the state is to promote a good and virtuous life. Augustine argued that this was in harmony with divine law—which, if adhered to, will prevent injustice. For Aquinas, steeped in the works of Plato and Aristotle, justice was the prime political virtue that underpinned his entire political philosophy, and the notion of justice was the key element in governance. Just laws were the difference that distinguished good government from bad, bestowing upon it the legitimacy to rule. It was also justice that determined the morality of the actions of the state, a »

Warfare for the protection of Christian values could be justified in Aquinas's thinking, including the First Crusade of 1096–1099, in which Jerusalem was captured and thousands massacred.

principle that can most clearly be seen in Aquinas's theory of a "just war."

Defining a just war
Using Augustine's arguments as his starting point, Aquinas agreed that although Christianity preached pacifism for its adherents, it was sometimes necessary to fight in order to preserve or restore peace in the face of aggression. However, such a war should be defensive, not preemptive, and waged only when certain conditions could be met. He called these conditions the *jus ad bellum*, or "right to war"—which were distinct from the *jus in bello*, the rules of just conduct in a war—and believed that they would ensure the justice of the war.

Aquinas identified three distinct basic requirements for just war: rightful intention, authority of the sovereign, and a just cause. These principles have remained the basic criteria in just-war theory to the present day. The "rightful intention" for the Christian meant one thing only—the restoration of peace—but it is in the other two conditions that we can see a more secular approach. The "authority of the sovereign" implies that war can only be waged by an authority such as the state or its ruler, while the "just cause" limits its power to fighting a war only for the benefit of the people rather than for personal gain or glory. For these criteria to be met, there must be a properly instituted government or ruler bound by laws that ensure the justice of its actions, and this in turn needs to be based on a theory of legitimate governance, taking into account the demands of both the Church and the state.

The Geneva Convention consists of four treaties signed between 1864 and 1949—broadly based on the concepts of just war—defining fair treatment of soldiers and civilians in wartime.

Natural and human laws
This recognition of the role of the state and its authority distinguished Aquinas's political philosophy from other thinkers of the time. His emphasis on justice as an essential virtue, influenced by his study of Plato and Aristotle, led him to consider the place of law in society, and this interest in law formed the basis for his political thinking. Unsurprisingly, given the increasing plurality of society at the time, this involved an examination of the differences between divine and human laws and by implication the laws of the Church and those of the state.

As a Christian, Aquinas believed that the universe is ruled by an eternal divine law and that humans—as the only rational creatures—have a unique relationship with it. Because of our ability to reason, we are subject to what he calls a "natural law," which we have arrived at by examining

The Right To War

For Aquinas, the only **rightful intention** of a just war is the restoration of peace.

A just war can only be waged under the **authority of the sovereign**.

For a war to be fought for a **just cause**, it must benefit the people.

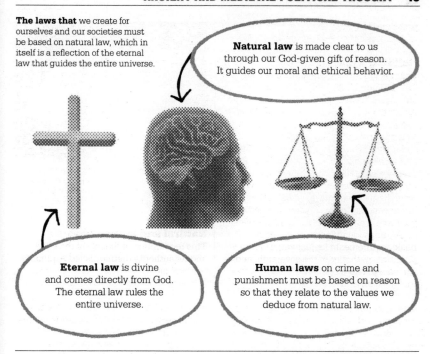

The laws that we create for ourselves and our societies must be based on natural law, which in itself is a reflection of the eternal law that guides the entire universe.

Natural law is made clear to us through our God-given gift of reason. It guides our moral and ethical behavior.

Eternal law is divine and comes directly from God. The eternal law rules the entire universe.

Human laws on crime and punishment must be based on reason so that they relate to the values we deduce from natural law.

human nature and inferring a moral code of behavior. Far from being a contradiction of God's law, however, Aquinas explained this as our participation in the eternal law.

Reason, he argues, is a God-given ability that enables us to devise for ourselves the natural law, which is, in effect, the way in which the eternal law applies to human beings in accordance with our nature as a social animal. However, natural law—which is concerned with morality and virtue—is not to be confused with the human laws that govern our day-to-day affairs, which we have created to enable the smooth running of our social communities. These man-made laws are, like their creators, by their very nature fallible, so they can lead to injustice, and their authority can only be judged by comparison with natural law.

The urge for community

While Aquinas attributes natural law to our propensity for rational thought, the emergence of human laws is explained by another aspect of human nature—

our need to form social communities. This idea is very much the same as proposed by Aristotle in Politics—which Aquinas had written a lengthy commentary on—that man is by nature a "political animal." The urge to form social communities is something that defines us as humans distinct from other animals. Like Aristotle, Aquinas recognizes that humans naturally form family units, which in turn come together as villages and ultimately form political societies such as city-states or nation-states, providing an ordered social framework. Although he agreed in principle with Aristotle that such a state was the perfect community, his conception of it was not the same as the ancient Greek understanding, which was not compatible with the views of the Church in the 13th century.

According to the Greek philosophers, the aim of such a society was to enable its citizens to lead a "good life" in accordance with virtue and reason. Aquinas's »

Thomas Aquinas

The son of the Count of Aquino, Aquinas was born in Roccasecca, Italy, and was schooled in Monte Cassino and the University of Naples. Although expected to become a Benedictine monk, he joined the new Dominican order in 1244 and moved to Paris a year later. In about 1259, he taught in Naples, Orvieto, and the new school in Santa Sabina and acted as a papal advisor in Rome.

He was sent back to Paris in 1269, probably due to a dispute over the compatibility of Averroes's and Aristotle's philosophies with Christian doctrine. In 1272, he set up a new Dominican university in Naples. While there, he had a mystical experience that prompted him to say that all he had written seemed "like straw" to him. Aquinas was summoned as an advisor to the Council of Lyons in 1274, but fell ill and died after an accident on the way.

Key works

1254–1256 *Commentary on the Sentences*
c.1258–1260 *Summa Contra Gentiles*
1267–1273 *Summa Theologica*

interpretation was subtly different, bringing it in line with Christian theology and his own ideas of natural law. For him, the role of political society was to enable its citizens to develop their powers of reason, and through this, to acquire an understanding of moral sense—in other words, the natural law. They would then be able to live well, in accordance with natural law, and—as Christians—in accordance with divine law.

Ruling justly

The question that followed was this: What form of government is best suited to ensuring the aspirations of this political society? Again, Aquinas takes his lead from Aristotle, classifying various types of regime by the number of rulers and, crucially, whether their rule is just or unjust. Rule by a single individual is known as monarchy when it is just, but tyranny when unjust; similarly, just rule by a few is known as aristocracy, but when unjust, as an oligarchy; and just rule by the people is called a republic or polity, as opposed to the unjust rule of a democracy.

What determines whether these forms of government are just or unjust are the laws through which order is brought to the state. Aquinas defined law as "an ordinance of reason, for the common good, promulgated by one who has the care of the community." This definition sums up his criteria for just rule. The laws must be based on reason rather than divine law imposed on the state by the Church in order that they satisfy our human need to deduce for ourselves the natural law.

Maintaining order

Aquinas goes on to explain that purely human laws are also necessary for the maintenance of order in society. Natural law guides our decisions of right and wrong and the moral code that determines what constitutes a crime or injustice, but it is human law that decides what would be a fitting punishment and how this should be enforced. These human laws are essential to ordered, civilized society and provide deterrents and incentives to potential wrongdoers to act with respect for the common good—and eventually to "do willingly what hitherto they did from fear, and become virtuous." The justice of human laws is judged by how well they measure up to natural law. If found to fall short, they should not be considered laws at all.

The second part of Aquinas's definition, however, is perhaps the deciding factor in judging the justice of a system of government. The laws imposed should be in the interests of the people as a whole and not those of the ruler or rulers. Only with such laws can the state provide a framework in which its citizens can freely pursue their intellectual and moral development. However, the question still remains: Who should rule? Aquinas, like Aristotle, believed that the majority did not have the reasoning power to fully appreciate the morality necessary for ruling, which implies that government should not be in the hands of the people, but a just individual, monarch, or aristocracy. But Aquinas also recognized the potential for these individuals to be corrupted and argued instead for some form of mixed constitution.

Surprisingly, in view of his notion of the state existing to promote life according to Christian principles, Aquinas does not dismiss the possibility of a legitimate non-Christian ruler. Although his rule would not be perfect, a pagan could rule justly and in accordance with human laws, allowing his citizens to develop their powers of reason and eventually come to deduce a moral code. Living then according to natural law, they would in time become a Christian society.

A radical thinker

When viewed from our modern standpoint nearly 900 years later, it might appear that Aquinas was simply rediscovering and repeating Aristotle's political theories. However, when considered fully in context against a background of medieval

The United Nations was established in 1945 after World War II with the intention of maintaining international peace and promoting principles that Aquinas would have called natural law.

Christianity, his views are revealed as a radical change in political thinking that challenged the conventional power of the Roman Catholic Church. Despite this, thanks to his scholarship and devoutness, his ideas were soon accepted by the established Church and have remained the basis for a large part of Catholic political philosophy to the present day.

In the criteria for a just war—rightful intention, authority of the sovereign, and just cause—we can see how these principles fit Aquinas's more general ideas of political justice based on natural law and the principle of reason rather than divine authority. As well as influencing much subsequent just-war theory, Aquinas's notion of natural law was embraced by both theologians and experts on law. Over the centuries, the necessity of human law would become a key issue in the increasing conflict between Church and secular powers in Europe as emerging nation-states asserted their independence from the papacy. ■

Aquinas's view of the requirements of a just war— rightful intention, authority, and just cause—still hold true today and motivate many involved in anti-war movements.

GOVERNMENT PREVENTS INJUSTICE, OTHER THAN SUCH AS IT COMMITS ITSELF

IBN KHALDUN (1332–1406)

IN CONTEXT

IDEOLOGY
Islam

FOCUS
Corruption of power

BEFORE

1027–256 BCE Historians in China during the Zhou dynasty describe the "Dynastic Cycle" of empires declining and being replaced.

c.950 Al-Farabi draws on Plato and Aristotle for *The Virtuous City*, his notion of an ideal Islamic state and the shortcomings of governments.

AFTER

1776 In *The Wealth of Nations*, British economist Adam Smith explains the principles behind the division of labor.

1974 US economist Arthur Laffer uses Ibn Khaldun's ideas on taxation to produce the Laffer curve, which demonstrates the relationship between rates of taxation and government revenue.

 When a nation has become the victim of a psychological defeat, then that marks the end of a nation.
Ibn Khaldun

D escribed by British anthropologist Ernest Gellner as the best definition of government in the history of political theory, Ibn Khaldun's assertion that "government prevents injustice, other than such as it commits itself" could be taken for a cynical modern comment on political institutions or for the realism of Machiavelli. In fact, this definition lies at the heart of an innovative 14th-century analysis of the causes of political instability.

Built on community

Unlike many other political thinkers of his time, Ibn Khaldun took a historical, sociological, and economic standpoint to examine the rise and fall of political institutions. Like Aristotle, he recognized that humans form social communities, which he ascribed to the Arabic concept of *asabiyyah*—which translates as "community spirit," "group solidarity," or simply "tribalism." This social cohesion gives rise to the institution of the state, whose purpose is to protect the interests of its citizens and defend them against attack.

Whatever form this government may take, it contains the seeds of its own destruction. As it gains more power, it becomes less concerned with the well-being of its citizens and begins to act more in its own self-interest, exploiting people and creating injustice and disunity. What had started as an institution to prevent injustice is now committing injustices itself. The *asabiyyah* of the community declines, so conditions are ripe for another government to emerge and take the place of the decadent regime. Civilizations rise and fall in this way, Ibn Khaldun argues, in a cycle of political dynasties.

Corruption leads to decline

Ibn Khaldun also points out the economic consequences of the existence of a powerful elite. At the beginning of a political society, taxes are only used to provide for necessities to maintain the *asabiyyah*, but as it becomes more civilized, the rulers impose higher taxes to maintain their own increasingly opulent lifestyles. Not only is this an injustice that threatens the unity of the state, but it is also counterproductive— overtaxing discourages production and leads in the long run to lower, not higher, revenues. This idea was rediscovered in the 20th century by US economist Arthur Laffer. Ibn Khaldun's theories on the division of labor and the labor theory of value also predate their "discovery" by mainstream economists.

Although he believed that the continuous cycle of political change was inevitable, Ibn Khaldun saw some forms of government as better than others. For him, *asabiyyah* is best maintained under a single ruler, such as a caliph in an Islamic state (which has the added benefit of religion to give social cohesion). It is maintained least satisfactorily under a tyrant. Government is a necessary evil, but since it implies an inherent injustice of control of men by other men, its power should be kept to a minimum. ∎

The unity of a political society comes from *asabiyyah*, or **community spirit**.

⬇

This is the **basis for government**, and prevents injustice.

⬇

As a society advances, social cohesion decreases and its **government becomes lax** …

⬇

… **exploiting its citizens** for its own advantage, causing injustice.

⬇

Eventually, **another government emerges** to take the place of the decadent regime.

⬇

Government prevents injustice, other than such as it commits itself.

Ibn Khaldun

Born in Tunis, Tunisia, in 1332, Ibn Khaldun was brought up in a politically active family and studied the Quran and Islamic law. He held official posts in the Maghreb region of North Africa, where he saw firsthand the political instability of many regimes. While working in Fez, he was imprisoned after a change of government, and after his release moved to Granada in southern Spain, where he led peace negotiations with the Castilian king, Pedro the Cruel. He later returned to serve in several North African courts but fled to the protection of a Berber tribe in the desert when his attempts at reform were rejected. In 1384, he settled in Cairo, where he completed his *History*. He made one final journey in 1401, to Damascus to negotiate peace between Egypt and the Mongol Khan Timur.

Key works

1377 *Introduction to History*
1377–1406 *History of the World*
1377–1406 *Autobiography*

A PRUDENT RULER CANNOT, AND MUST NOT, HONOR HIS WORD
NICCOLÒ MACHIAVELLI (1469–1527)

IN CONTEXT

IDEOLOGY
Realism

FOCUS
Statecraft

BEFORE
4th century BCE Chanakya advises rulers to do whatever is necessary to achieve the well-being of the state.

3rd century BCE Han Fei Tzu assumes it is human nature to seek personal gain and avoid punishment, and his Legalist government makes strict laws.

51 BCE Roman politician Cicero advocates republican rule in *De Republica*.

AFTER
1651 Thomas Hobbes's *Leviathan* describes life in a state of nature as "nasty, brutish, and short."

1816–1830 Carl von Clausewitz discusses the political aspects of warfare in *On War*.

W ritten by probably the best known (and most often misunderstood) of all political theorists, Niccolò Machiavelli's work gave rise to the term "Machiavellian," which epitomizes the manipulative, deceitful, and generally self-serving politician who believes that "the end justifies the means." However, this term fails to encapsulate the much broader and innovative political philosophy Machiavelli proposed in his treatise *The Prince*.

Machiavelli lived in turbulent political times at the beginning of the period that would come to be known as the Renaissance. This was a turning point in European history, when the medieval concept of a Christian world ruled with divine guidance was replaced by the idea that humans could control their own destiny. As the power of the Church was being eroded by Renaissance humanism, prosperous Italian city-states, such as Machiavelli's native Florence, had been established as republics. However, they were repeatedly threatened and taken over by rich and powerful families, such as the Medicis, seeking to extend their influence. Through his firsthand experience in public office for the Florentine Republic as a diplomat, and influenced by his study of classical Roman society and politics, Machiavelli developed an unconventional approach to the study of political theory.

A realistic approach
Rather than seeing society in terms of how it ought to be, Machiavelli tried to "go directly to the effectual truth of the thing rather than to the imagination of it," meaning that he sought to get to the heart of the matter and treat politics not as a branch of moral philosophy or ethics, but rather in purely practical and realistic terms.

Unlike previous political thinkers, he does not see the purpose of the state as

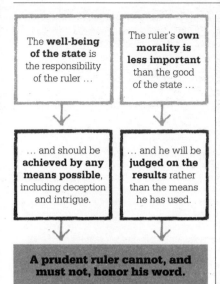

The **well-being of the state** is the responsibility of the ruler …

The ruler's **own morality is less important** than the good of the state …

↓ … and should be **achieved by any means possible**, including deception and intrigue.

↓ … and he will be **judged on the results** rather than the means he has used.

↓ ↓

A prudent ruler cannot, and must not, honor his word.

At the center of his political philosophy is the Renaissance idea of viewing human society in human terms, completely separated from the religious ideals imposed by the Christian Church. To achieve this, his starting point is an analysis of human nature based on his observations of human behavior throughout history, which brings him to the conclusion that the majority of people are by nature selfish, short-sighted, fickle, and easily deceived. His view is realistic, if somewhat cynical, and very different from those of previous political thinkers. While they might appear to be an obstacle to creating an efficient, stable society, Machiavelli argues that some of these human failings can in fact be useful in establishing a successful society, though this requires the correct leadership.

Using human nature

Man's innate self-centeredness, for example, is shown in his instinct for self-preservation. However, when threatened by aggression or a hostile environment, he reacts with acts of courage, hard work, and cooperation. Machiavelli draws a distinction between an original, fundamental human nature that has no virtues and a socially acquired nature that acts in a virtuous manner and is beneficial to society. Other negative human traits can also be turned to the common good, such as the tendency to imitate rather than think as individuals. »

nurturing the morality of its citizens, but rather as ensuring their well-being and security. Consequently, he replaces the concepts of right and wrong with notions such as usefulness, necessity, success, danger, and harm. By placing utility above morality, his ideas for the desirable qualities of a successful leader are based on effectiveness and prudence rather than any sort of ideology or moral rectitude.

Instinct for **self-preservation**

Credulity

Lack of individuality

Fickleness

An effective leader can harness the weaker traits of humanity in his people to great effect, in the same way that a sheepdog can manipulate a herd of sheep.

This, Machiavelli notes, leads people to follow a leader's example and act cooperatively. Further, traits such as fickleness and credulity allow humans to be easily manipulated by a skillful leader to behave in a benevolent way. Qualities such as selfishness, manifested in the human desire for personal gain and ambition, can be a powerful driving force if channeled correctly and are especially useful personal qualities in a ruler.

The two key elements to transforming the undesirable, original human nature into a benevolent social nature are social organization and what Machiavelli describes as "prudent" leadership, by which he means leadership that is useful to the success of the state.

Advice for new rulers

Machiavelli's famous (and now infamous) treatise *The Prince* was written in the style of the practical guides for leaders known as "Mirrors of Princes," which were common in the Middle Ages and the Renaissance. It is addressed to a new ruler—and is dedicated to a member of the powerful Medici family—with advice on how basic human nature can be engineered and manipulated for the good of the state. Later interpretations, however, hint that Machiavelli was using the genre somewhat cleverly by exposing

to a wider audience the secrets already known to the ruling classes. Having explained man's essentially self-centered but malleable nature, he then turns his attention to the qualities that are necessary for a ruler to govern prudently.

Leadership qualities

Confusingly, Machiavelli uses the word *virtù* to describe these leadership qualities, but this is very different from our modern idea of moral virtue, as well as the concept of virtue as understood by the Church. Machiavelli was a Christian, and as such he advocates Christian virtues in day-to-day life, but when dealing with the actions of a ruler, he believes that morality must take a backseat to utility and the security of the state. In this respect, his ideas hark back to the Roman quality of "virtue" embodied by the military leader who is motivated by ambition and the pursuit of glory, properties that are almost the exact opposite of the Christian virtue of modesty. Machiavelli notes, however, that these motivations are also a manifestation of human nature's inherent self-interest, and similarly can be harnessed for the common good.

Machiavelli takes the analogy between military and political leaders further, pointing out other aspects of *virtù*, such as boldness, discipline, and organization.

He also stresses the importance of analyzing a situation rationally before taking action and basing that action not on how people should ideally behave but on how they will behave (meaning in their own self-interest). In Machiavelli's opinion,

Sandro Botticelli's *Adoration of the Magi*, painted in 1475, includes representations of the powerful Medici family, who ruled Florence at the time Machiavelli wrote *The Prince*.

> In judging policies, we should consider the results that have been achieved through them rather than the means by which they have been executed.
> **Niccolò Machiavelli**

social conflict is an inevitable result of the selfishness of human nature. (This is in contrast to the medieval Christian view that selfishness was not a natural condition.) In order to deal with this selfishness, a leader needs to employ the tactics of war.

Although Machiavelli believes that to a large extent man is master of his own fate, he recognizes that there is also an element of chance at play, which he refers to as *fortuna*. The ruler must battle against this possibility, as well as against the fickleness of human nature, which also corresponds to *fortuna*. He sees that political life in particular can be seen as a continuous contest between the elements of *virtù* and *fortuna*, and in this regard is analogous to a state of war.

Conspiracy is useful

By analyzing politics using military theory, Machiavelli concludes that the essence of most political life is conspiracy. Just as success in war is dependent on espionage, intelligence, counterintelligence, and deception, political success requires secrecy, intrigue, and deceit. The idea of conspiracy had long been known to military theorists and was practiced by many political leaders, but Machiavelli was the first in the West to explicitly propose a theory of political conspiracy. Deceit was considered contrary to the idea that a state should safeguard the morality of its citizens, and Machiavelli's suggestions were a shocking departure from conventional thinking.

According to Machiavelli, while intrigue and deceit are not morally justifiable in private life, they are prudent for successful leadership and excusable when used for

the common good. More than that, Machiavelli asserts that in order to mold the undesirable aspects of human nature, it is essential that a ruler is deceitful and—out of prudence—does not honor his word, since to do so would jeopardize his rule, threatening the stability of the state. For the leader, then, compelled to deal with the inevitable conflicts that face him, the ends do justify the means.

The end is what counts

A prince's success as a ruler is judged by the consequences of his actions and their benefit to the state, not by his morality or ideology. As Machiavelli puts it in *The Prince*, "In the actions of all men, especially princes, where there is no recourse to justice, the end is all that counts. A prince should only be concerned with conquering or maintaining a state, for the means will always be judged to be honorable and praiseworthy by each and every person, because the masses always follow appearances and the outcomes of affairs, and the world is nothing other than the masses." He does, however, stress that this is a matter of expediency and not a model for social behavior. It is only excusable when done for the public good. It is also important that the methods of intrigue and deception should be a means to an end and not become an end in themselves, so these methods need to be restricted to political and military leaders and strictly controlled.

Another tactic Machiavelli borrows from the military is the use of force and violence, which again is morally indefensible in private life but excusable when employed for the common good. Such a policy creates fear, which is a means of ensuring the security of the ruler. Machiavelli tackles the question of whether it is better for a leader to be feared or loved with characteristic pragmatism. In an ideal world, he should be both loved and feared, but in reality, the two seldom go together. Fear will keep the leader in a much stronger position and is therefore better for the well-being of the state. Rulers who have gained power through exercising their »

The goal of the ruler is to **ensure the well-being** and **security** of his citizens ...

... but to do this effectively, he must sometimes **use deceit, treachery, and secrecy**.

Though Machiavelli did not sanction the use of questionable methods to get things done in private life, he argued that the ruler should use all means necessary to secure the future of the state.

virtù are in the most secure position, having defeated any opposition and earned respect from the people. But to maintain this support and hold onto power, they must continually assert their authority.

An ideal republic

While *The Prince* is addressed to the would-be successful ruler, Machiavelli was a statesman in the Republic of Florence, and in his less well-known work, *Discourses on Livy*, he strongly advocated republicanism rather than any form of monarchy or oligarchy. Despite remaining a lifelong Catholic, he was also opposed to any interference in political life by the Church. The form of government he favored was modeled on the Roman Republic, with a mixed constitution and participation by its citizens, protected by a properly constituted citizens' army as opposed to a militia of hired mercenaries. This, he argued, would protect the liberty of the citizens and minimize any social conflict between the common people and a ruling elite. However, to found such a republic, or reform an existing state, requires the leadership of an individual who possesses the appropriate *virtù* and prudence. Though it may require a strong leader and some scurrilous means to begin with, once a political society is established, the ruler can then introduce the necessary laws and social organization to enable it to continue as an ideal republic—this would be a pragmatic means to achieve a desirable end.

Machiavelli's philosophy, based on personal experience and an objective study of history, challenged the dominance of the Church and conventional ideas of political morality and led to his works being banned by the Catholic authorities. By treating politics as a practical and not a philosophical or ethical subject of study, he replaced morality with utility as the purpose of the state and shifted the emphasis from the moral intention of a political action to focus primarily on its consequences.

Enduring legacy

The Prince was very influential in the centuries following Machiavelli's death, particularly among leaders such as Henry VIII of England, Holy Roman Emperor Charles V, Oliver Cromwell, and Napoleon, and the book was acknowledged as an inspiration by such diverse figures as Marxist theorist Antonio Gramsci and Fascist dictator Benito Mussolini.

Machiavelli's critics, too, came from all sides of the political spectrum, with Catholics accusing him of supporting the Protestant cause, and vice versa. His importance to mainstream political thinking was immense. He was clearly very much a product of the Renaissance, with its emphasis on humanism rather than religion and empiricism rather than faith and dogma, and he was the first to take an objective, scientific approach to political history.

This objectivity also underlies his perhaps cynical analysis of human nature, which was a precursor to Thomas Hobbes's brutal description of life in a state of nature. His concept of utility became a mainstay of 19th-century liberalism. In a more general sense, by divorcing morality and ideology from politics, his work was the basis for a movement that later became known as political realism, with particular relevance in international relations.

"Machiavellian" behavior

The term "Machiavellian" is in common usage today and is usually applied pejoratively to politicians who are perceived (or discovered) to be acting manipulatively and deceitfully. President Richard Nixon, who attempted to cover up a break-in and wiretapping of his opponent's headquarters and was forced to resign over the scandal, is a modern-day example of such underhanded behavior. It is also possible that Machiavelli may have been making a less obvious point in *The Prince*: perhaps he was saying that those who have been successful rulers may have behaved in just as "Machiavellian" a way, but their actions have not been as closely examined. How they achieved their success has been overlooked because the focus has shifted to what they achieved. It seems that we tend to judge leaders on their results rather than the means used to achieve them.

Expanding this argument further, we might consider how often the losers of a war are found to be morally questionable, while the victors are seen as above reproach—the notion that history is written by the victors. Criticizing Machiavelli leads us to examine ourselves and the extent to which we are prepared to overlook the dubious machinations of our governments if the outcome works in our favor. ∎

Richard Nixon resigned as president in 1974. He authorized a break-in and wiretap at the Democratic National Committee headquarters, actions described as "Machiavellian."

Niccolò Machiavelli

Born in Florence, Niccolò Machiavelli was the son of a lawyer and is believed to have studied at the University of Florence, but little is known of his life until he became a government official in 1498 in the government of the Republic of Florence. He spent the next 14 years traveling around Italy, France, and Spain on diplomatic business.

In 1512, Florence was attacked and returned to the rule of the Medici family. Machiavelli was imprisoned and tortured unjustly for conspiring against the Medici, and when released, he retired to a farm outside Florence. There, he devoted himself to writing, including *The Prince* and other political and philosophical books. He tried to regain favor with the Medici, with little success. After they were overthrown in 1527, he was denied a post with the new republican government because of his links with the Medici. He died later that year.

Key works

c.1513 (pub. 1532) *The Prince*
c.1517 (pub. 1531) *Discourses on Livy*
1519–1521 *The Art of War*

THE EARLY MODERN PE

1515–1848

The invention of the printing press, the rise of nation-states, and the discovery of the Americas were some of the factors that influenced the transition from the Middle Ages to the "Age of Reason," during which the authority of the Church was increasingly questioned and modern Western political thought began to develop.

In the absence of religious doctrine, and faced with the conflict between civil and religious governance, people needed a new way to organize and legitimize political order. Two concepts became fundamental: the "divine right of kings" and "natural law," which analyzed human behavior to arrive at valid moral principles. Increasingly, the analysis was based not on theology, but on reason.

The social contract

In France, Jean Bodin argued in favor of a strong central power with absolute sovereignty to quell the unrest following the decline of papal authority in Europe. Thomas Hobbes, writing during a time of civil war in England, agreed with Bodin on the need for a strong sovereign but not on the divine right of kings. For Hobbes,

the power to rule was granted not by God but via a social contract with the ruled. The idea that the power to govern is granted by the people via an implicit or explicit contract—and that rulers can legitimately be removed from power if they break the contract—is still central to modern understandings of political systems.

While Bodin and Hobbes used the concept of natural law to argue for absolutism, others used it to assert that humans had natural rights. Hugo Grotius, for example, placed liberty and rights firmly in the possession of individuals, as opposed to thinking of them as qualities bestowed by God. This idea was key to the development of liberalism.

Like Hobbes, John Locke believed in the social contract, but his more optimistic view of human nature persuaded him that government should not be absolute, but limited to protection of individual rights and freedom. Jean-Jacques Rousseau, for his part, used the social contract to offer a radical new view of how politics could function in the modern age. Whereas many Enlightenment thinkers encouraged enlightened despots to rule wisely and were against the rule of the mob, Rousseau

RIOD

argued that true sovereignty resided only with the people.

Revolutionary thoughts

Enlightenment ideals began to shape events, most spectacularly in the American and French revolutions of the 1770s and 1780s. For example, Thomas Paine's simple argument for independence, a republic, and democracy in *Common Sense* popularized the demands of the American revolutionaries. The pamphlet became an instant bestseller, inspiring the American Declaration of Independence, just as Rousseau inspired the French Revolution of 1789—often seen as the culmination of the European Enlightenment—with ideals of human rights, freedom, checks and balances, international law, representative democracy, and reason.

Belief that society could be radically reconstructed in a rational fashion was gaining ground at the beginning of the 19th century, and by the 1850s, had inspired revolutionary movements around the world. British writer Mary Wollstonecraft helped expand the argument that the ideals of Enlightened freedom should not exclude half of humanity and that women's rights were an integral part of a just society.

New conservatism

The bloody Reign of Terror that followed the revolution in France demonstrated the failings of radicalism and provoked a reaction that inspired a new, sophisticated style of conservative thought. Using the language of freedom and rights, Edmund Burke advocated government by established wise rulers, arguing that it was more important to maintain social stability than to attempt radical reform and that healthy societies could only develop over many generations.

Meanwhile, a distinctive style of liberal argument in defense of rights also began to develop. Proceeding on the basis of simple claims about humanity's desire for happiness, English philosopher Jeremy Bentham constructed a justification for limited democratic freedoms that respected property and identified the limits of government. A more ambiguous variant of the same conclusions was provided by German philosopher Georg Hegel, who argued for the need to understand freedom as possible only in a fully developed civil society. His complex arguments provided a framework with which the next generation of thinkers would attempt to understand the failings of the postrevolutionary world. ∎

THE CONDITION OF MAN IS A CONDITION OF WAR
THOMAS HOBBES (1588–1679)

IN CONTEXT

IDEOLOGY
Realism

FOCUS
Social contract

BEFORE
1578 The concepts of sovereignty and the divine right of kings emerge, influenced by *The Six Books of the Republic* by Jean Bodin.

1642–1651 The English Civil War temporarily establishes the precedent that the monarch cannot rule without the consent of Parliament.

AFTER
1688 The Glorious Revolution in England leads to the 1689 Bill of Rights, which limits the powers of the monarch in law.

1689 John Locke opposes absolutist rule, arguing that government should represent the people and protect their rights to life, health, liberty, and possessions.

The Enlightenment period that followed the Middle Ages in Europe introduced new views on human nature that were not based on religious doctrine, but were instead founded on rational thought. Disagreement between some Enlightenment thinkers often derived from differences in opinion concerning the true nature of the human condition and human behavior. To settle such abstract, fundamental differences, scholars began to state their views on the so-called "state of nature"—the theoretical condition of mankind before the introduction of social structures and norms.

Many thinkers believed that by analyzing the human "instincts" and behaviors of this state of nature, one could design a system of government that met the needs of its citizens and would promote good behaviors and counteract bad ones. For example, if humans were able to see beyond narrow self-interests and work for the public good, then they could enjoy the benefits of democratic rights. However, if they mainly cared about their own interests and maximizing their own power, then a strong, controlling authority was required in order to prevent chaos. English writer Thomas Hobbes was one of the first Enlightenment philosophers to base his argument explicitly on an articulated view of the state of nature. Hobbes's view was that human beings needed to be ruled by government, as the state of nature was a terrible, "dog-eat-dog" world.

The cruel state of nature
In his most famous work, *Leviathan*, Hobbes portrays humans as rational agents who seek to maximize power and act according to self-interest, because acting otherwise would threaten their self-preservation. The title is suggestive of Hobbes's views on the state and human

Left ungoverned, men will terrorize each other in a **state of nature** ...

→

... in which individuals will stop at nothing to ensure their own **self-preservation or self-promotion**.

↓

In the state of nature, the condition of man is a condition of war of everyone against everyone.

↓

To avert a descent into the state of nature, men must **enter into a social contract**, submitting to the authority and protection of a sovereign.

→

The sovereign must be an absolute ruler with **indivisible and unlimited power** to prevent factional strife and chaos.

↓

If a sovereign fails in their duty, the **social contract is broken** and individuals may take action, leading back to a state of nature.

---

nature. Leviathan is the name of a monster in the biblical book of Job, and for Hobbes, the state is the "great Leviathan ... which is but an Artificial Man; though of greater stature and strength than the Natural, for whose protection and defense it was intended; and in which, the Sovereignty is an Artificial Soul, as giving life and motion to the whole body." The state is thus a cruel, artificial construct but is necessary nonetheless for the sake of the protection of its citizens.

The book was written during the English Civil War (1642–1651) and argues against challenges to royal authority. The state of nature—the warring of all against one another—was for Hobbes comparable to civil war and could only be avoided if men handed over their arms to a third party—the sovereign—via a social contract that ensured that all others would do the same. The reason rational agents would surrender their freedom to an absolute ruler was that life in the state of nature was so "solitary, poor, nasty, brutish, and short" that freedom would always be a secondary concern, an ill-afforded luxury. Hobbes stated that while people would

The frontispiece of *Leviathan* depicts a ruler composed of tiny faces rising up over the land and holding a sword and scepter, symbolizing earthly and ecclesiastical powers respectively.

have natural rights in such a state of nature, the overriding concern would be to do whatever was necessary to secure survival. All actions could be justified— rights would not protect the individual.

Rule by social contract
With no common authority to solve disputes or protect the weak, it would be up to each individual to decide what he or she needs—and needs to do—to survive. In the state of nature, men are naturally »

free and independent, with no duties to others. Hobbes assumes that there will always be a scarcity of goods and that people are equally vulnerable. Some people will go into conflict to secure food and shelter, while others will be willing to do so in order to obtain power and glory. A state of constant fear will ensue, leading to preemptive attacks.

Hobbes sees this state of war and chaos as the natural end point of uncontrolled human freedom. In order to prevent it, the state needs to have indivisible power and authority to control its subjects. This is similar to a description of sovereignty by French jurist Jean Bodin, which was also born out of a period of civil war. However, Hobbes did not base authority on the divine right of kings, but on the idea of a social contract that all rational people would agree upon.

While the concept of man's state of nature was deeply influential among Hobbes's contemporaries and future political theorists, it was often interpreted differently. Hobbes used the state of nature to refer to a hypothetical situation, a sort of rational reconstruction of how life without order and government would be. This differed from the way later thinkers, including John Locke and Jean-Jacques Rousseau, would use the

Hobbes wrote *Leviathan* as the English Civil War was waged. His view of the "state of nature" that a sovereign protected against seemed to be borne out by the savagery of the war.

concept in their own works on the social contract and ideal forms of government. Locke and Rousseau did not consider the state of nature to be a rational construct, but an actual state of affairs.

A necessary evil

Enlightenment thinkers referred to the concept of a social contract between the ruled and the ruler to answer questions of the political legitimacy of various modes of governance. To rule legitimately, there must be either an explicit or tacit

---

Thomas Hobbes

Born in 1588, Thomas Hobbes was educated at Oxford University in England and would later work as a tutor for William Cavendish, Earl of Devonshire. Due to the English Civil War, he spent a decade in exile in Paris, where he wrote *Leviathan*, which has had a profound influence on the way we perceive the role of government and the social contract as a basis for legitimacy to govern. Hobbes's political philosophy was influenced by his interest in science and his correspondence with philosophers, including René Descartes (1596–1650). Drawing from scientific writings, Hobbes believed that everything could be reduced to its primary components—even human nature. He was inspired by the simplicity and elegance of geometry and physics and revolutionized political theory by applying such scientific method to its reasoning. He returned to England in 1651 and died in 1679.

Key works

1628 *History of the Peloponnesian War*
1650 *Treatise on Human Nature*
1651 *Leviathan*

Hobbes saw the state of nature as undesirable, stating that the people must willingly subject themselves to a ruler or sovereign in order to protect society.

In the state of nature, all **men are at war** with each other and live in a constant **state of fear** of their fellow beings.

With the social contract, people invest all power in a third party, the sovereign, in exchange for **safety and the rule of law**.

agreement that the sovereign will protect his citizens and their natural rights if they agree to surrender their individual freedom and submit to subordination.

Hobbes argued that humans had two principal choices in life: they could either live without government (the state of nature) or with government. For Hobbes, a social contract bestowing indivisible authority to a sovereign was a necessary evil to avoid the cruel fate that awaited man if a strong power could not keep the destructive impulses of individuals in check. Hobbes believed that, "During the time men live without a common power to keep them all in awe, they are in that condition called war; and such a war, as is of every man, against every man." However, unlike earlier scholars who had argued for the divine right of kings to rule, Hobbes truly saw the relationship between the ruled and the ruler as contractual. The contract was primarily made between the individuals in a society, while the sovereign was an outside third party.

Collective action
Because people are rational, they can see that the state of nature is undesirable and that peace is good. However, because each individual has to protect their own interests in the state of nature, a "collective

action problem" arises. Although Hobbes did not coin this term, his dilemma of individuals in the state of nature not trusting each other to lay down arms is very similar to this modern concept, where a problem exists that can only be overcome if individuals—all of whom stand to gain from the successful outcome—act collectively. Hobbes's solution was radical: invest all power in a third party—the sovereign. Contemporary scholars have identified many ways in which individuals overcome collective action problems without the need for a strong government. British philosopher Margaret Gilbert has suggested that collective action involves joint commitment to a course of action in which, in effect, people act as parts of one person with one aim. Nevertheless, governments are still the main regulators of conflict and providers of public goods.

Hobbes's contractual view of government authority also affected the duties of the sovereign. Only so long as the sovereign could protect his subjects were they bound by the social contract. However, Hobbes did not encourage popular revolutions, nor religious influence on state matters, and he did not favor democratic rule. The main aim of government was stability and peace, not individual freedom. »

Oliver Cromwell led the anti-Royalist forces that deposed King Charles I in 1649. Hobbes believed the social contract was still intact, since rule had passed unbroken to Parliament.

Pragmatic politics

Hobbes's views on the social contract did legitimize changes in government. When the English king Charles I was dethroned in 1649 by Oliver Cromwell, according to Hobbes's thinking, the social contract was held intact, since one ruler was merely replaced with another. In other words, Hobbes was an antidemocrat and an absolutist, but also a pragmatist. Although he did not take a decisive stance on which mode of government was best, he clearly preferred Charles I's monarchy as a good, stable form of government. However, he also regarded parliamentary sovereignty as a suitable form of government, as long as the legislative assembly contained an odd number of members to prevent a situation of political stalemate.

The logic behind Hobbes's version of the social contract was questioned by many scholars. John Locke provided a sarcastic critique by questioning why one would believe that "Men are so foolish that they take care to avoid what Mischiefs may be done to them by Pole-cats, or Foxes, but are content, nay think it Safety, to be devoured by Lions." For Locke, authoritarian rule is just as dangerous as civil disorder—he preferred the state of nature to subordination. Hobbes believed, however, that only governments with indivisible and unlimited power would prevent the otherwise inevitable disintegration of society into civil war. For Hobbes, anyone arguing for individual freedoms and rights had not grasped that the basic security that civilized life took for granted would only endure as long as strong, centralized rule existed. Political obedience was needed to keep the peace. Citizens had a right to defend themselves if their lives were threatened, but in all other questions, the government was to be obeyed to prevent factional strife or political paralysis.

Against a state of nature

Hobbes delivered a strong argument for absolutism based on his deliberations on the nature of man. His opponents—arguing against absolutism—responded by challenging his portrayal of human beings as hungry for power and strife. Jean-Jacques Rousseau saw the life of man in the state of nature in a romantic light, as a life of innocence and simplicity, in contrast to life in modern society, which was dishonest. Therefore, one should not try to escape from the state of nature; rather, it should be recreated as best as possible in the mode of government. Rousseau therefore advocated direct democracy in small communities. While Hobbes lived his life with the English Civil War as a reference point, Rousseau lived in the tranquil city

The Social Contract

We, the people, agree to obey the law and to respect the authority of the sovereign, whose power is indivisible and unlimited.

The Triumph of Death (1562) by Pieter Bruegel the Elder depicts anarchy breaking out as Death comes to rich and poor alike. Hobbes saw the state of nature as similarly anarchic and brutal.

of Geneva, Switzerland. It is telling how their different backgrounds shaped their political theories. Unlike Hobbes, Rousseau regarded the state of nature as a historical description of man in a presocial state of nature. Political theorists have since vacillated between the extremes of Hobbes and Rousseau, viewing the condition of man either as a condition of war or as people living in accordance with nature.

Two other influential philosophers— Locke and Scottish philosopher David Hume—also criticized Hobbes. Locke writes on the state of nature in his two treatises of government (1690) and refers to the laws of nature that govern this condition. In contrast to Hobbes, he states that even in the state of nature, no man has the right to harm another. Hume adds to the debate by stating that human beings are naturally social and that the savage condition described by Hobbes is therefore improbable.

The Hobbes method

Today, scholars continue to use Hobbes's method and the concept of a state of nature to argue for and against different political systems. John Rawls used Hobbes's notion of what made a stable society when formulating what rational people would be able to agree upon. In *A Theory of Justice* (1971), Rawls argues that people would choose a condition where everyone had some basic rights and economic safeguards if forced to choose under a "veil of ignorance," not knowing whether they would have a privileged position in this imagined society. Hobbes did not, however, theorize on the ideal society, but on the necessity of strong government. While most scholars today would consider Hobbes's view of the human condition to be pessimistic, he maintains a significant influence on political thought. The realist tradition in international relations, which stresses the study of power, departs from Hobbes's premise that the condition of man is a condition of war. Nevertheless, the anarchical condition that Hobbes described in the state of nature is also taken to be true for the international system, where states are the main actors.

Realist views of the international system still dominate today, despite the end of the Cold War. The main difference from Hobbes's theory is that, at the international level, it is not possible to rely on the *"Leviathan"* of the state to subdue destructive pursuits of power and self-interest. States cannot trust each other and are therefore doomed to arms races and wars. ∎

 Without a common power to keep them all in awe, they [men] are in that condition called war.
Thomas Hobbes

THE END OF LAW IS TO PRESERVE AND ENLARGE FREEDOM
JOHN LOCKE (1632–1704)

IN CONTEXT

IDEOLOGY
Liberalism

FOCUS
The rule of law

BEFORE
1642 A series of conflicts known as the English Civil War breaks out due to concerns that Charles I would attempt to introduce absolutism in England.

1661 Louis XIV begins his personal rule of France and embodies absolutism phrase *"L'état, c'est moi,"* that he is the state.

AFTER
1689 The English Bill of Rights secures the rights of Parliament and elections free of royal interference.

18th century Popular revolutions in France and North America lead to the establishment of republics based on liberalist principles.

 In all the states of created beings capable of law, where there is no law, there is no freedom.
John Locke

A n important question in political theory concerns the role of government and the functions it should perform. Equally important is the question of what gives the government a right to govern and where the boundaries of government authority should be. Some medieval scholars argued that kings had

a right to rule that had been bestowed upon them by God, while others proclaimed that the nobility had a birthright to rule. Enlightenment thinkers started to challenge these doctrines. But if the power to rule was not to be granted by divine will or by birth, other sources of legitimacy had to be found.

English philosopher John Locke was the first to articulate the liberal principles of government: namely that the purpose of government was to preserve its citizens' rights to freedom, life, and property; to pursue the public good; and to punish people who violated the rights of others. Lawmaking was therefore the supreme function of government. For Locke, one of the main reasons people would be willing to enter into a social contract and submit to being ruled by a government is that they expect the government to regulate disagreements and conflicts in a neutral manner. Following this logic, Locke was also able to describe the characteristics of an illegitimate government. It followed that a government that did not respect and protect people's natural rights—or unnecessarily constrained their liberty—

was not legitimate. Locke was therefore opposed to absolutist rule. Unlike his contemporary Thomas Hobbes, who believed that an absolute sovereign was required to save people from a brutal "state of nature," Locke maintained that the powers and functions of government had to be limited.

The centrality of laws

Much of Locke's writing on political philosophy centered on rights and laws. He defined political power as "a Right of making Laws with Penalties of Death." He contended that one of the primary reasons why people would voluntarily leave the lawless state of nature was that no independent judges existed in such a situation. It was preferable to grant government a monopoly on violence and sentencing to ensure fair rule of law. Moreover, for Locke, a legitimate government upholds the principle of separation of the legislative and executive powers. The legislative power is superior to the executive—the former has supreme power to establish general rules in the affairs of government, while the latter is only responsible for enforcing the law in specific cases.

One reason for the centrality of laws in Locke's writings is that laws protect liberty. The purpose of law is not to abolish or restrain, but to preserve and enlarge freedom. In political society, Locke believes

---

Humans are **rational, independent agents** with natural rights.

↓

They join political society **to be protected** by the rule of law.

↓

The end of law should be to preserve and enlarge freedom.

---

that "where there is no law, there is no freedom." Laws, therefore, both constrain and enable freedom. To live in freedom is not to live without laws in the state of nature. Locke points out that "freedom is not, as we are told, liberty for every man to do what he lists (for who could be free when every other man's humor might domineer over him?), but a liberty to dispose, and order as he lists, his person, actions, possessions, and his whole property, within the allowance of those laws." In other words, laws can not only preserve, but also enable liberty to be exercised. Without »

John Locke

John Locke lived in—and shaped—one of the most transformative centuries in English history. A series of civil wars pitted Protestants, Anglicans, and Catholics against each other, and power vacillated between the king and Parliament. Locke was born in 1632 close to Bristol, England. He lived in exile in France and Holland for large periods of time due to suspicions that he was involved in an assassination plot against King Charles II. His book *Two Treatises of Government* provided the intellectual foundation for the Glorious Revolution of 1688, which transferred the balance of power permanently from the king to Parliament. He promoted the idea that people are not born with innate ideas, but with a mind like a blank slate—a very modern way of viewing the self.

Key works

1689 *Two Treatises of Government*
1689 *A Letter Concerning Toleration*
1690 *An Essay Concerning Human Understanding*

The Role Of Government

Governments must **craft good laws** ...

... that **protect the rights** of the people ...

... and **enforce them** with the public good in mind.

laws, our freedom would be limited by an anarchical, uncertain state of nature, and in practice there may be no freedom at all.

Man's initial condition

Locke says that laws should be designed—and enforced—with man's initial condition and nature in mind. Like most social contract theorists, he considers men to be equal, free, and independent. According to Locke, the state of nature is a situation in which people coexist, often in relative harmony, but there is no legitimate political power or judge to settle disputes in a neutral way. Locke writes that "men living according to reason, without a common superior on Earth to judge between them, is properly the state of nature."

Unlike Hobbes, Locke does not equate the state of nature with war. A state of war is a situation in which people do not uphold natural law, or the law of reason as Locke calls it. Where Hobbes would see human beings acting as "power maximizers,"

Opposed to absolutist rule, Locke as a child had witnessed the execution of King Charles I in 1649 for being "a tyrant, traitor, murderer, and public enemy to the good of this nation."

mainly concerned with self-preservation, Locke finds that people can act according to reason and with tolerance in the state of nature. Conflicts are therefore not necessarily common in a state of nature. However, when population density increases, resources become scarce. The introduction of money leads to economic inequality, conflicts increase, and human society begins to need laws, regulators, and judges to settle disputes in an objective manner.

The purpose of government

The question of legitimacy was at the heart of Locke's political thinking. Following the example of Hobbes, he sought to deduce the legitimate role of government based on an understanding of the human state of nature.

Locke agrees with Hobbes that a legitimate government is based on a social contract between individuals in a society. The problem with the state of nature is that there are no judges or police to enforce the law. People are willing to enter civil society in order for government to take up this role. This is, therefore, a legitimate role for government. Another important aspect of legitimate government is rule by consent of the people. For Locke, this did not have to mean democracy—a majority of people could reasonably decide that a monarch, aristocracy, or a democratic assembly should rule. The important point was that the people granted the right to rule and were entitled to take back this privilege.

Locke argued against a strong, absolutist sovereign—as advocated by Thomas Hobbes—since such a powerful figure would limit individual freedom unnecessarily. For

Locke, total subordination was dangerous. He wrote, "I have reason to conclude that he who would get me into his power without my consent would use me as he pleased when he got me there, and destroy me too when he had a fancy to it; for nobody can desire to have me in his absolute power unless it be to compel me by force to that which is against the right of my freedom, i.e., make me a slave."

Rather, Locke favors a limited role for government. Government should protect people's private property; keep the peace; secure public commodities for the whole people; and, as far as possible, protect citizens against foreign invasions. For Locke, "This is the original, this is the use, and these are the bounds of the legislative (which is the supreme) power in every commonwealth." The purpose of government is to do what is missing in the state of nature to ensure people's freedom and prosperity. There is no need to enslave people under absolute rule. The primary function of government is to craft good laws to protect people's rights and to enforce those laws with the public good in mind.

The right to revolt

Locke's distinction between legitimate and illegitimate governments also carries with it the idea that opposition to illegitimate

For a government to be legitimate, according to Locke, assemblies of elected representatives of the people, such as the House of Commons, must be allowed to meet and debate.

 A Bill of Rights is what the people are entitled to against every government, and what no just government should refuse, or rest on inference.
Thomas Jefferson

rule is acceptable. Locke describes a range of scenarios in which people would have a right to revolt in order to take back the power they had given the government. For example, people can legitimately rebel if: elected representatives of the people are prevented from assembly; foreign powers are bestowed with authority over people; the election system or procedures are changed without public consent; the rule of law is not upheld; or the government seeks to deprive people of their rights. Locke regarded illegitimate rule as tantamount to slavery. He even went as far as to condone regicide—the execution of a monarch—in circumstances where the monarch has broken the social contract with his people. As the son of Puritans who had supported the Parliamentarian cause in the English Civil War, this was no mere theoretical concern—Locke's writing gives a clear justification for the execution of Charles I.

Locke's legacy

The political philosophy of John Locke has, since his time, become known as "liberalism"—the belief in the principles of liberty and equality. The revolutions in France and North America near the end of the 18th century were founded on liberal ideas. In fact, Thomas Jefferson, one of the architects of the US Constitution and the Declaration of Independence, revered Locke and used many of his phrases in the founding documents. The emphasis on protection of "life, liberty, or property" found in the Bill of Rights in the Constitution and the inalienable rights to "Life, Liberty, and the pursuit of Happiness" in the Declaration can all be traced directly back to John Locke's philosophy a century earlier. ■

TO RENOUNCE LIBERTY IS TO RENOUNCE BEING A MAN
JEAN-JACQUES ROUSSEAU (1712–1778)

IN CONTEXT

IDEOLOGY
Republicanism

FOCUS
The general will

BEFORE
1513 Niccolò Machiavelli's *The Prince* offers a modern form of politics in which a ruler's morality and the concerns of state are strictly separate.

1651 Thomas Hobbes's *Leviathan* argues for the foundation of the state on the basis of the social contract.

AFTER
1789 The Jacobin Club begins meeting in Paris. Its extremist members attempt to apply Rousseau's principles to revolutionary politics.

1791 In Britain, Edmund Burke blames Rousseau for the "excesses" of the French Revolution.

For centuries in Western Europe, a certain style of thinking about human affairs prevailed. Under the sway of the Catholic Church, the writings of ancient Greece and Rome had been steadily studied and rehabilitated, with outstanding intellectuals such as Augustine of Hippo and Thomas Aquinas rediscovering ancient thinkers. A scholastic approach, treating history and society as essentially unchanging and the higher purpose of morality as fixed by God, had come to dominate the ways in which society was considered. It took the upheavals associated with the development of capitalism and urban life to begin to tear this approach apart.

Rethinking the status quo

In the 16th century, Niccolò Machiavelli, in a radical departure with the past, had turned the scholastic tradition on its head in *The Prince*, drawing on ancient examples not to act as a guide to a moral life, but to demonstrate how an effective statecraft or politics could be cynically performed. Thomas Hobbes, writing his *Leviathan* during the English Civil War of the mid-17th century, used the scientific method of deduction rather than the reading of ancient texts to argue for the necessity of a strong state to preserve security among the people.

However, it was Jean-Jacques Rousseau, an idiosyncratic Swiss exile from Geneva whose personal life scandalized polite society, who proposed the most radical break with the past. Rousseau's autobiographical *Confessions*, published after his death, reveal that it was during his time in the Italian island-port of Venice—while working as an underpaid ambassadorial secretary—that he decided "everything depends entirely on politics." People were not inherently evil but could become so under evil governments. The virtues he saw in Geneva and the vices in Venice—in particular, the sad decline

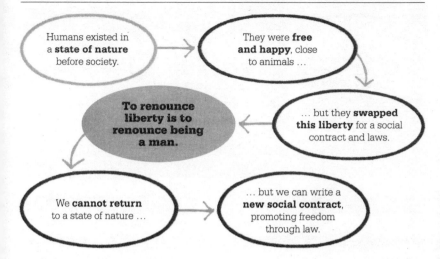

Humans existed in a **state of nature** before society.

They were **free and happy**, close to animals …

… but they **swapped this liberty** for a social contract and laws.

To renounce liberty is to renounce being a man.

We **cannot return** to a state of nature …

… but we can write a **new social contract**, promoting freedom through law.

of the city-state from its glorious past—could be traced not to human character, but to human institutions.

Society shaped by politics
In his *Discourse on Inequality* of 1754, Rousseau broke with previous political philosophy. The ancient Greeks and others writing on society—including Ibn Khaldun in the 14th century—viewed political processes as subject to their own laws, working with an unchanging human nature. The Greeks, in particular, had a cyclical view of political change in which

The corruption Rousseau found in Venice exemplified for him the way in which bad government causes people to be bad. He contrasted this with the propriety of his hometown, Geneva.

good or virtuous modes of government—whether monarchy, democracy, or aristocracy—would degenerate into various forms of tyranny before the cycle was renewed again. Society, as such, did not change—merely its form of government.

Rousseau disagreed. If, as he argued, society could be shaped by its political institutions, there was (in theory) no limit to the ability of political action to reshape society for the better.

This assertion marked Rousseau as a distinctively modern thinker. Nobody before Rousseau had systematically thought of society as something distinct from its political institutions, as an entity that was itself capable of being studied and acted upon. Rousseau was the first, even among the philosophers of the Enlightenment, to reason in terms of social relations among people.

This new theory begged an obvious question: If human society was open to political change, why, then, was it so obviously imperfect?

On property and inequality
Rousseau provided, again, an exceptional answer—one that scandalized his fellow philosophers. As his starting point, he asked that we consider humans without society. Thomas Hobbes had argued such people would be savages, living lives »

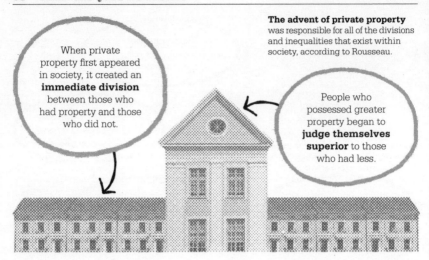

When private property first appeared in society, it created an **immediate division** between those who had property and those who did not.

The advent of private property was responsible for all of the divisions and inequalities that exist within society, according to Rousseau.

People who possessed greater property began to **judge themselves superior** to those who had less.

that were "poor, nasty, brutish, and short," but Rousseau asserted quite the opposite. Human beings free from society were well-disposed, happy creatures, content in their state of nature. Only two principles guided them: the first, a natural self-love and desire for self-preservation; the second, a compassion for their fellow human beings. The combination of the two ensured that humanity reproduced itself, generation after generation, in a state close to that of other animals.

This happy condition was, however, brutally brought to a close by the creation of civil society and, in particular, the development of private property. The arrival of private property imposed an immediate inequality on humanity that did not previously exist—between those who possessed property and those who did not. By instituting this inequality, private property provided the foundations of further divisions in society—between those of master and slave, and then in the separation of families. On the foundation of these new divisions, private property then provided the mechanism by which a natural self-love turned into destructive love of self, now driven by jealousy and pride and capable of turning against other human beings. It became possible to possess and acquire and to judge

oneself against others on the basis of this material wealth. Civil society was the result of division and conflict working against a natural harmony.

The loss of liberty

Rousseau built on this argument in *The Social Contract*, published in 1762. "Man was born free, and he is everywhere in chains," he wrote. While his earlier writings had been resolutely bleak in their opposition to conventional society, *The Social Contract* sought to provide the positive foundations for politics. Like Thomas Hobbes before him, Rousseau saw the emergence of a sovereign power in society as the result of a social contract. People could choose to forfeit their own rights to a government, handing over their full liberty to a sovereign in return for the king—in Hobbes's account—providing security and protection. Hobbes argued that life without a sovereign pushed humanity back to a vile state of nature. By handing over a degree of liberty—in particular, liberty to use force—and swearing obedience, a people could guarantee peace, since the sovereign could end disputes and enforce punishments.

Rousseau rejected this. It was impossible, he thought, for any person or persons to hand over their liberty without also handing over their humanity and therefore destroying morality. A sovereign could not hold absolute authority, since it was impossible for a free man to enslave himself. Establishing a ruler superior to the rest of society transformed humanity's natural equality into a permanent, political inequality. For Rousseau, the social contract envisioned by Hobbes was a form of hoax by the rich against the poor; there was no other way that the poor would agree to a state of affairs in which the social contract preserved inequality.

The societies that existed, then, were not formed in the state of nature, deriving their legitimacy from improvement over that time. Rather, Rousseau argued, they were formed after we had left the state of nature and property rights—with the resultant inequalities—had been established. Once property rights were in place, conflicts could ensue over the distribution of those rights. It was civil society and property that led to war, with the state as the agency through which war could be pursued.

Revising the social contract

What Rousseau offered in *The Social Contract* was the possibility of this dire situation transforming into its opposite. The state and civil society were burdens on individuals, depriving them of a natural freedom. But they could be changed into positive extensions of our freedom, if political institutions and society were organized effectively. The social contract, instead of being a pact written in fear of our evil natures, could be a contract written in the hope of improving ourselves. The state of nature might have been free, but it meant people had no greater ideals than that of their animal appetites. More sophisticated desires could only appear outside the state of nature, in civil society. To achieve this, a new kind of social contract would be written.

Where Hobbes saw law only as a restraint and freedom existing only in the absence of law, Rousseau argued that laws could become an extension of our freedom, provided that those subject to the law also prescribed the law. Freedom could be won within the state rather than against it. To achieve this, the whole people must become sovereign. A legitimate state is one that offers greater freedom than is obtainable in the raw state of nature. To secure that positive freedom, a people must also be equal. In Rousseau's new world, liberty and equality march together rather than in opposition.

Popular sovereignty

In *The Social Contract*, Rousseau laid down, in outline, many of the claims that would underlie the development of the left in politics over subsequent »

Hobbes and Rousseau compared			
	In the state of nature ...	**The social contract ...**	**Freedom ...**
Hobbes	... life is nasty, brutish, and short.	... is necessary to guarantee peace and avoid the state of nature.	... can exist only in the absence of law.
Rousseau	... people are contented, happy creatures.	... preserves inequalities and destroys a person's humanity.	... can be won within the bounds of law.

centuries: a belief that freedom and equality were partners, not enemies; a belief in the ability of law and the state to improve society; and a belief in the people as a sovereign entity from which the state gained its legitimacy. Despite the vehemence of his attack on private property, Rousseau was not a socialist. He believed that the total abolition of private property would pitch liberty and equality into conflict, while a moderately fair distribution of property could enhance freedom. In fact, he later went on to argue for an agrarian republic of small-scale farmers. Nonetheless, Rousseau's ideas were, for the time, dramatically radical. By investing the whole people with sovereignty and by identifying sovereignty with equality, he offered a challenge to an entire existing tradition of Western political thought.

A new contract

Rousseau did not equate this idea of popular sovereignty with democracy as such, fearing that a directly democratic government, requiring all citizens to participate, was uniquely prone to corruption and civil war. Instead, he envisioned sovereignty being invested in popular assemblies capable of delegating the tasks of government—via a new social contract, or a constitution—to an executive. The sovereign people would embody the "general will," an expression of popular assent. Day-to-day government, however, would depend on specific decisions, requiring a "particular will."

It was in this very distinction, Rousseau thought, that conflict between the "general will" and the "particular will" opened up, paving the way for the corruption of the sovereign people. It was this corruption that so marked the world of Rousseau's time, in his view. Instead of acting as a collective, sovereign body, the people were consumed by the pursuit of private interests. In place of the freedom of popular sovereignty, society had pushed people into separate, private spheres of endeavor, whether in the arts, science, or literature or in the division of labor. This numbed people into habitual deference and instilled a spirit of passivity.

To ensure the government was an authentic expression of the popular, general will, Rousseau believed that participation in its assemblies and procedures should be compulsory, removing—as far as possible—the temptations of the private will. But this belief in the necessity of combating private desires is exactly where Rousseau's later, liberal critics have found the deepest fault.

Jean-Jacques Rousseau

Jean-Jacques Rousseau was born in Geneva, Switzerland. The son of a freeman entitled to vote in city elections, he never wavered in his appreciation of Geneva's liberal institutions. Inheriting a large library and a voracious appetite for reading, Rousseau received no formal education. At the age of 15, an introduction to the noblewoman Françoise-Louise de Warens led to his conversion to Catholicism, exile from Geneva, and disownment by his father.

Rousseau began studying in earnest in his 20s and was appointed secretary to the ambassador to Venice in 1743. He left soon after for Paris, where he built a reputation as a controversial essayist. When his books were banned in France and Geneva, he fled briefly to London but soon returned to France, where he spent the rest of his life.

Key works

1754 *Discourse on the Origin and Basis of Inequality Among Men*
1762 *Emile*
1762 *The Social Contract*
1770 *Confessions*

Private vs. general will

The "general will," however desirable in theory, could easily be vested in deeply oppressive arrangements. Not least was the difficulty in actually ascertaining the "general will." The road for an individual or a group claiming to express the general will when merely exercising their own particular wills was clearly wide open. Rousseau, in desiring to make the people sovereign, could be presented as the forefather of totalitarianism. What repressive regime since his time has not attempted to claim the support of "the people"?

Indeed, Rousseau's provisions against factions and divisions among the people—which he, like Machiavelli, saw as undermining the state—could certainly turn into a tyranny of the majority, in which unpopular minorities suffer at the hands of those exercising the "general will." Rousseau's recommendation for dealing with this dilemma was to recognize the inevitability of factions and to multiply them indefinitely—making so many particular wills that no one of them would stand a chance of representing the general will, nor would any one faction be dominant enough to oppose the general will.

States formed under illegitimate social contracts based on the fraud of the powerful were not capable of expressing this will precisely because their subjects were bound to them only by deference to authority, not by mutual assent. However, if the apparent contracts between rulers and ruled were illegitimate, based on a denial of people's sovereignty rather than its expression, it would follow that the people had every right to depose their rulers. That, at least, is how the more

The French Revolution began when an angry mob stormed the Bastille in Paris on July 14, 1789. The medieval fortress and prison was a symbol of royal power.

radical of Rousseau's later followers came to interpret him. Rousseau himself was at best ambiguous on the issue of outright revolt, frequently denouncing violence and civil unrest and urging respect for existing laws.

A revolutionary icon

Rousseau's belief in the sovereignty of the people and the perfectibility of both people and society has had an immense impact. In the French Revolution, the Jacobins adopted him as a figurehead for their own belief in the necessity of a ruthlessly complete, egalitarian transformation of French society. In 1794, he was reinterred in the Panthéon, Paris, as a national hero. Over the next two centuries, Rousseau's work also acted as a touchstone for all those who wished to see society radically overhauled for the common good, from Karl Marx onward.

Similarly, the arguments against Rousseau, during his life and after, have helped to shape both conservative and liberal thought. In 1791, Edmund Burke, one of the founders of modern conservatism, held Rousseau to be almost personally responsible for the French Revolution and what he saw as its excesses. Writing almost 200 years later, the radical-liberal philosopher Hannah Arendt believed the errors in Rousseau's thinking helped to drive the Revolution away from its liberal roots. ∎

> ❝ The mere impulse of appetite is slavery, while obedience to the law we prescribe to ourselves is liberty.
> **Jean-Jacques Rousseau** ❞

72

NO GENERALLY VALID PRINCIPLE OF LEGISLATION CAN BE BASED ON HAPPINESS
IMMANUEL KANT (1724–1804)

IN CONTEXT

IDEOLOGY
Freedom

FOCUS
Personal responsibility

BEFORE
380 BCE Plato argues in the *Republic* that the state's main aim is to ensure the happiness of all people.

1689 In his *Second Treatise on Government*, John Locke states that by a "social contract," people delegate their right of self-protection to government.

AFTER
1851 Pierre-Joseph Proudhon argues that the social contract should be between individuals, not between individuals and government.

1971 In his book *A Theory of Justice*, John Rawls combines Kant's idea of autonomy with Social Choice theory.

Happiness is gained and felt in **different ways** by different people.

This means that it **cannot** be used to **generate fixed principles** that are equally applicable to everyone.

Since **laws** must be agreed as **applicable to all** and reflective of the **common will** …

… **no generally valid principle of legislation can be based on happiness.**

In 1793, the great German philosopher Immanuel Kant wrote an essay entitled "On the Common Saying: 'That may be right in theory, but it does not work in practice,'" which is often now referred to simply as *Theory and Practice*. The essay was written in a year of momentous political change: George Washington became the first president of the US, the German city of Mainz declared itself an independent republic, and the French Revolution reached its height with the execution of King Louis XVI and Marie Antoinette. Kant's essay examined not only political theory and practice, but also the legitimacy of government itself. This was a topic that had become literally a matter of life or death.

King Louis XVI of France was executed in 1793. For Kant, the French Revolution was a warning to all governments that they must rule for the good of all the people.

In stating that "no generally valid principle of legislation can be based on happiness," Kant argues with a position taken by the Greek philosopher Plato some 2,000 years earlier. Kant's essay states that happiness does not work as a basis for law. No one can, nor should, try to define what happiness is for someone else, so a rule based on happiness cannot be applied consistently. "For ... the highly conflicting and variable illusions as to what happiness is," Kant wrote, "... make all fixed principles impossible, so that happiness alone can never be a suitable principle of legislation." What is crucial instead, he believed, is that the state ensures people's freedom within the law "so that each remains free to seek his happiness in whatever way he thinks best, so long as he does not violate the lawful freedom and rights of his fellow subjects at large."

Kant considers what would happen in a society where people live "in a state of nature," free to pursue their own desires. He sees the main problem as a conflict of interests. What do you do, for instance, if your neighbor moves into your house and throws you out, and there are no laws to stop him or give you any redress? Kant claims that a state of nature is a recipe for anarchy, in which disputes cannot be settled peacefully. For this reason, people willingly "abandon the state of nature ... in order to submit to external public and lawful coercion." Kant's position follows on from the English philosopher John Locke's earlier idea of the social contract, which says that people make a contract with the state in which they each freely consent to give up some of their freedom in exchange for the state's protection.

The consent of all

Kant asserts that governments must remember that they govern only by the people's consent—not the consent of a few people, nor even a majority, but of the entire population. What counts is that no one among the population might potentially object to a proposed law. "For if the law is such that a whole people could not possibly agree to it, it is unjust; but if it is at least possible that a people could agree to it, it is our duty to consider the law just."

Kant's idea acts as an important guide for the citizen, as well as the government, because he is also saying that if a government passes a law that you consider wrong, it is still your moral duty to obey it. You might think it is wrong to pay taxes to your government to fund a war, but you should not withhold your taxes because you feel the war is unjust or unnecessary, because "it is at least possible that the war is inevitable and the tax indispensable."

However, for Kant, although subjects have a duty to obey the law, they also have to take individual responsibility for their moral choices. He says that morals have a "categorical imperative." By this, he means that an individual should only follow rules or maxims that they believe should apply to everyone. Each person, he says, must act as though they were lawmakers through each of the moral choices they make. »

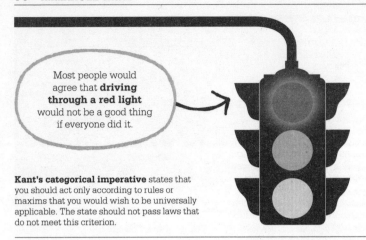

Most people would agree that **driving through a red light** would not be a good thing if everyone did it.

Kant's categorical imperative states that you should act only according to rules or maxims that you would wish to be universally applicable. The state should not pass laws that do not meet this criterion.

The will of the people

At the heart of Kant's philosophy—and applicable to both morality and politics—is the notion of autonomy. This is the idea that the human will is and must be wholly independent. Freedom is not being unbound by any law, but being bound by laws of one's own making. The link between morals and state laws is direct. The legitimacy of both morality and laws is that they are based on the rational desires of the people; the social contract is "based on a coalition of the wills of all private individuals in a nation." State laws must be literally "the will of the people." So, if we agree to be governed, we must rationally agree to obey every law the government passes. By the same token, though, the laws of an external government, such as an occupying force or colonial power, have no legitimacy.

Kant asks whether a government has a role in promoting the happiness of its people. He is clear that since only an individual can decide what makes him happy, any legislation designed to improve people's situation must be based on their actual wishes, not what the government believes will be good for them. Nor should a government compel individuals to make other people happy. It cannot, for example, force you to go and see your grandmother regularly, even though it might be good for the country's general happiness if grandmothers were properly appreciated.

A state without happiness?

Some commentators have argued that Kant does not see happiness as playing any part in government thinking. If this were the case, however, the state would do no more than protect its citizens physically. It would have no business providing education; building things such as hospitals, art galleries, and museums, or roads and railways; or looking after people's welfare in any way. This position may be logically consistent, but it is not a recipe for a state where very many of us would want to live.

All the same, in the last 50 years, some thinkers have used this interpretation of Kant as a basis for the privatization of state industries and for the dismantling of the welfare system on the grounds that it is an infringement of individual freedom to expect people to pay taxes for other people's happiness. However,

 No one can compel me to be happy in accordance with his conception of the welfare of others.
Immanuel Kant

> 66 All right consists solely in the restriction of the freedom of others.
> **Immanuel Kant** 99

other commentators believe this is a misunderstanding of Kant's position. They claim that Kant is not necessarily saying the promotion of happiness should not play a part in the thinking of the state—just that happiness cannot be the sole criterion. In addition, Kant points out that happiness can only be found after a solid constitution, outlining the role of the state, is already in place. In *Theory and Practice*, he says "the doctrine that 'the public welfare is the supreme law of the state' retains its value and authority undiminished; but the public welfare which demands first consideration lies precisely in that legal constitution which guarantees everyone his freedom within the law."

Intervention in Afghanistan may be unpopular with the public in the US and Europe but, according to Kant, this discontent does not give individuals the right to withhold their taxes.

Rights and happiness

Two years before *Theory and Practice*, in an essay entitled *Perpetual Peace*, Kant wrote that governments have two sets of duties: to protect the rights and liberties of the people as a matter of justice, and to promote the happiness of the people,

as long as they can do this without diminishing the rights and freedom of the people.

In recent years, commentators have wondered whether governments have concentrated too much on economics and left happiness out of the picture. Responding to these criticisms, in 2008, France's then-president Nicolas Sarkozy commissioned an inquiry from a team led by US economist Joseph Stiglitz to assess how economic progress should be measured. Their 2009 report called for the use of indicators beyond GDP. ■

Immanuel Kant

The German philosopher Immanuel Kant was born in Königsberg, Prussia (now Kaliningrad in Russia), and lived there his whole life. The fourth of nine children of Lutheran parents, he was educated at a Lutheran school, where he gained a love of Latin but took a strong dislike to religious introspection. At the age of 16, he enrolled as a theology student but soon became fascinated by philosophy, mathematics, and physics.

Kant worked at the University of Königsberg as an unpaid lecturer and sublibrarian for 15 years before becoming a professor of logic and metaphysics at the age of 46. He gained international fame with the publication of his *Critiques* and continued to teach for the rest of his life. He is considered by many to be the greatest thinker of the 18th century.

Key works

1781 *Critique of Pure Reason* (revised 1787)
1788 *Critique of Practical Reason*
1793 *Theory and Practice*

THE PASSIONS OF INDIVIDUALS SHOULD BE SUBJECTED
EDMUND BURKE (1729–1797)

IN CONTEXT

IDEOLOGY
Conservativism

FOCUS
Political tradition

BEFORE
1688 English landowners force the abdication of James II in the Glorious Revolution.

1748 Montesquieu asserts that liberty is maintained in England by a balance of power in different parts of society.

AFTER
1790–1791 Paine's *Rights of Man* and Wollstonecraft's *A Vindication of the Rights of Woman* counter Burke's work.

1867–1894 Marx's *Capital* states that the overthrow of the status quo is inevitable.

1962 Michael Oakeshott upholds the importance of tradition in public institutions.

 The social contract...
is between those who are
living, those who are dead,
and those who are to be born.
Edmund Burke

In 1790, British statesman and political theorist Edmund Burke wrote one of the first and most cogent criticisms of the revolution in France, which had begun the previous year. His pamphlet, entitled "Reflections on the French Revolution," suggested that the passions of individuals should not be allowed to dictate political judgments.

When the revolution began, Burke had been surprised by it but not overtly critical. He was shocked by the ferocity of the insurgents but admired their revolutionary spirit—much as he had admired the American revolutionaries in their quarrel with the English crown. By the time Burke was writing his pamphlet, the revolution had gathered momentum. Food was scarce, and rumors abounded that the king and aristocrats were set to overthrow the Third Estate (the rebellious people). Peasants rose up against their ruling lords, who—in fear for their lives—granted them their freedom through the Declaration of the Rights of Man and of the Citizen. This affirmed that all people had "natural rights" to liberty, property, and security and to resist oppression.

However, the king refused to sanction the Declaration, and on October 5, 1789, crowds of Parisians marched to Versailles to join the peasants in forcing the king and his family back to Paris. For Burke, this was a step too far, and it provoked him to write his critical pamphlet—which

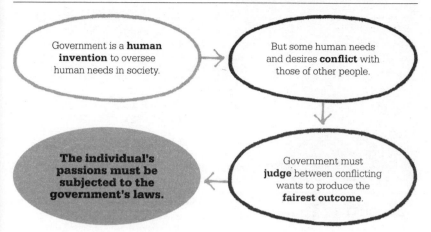

Government is a **human invention** to oversee human needs in society.

But some human needs and desires **conflict** with those of other people.

Government must **judge** between conflicting wants to produce the **fairest outcome**.

The individual's passions must be subjected to the government's laws.

has been seen ever since as the classic rebuttal to would-be revolutionaries.

Government as organism

Burke was a Whig, a member of a British political party that favored the gradual progress of society—as opposed to the Tory party, which strove to maintain the status quo. Burke championed emancipation for Catholics in Ireland and for India from the corrupt East India Company. But, unlike other Whigs, he believed the continuity of government was sacrosanct. In *Reflections*, he argues that government is like a living thing, with a past and a future. We cannot kill it and start anew, as the French revolutionaries aimed to do.

Burke sees government as a complex organism that grows over time into the subtle, living form that it is today. The nuances of its political being—from the behavior of monarchs to the inherited aristocratic codes of behavior—have developed over generations in such an elaborate way that nobody can understand how it all works. The habit of government is so deep-rooted among the ruling class, he says, that they barely have to think about it. Anyone believing they can use their powers of reason to destroy society and build a better one from scratch—such as Enlightenment thinker Jean-Jacques Rousseau—is foolish and arrogant.

Abstract rights

Burke is particularly damning of the Enlightenment concept of natural rights. They may be all very well in theory, he says, but that's where the problem lies: "their abstract perfection is their practical defect." Also, for Burke, a theoretical right to a good or service is of no use whatsoever if there »

John Bull is tempted by the devil, who hangs from the Tree of Liberty, symbolizing the fear of French revolutionary zeal spreading to England at the time of Burke's writings.

Edmund Burke

Born in Dublin, Ireland, in 1729, Burke was raised as a Protestant, while his sister, Juliana, was raised a Catholic. He initially trained as a lawyer but soon gave up law to become a writer. In 1756, he published *A Vindication of Natural Society*, a satire of Tory leader Lord Bolingbroke's views on religion. Soon after, he became private secretary to Lord Rockingham, the Whig prime minister.

In 1774, Burke became a Member of Parliament, later losing his seat due to the unpopularity of his views on the emancipation of Catholics. His fight for the abolition of capital punishment earned him a reputation as a progressive. However, his criticism of the French Revolution caused a split with the radical wing of his Whig party, and today he is remembered more for his conservative philosophy than his liberal views.

Key works

1756 *A Vindication of Natural Society*
1770 *Thoughts on the Cause of the Present Discontents*
1790 *Reflections on the Revolution in France*

is no means to procure it. There is no end to what people may reasonably claim as rights. In reality, rights are simply what people want, and it is the government's task to mediate between the wants of people. Some wants can even include restraint on the wants of others.

It is a fundamental rule of any civil society, Burke says, "that no man should be judge in his own cause." To live in a free and just society, a man must give up his right to determine many things he deems essential. In claiming that "the passions of individuals should be subjected," Burke means that society must control the unruly will of the individual for the good of the rest. If everyone is allowed to behave as he wishes, expressing every passion and whim, the result is chaos. In fact, not just individuals, but the masses as a whole must be so constrained "by a power out of themselves."

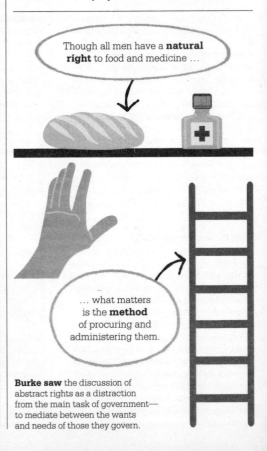

Though all men have a **natural right** to food and medicine ...

... what matters is the **method** of procuring and administering them.

Burke saw the discussion of abstract rights as a distraction from the main task of government—to mediate between the wants and needs of those they govern.

This refereeing role requires "a deep knowledge of human nature and human necessities" and is so complex that theoretical rights are a distraction.

Habit and prejudice

Burke was skeptical of individual rights, arguing instead for tradition and habit. He viewed government as an inheritance to be carried forward safely into the future and made a distinction between England's Glorious Revolution of 1688 and France's ongoing turmoil. The English revolution, which replaced the Catholic-leaning King James II with the Protestant William and Mary, was about preserving the status quo against a wayward monarch, not fabricating a new government, which would fill Burke with "disgust and horror."

Burke defended an unthinking emotional response to respect the king and parliament as "the general bank and capital of nations." He saw this as far superior to the vagaries of individual reason, but regarded prejudice as an age-old wisdom that could produce a fast, automatic response in emergencies that left the rational man hesitating.

The consequences of ignoring these traditions may be dire, Burke warned. New men entering the political fray would not be able to run an existing government, let alone a new one. Struggles between factions trying to step into the power vacuum would inevitably lead to bloodshed and terror—and a chaos so consuming that the military would have to take over.

The Burke revolution

Burke's prediction of both the Terror in the French Revolution, which occurred in 1793 and 1794, and the rise of Napoleon Bonaparte in 1799, earned him a reputation as something of a seer. His arguments appealed to those on the right but were also a surprise to those on the left. Thomas Jefferson, then living in France as a US diplomat, wrote, "The Revolution in France does not astonish me as much as the revolution in Mr. Burke." In England, Thomas Paine immediately wrote *The Rights of Man*—published in 1791—to challenge Burke's argument against natural rights.

Napoleon Bonaparte swept to power in 1799, fulfilling Edmund Burke's 1790 prediction that a military dictatorship would follow the revolutionary overthrow of the monarchy in France.

The power of property

Burke believed that society's stability was underpinned by inherited property— the massive inherited properties of the landowning aristocracy. Only such rich landowners had the power, self-interest, and inherited political skill, Burke asserted, to prevent the monarchy from overreaching itself. The great size of their landholdings also acted as a natural protection for the lesser properties around them. In any case, he argued, the redistribution from the few to the many could only ever result in "inconceivably small" gains.

Although Napoleon was eventually defeated, the revolutions that rolled on through Europe long after Burke's death gave his ideas a special place in the hearts of those frightened by the uprisings. Burke's plea for the continuity of government and society seemed to some to be a beacon of sanity in a mad world. However, for Karl Marx—who was particularly critical of Burke's ideas on property—and many others, Burke's defense of inequality was unacceptable. Burke argued persuasively against the trashing of tradition, but according to his critics, this leads ultimately to the defense of societies in which the majority are kept in a life of servitude, with no prospect of betterment and no say in their future. Burke's defense of prejudice, intended as a call for sympathy for people's natural inclinations, can end up as an argument for blind bigotry. His assertion that the passions of individuals should be subjected is potentially a justification for censorship, the persecution of dissenters, and a police state. ∎

RIGHTS DEPENDENT ON PROPERTY ARE THE MOST PRECARIOUS
THOMAS PAINE (1737–1809)

IN CONTEXT

IDEOLOGY
Republicanism

FOCUS
Universal male suffrage

BEFORE
508 BCE Democracy in Athens gives all male citizens a vote.

1647 A radical part of Oliver Cromwell's New Model Army calls for universal male suffrage and an end to monarchy.

1762 Jean-Jacques Rousseau publishes *The Social Contract*, arguing that sovereignty lies with the whole people.

AFTER
1839–1848 Chartism, a mass movement in Britain, calls for universal male suffrage.

1871 A newly united German Empire grants universal male suffrage.

1917–1919 As World War I ends, democratic republics replace monarchies across Europe.

Current rights to vote depend on **ownership of property**.

⬇

Property owners **abuse their position of privilege** to run society for their **own benefit**.

⬇

This breeds resentment among the poor, who will **rise up against the rich** if their needs are neglected.

⬇

Rights dependent on property are the most precarious.

⬇

Rights should be granted without property qualification.

The English Revolution, which reached the peak of its radicalism with the trial and execution of King Charles I in 1649, had fizzled out by the end of the 17th century. The "Glorious Revolution" of 1688 had seen the restoration of the monarchy, now subordinate to Parliament, and the stabilization of the British state. No formal constitution was written, and the brief experiment with a republic under Oliver Cromwell was over. The new government was a hybrid made of

When we are planning
for posterity, we ought
to remember that virtue
is not hereditary.
Thomas Paine

a corrupt and unrepresentative Lower House in the Commons, a corrupt and unelected Upper House in the Lords, and a monarch who was still nominally head of state.

The 1689 Bill of Rights that set out the parameters for the new government was a compromise that satisfied few, least of all those most obviously excluded from it: the Irish, Catholics, and nonconformists; the poor and the artisans; even the more prosperous middle classes and employees of the state. It was from this milieu that Thomas Paine emerged, after emigrating to America in 1774. In a series of incendiary and wildly popular pamphlets, he sought to reclaim arguments for democracy and republicanism that had been made during Cromwell's time.

The case for democracy

In *Common Sense*, published anonymously in Philadelphia in 1776, Paine made the case for a radical break by Britain's North American colonists from both the British Empire and constitutional monarchy. Like Hobbes and Rousseau before him, he argued that people come to form natural attachments to each other, creating a society from individuals. As these attachments of family, friendship, or trade become more complex, they in turn create a need for regulation. These regulations are systematized into laws, and a government is erected to create and enforce those laws. These laws are intended to act for the people, but there are too many people to make collective decisions. Democracy is required to elect representatives.

Democracy, Paine held, was the most natural way to balance the needs of society with those of government. Voting would act as the regulating instrument between society and government, allowing society to shape government so that it more closely corresponded to social needs. Institutions such as monarchy were unnatural, since the hereditary principle stood apart from society as a whole and monarchs could act in their own interests. Even a mixed state with a constitutional monarchy, as advocated by John Locke, would be dangerous, since a monarch could easily obtain more power and circumvent laws. Paine believed it was better to do away with the monarch entirely.

It followed that America's best course of action in its war with the British Empire was to refuse any compromise on the issue of the monarchy. Only with full independence could a democratic society be built. Paine's clear and unequivocal call for a democratic republic was an immediate success in the midst of the Revolutionary War against the British Empire. Returning to England in 1787, he visited France 2 years later and became a firm supporter of the French Revolution.

Reflections on revolution

On returning from France, Paine had a rude awakening. Edmund Burke, a politician and one of the founders of modern conservative thought, had strongly supported the rights of American colonies to independence. Burke and Paine had been on friendly terms since Paine's arrival back in England, but Burke had ferociously denounced the French Revolution, claiming in his 1790 *Reflections on the Revolution* in France that by its »

The inattentive judges in William Hogarth's satirical *The Bench* (1758) are portrayed as members of an idle, incompetent, and venal judiciary that has little regard for society's rights.

The French National Assembly has its roots in the French Revolution's National Convention, which was the country's first governing assembly to be elected by universal male suffrage.

had published the royal proclamation against "seditious libel"—the writing and printing of texts that attacked the state. Paine, denouncing this and other abuses as a new tyranny, called for an elected National Convention to draft a new, republican constitution for England. This was a direct call for revolution in all but name, taking France's republican National Convention as its model. Paine had returned to France shortly before the *Address* was published, and in his absence was found guilty of seditious libel.

The argument in the *Address* is brief but tackles Burke head on. Although England's Bill of Rights of 1689 gave guarantees about the rights all subjects would enjoy in a constitutional monarchy, it was open to abuse. Paine detailed some of the most obnoxious instances of corruption, but he wanted to go further and tackle the system

radicalism it threatened the very order of society. Burke viewed society as an organic whole, not amenable to sudden change. The Revolutionary War and Britain's "Glorious Revolution" did not directly threaten long-established rights but merely corrected some clear deformities in the system. In particular, they did not threaten the rights of property. But the situation in France, with its violent overthrow of the *ancien regime*, was clearly different.

Burke's opposition caused Paine to defend his position. He replied with *The Rights of Man*, printed in early 1791. Despite official censorship, it became the best-known and widest-circulated of all English defenses of the revolution in France. Paine argued for the rights of every generation to remake its political and social institutions as it saw fit, not bound by existing authority. A hereditary monarch had no claim to superiority over this right. Rights, not property, were the only hereditary principle, transmitted across the generations. A second part to the pamphlet, published in 1792, argued for a major program of social welfare. By the end of the year, the two volumes had sold 200,000 copies.

An end to monarchy

Under threat of prosecution, and with "Church and King" mobs burning his figure in effigy, Paine offered a still more radical step. *His Letter Addressed to the Addressers on the Late Proclamation* was written against "the numerous rotten boroughs and corporation addresses" that

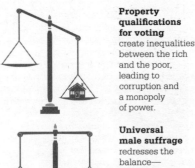

Property qualifications for voting create inequalities between the rich and the poor, leading to corruption and a monopoly of power.

Universal male suffrage redresses the balance— the rights of the rich and the poor must then be considered in the creation of policies.

itself. By defending hereditary property as the supreme law, this system drove the corruption and abuse. The tyranny of William Pitt's government was a direct result of its defense of property. At the top of the regime was a hereditary monarch, and Parliament acted merely as a defense of Crown and property. Reform of the corrupt Parliament was not enough: the whole system had to be transformed, from the top down.

Universal male suffrage

Paine asserted that sovereignty should not lie with the monarch, but with the people, who have an absolute right to make or unmake laws and governments as they see fit. The existing system contained no mechanism to allow the people to change the government. It was therefore necessary, Paine argued, to sidestep the system by electing a new assembly—a National Convention, as in France.

Paine attempted to popularize an argument made by Rousseau: that the "general will" of the people should be sovereign in a nation, and that with transparent and fair elections to the Convention, private interests and corrupt practices would be squeezed out. Universal male suffrage would determine the delegates to the Convention, and these delegates would be charged with drafting a new constitution for Britain. It was

England's property qualification for voting that Paine held most responsible for the corruption and venality of the electoral system. Only in a system where the rights of both rich and poor were equally considered would each respect the other, and neither seek to rob the other.

A legacy for reform

Paine's short pamphlet never quite achieved the success of either *Common Sense* or *The Rights of Man*, but the radical argument presented in the *Address*—for a republic, a new constitution, and a National Convention elected by universal male suffrage—formed the core of reformers' demands in Britain for the next 50 years. The London Corresponding Society, from the 1790s onward, called for a National Convention; the Chartists of the 1840s actually held a National Convention, which thoroughly alarmed the authorities; and the hated property qualification for voting was eventually removed in the 1867 Second Reform Act.

It was in Paine's adopted countries of America and France that his ideas had the most impact—perhaps especially in the United States, where he is credited as one of the Founding Fathers of independence and the Constitution and where his writings swayed thousands toward the cause of democracy and republicanism. ∎

Thomas Paine

Thomas Paine was born in Thetford, England. He emigrated to America in 1774, having lost his job as a tax collector after

agitating for better pay and conditions. With a recommendation from Benjamin Franklin, he became editor of a local magazine in Pennsylvania.

Common Sense was published in 1776, selling 100,000 copies in 3 months among a colonial population of 2 million. In 1781, Paine helped negotiate large sums from the French king for the Revolutionary War. Returning to London in 1790, and inspired by the French Revolution, he wrote *The Rights of Man*, which led to a charge of

seditious libel. After fleeing to France, he was elected to the National Convention there and avoided execution during the Terror. He returned to America in 1802 at President Jefferson's invitation and died 7 years later in New York.

Key works

1776 *Common Sense*
1791 *The Rights of Man*
1792 *Letter Addressed to the Addresses on the Late Proclamation*

ALL MEN ARE CREATED EQUAL
THOMAS JEFFERSON (1742–1826)

IN CONTEXT

IDEOLOGY
Nationalism

FOCUS
Universal rights

BEFORE
1649 England's King Charles I is tried and executed for acting "against the public interest, common right, liberty, justice, and peace of the people."

1689 John Locke refutes the divine right of kings and insists sovereignty lies in the people.

AFTER
1789 The French Revolution's *Declaration of the Rights of Man and Citizen* asserts that all men "are born and remain free with equal rights."

1948 The UN adopts the *Universal Declaration of Human Rights*.

1998 DNA evidence suggests that Jefferson may have fathered the children of his slave Sally Hemings.

T he American Declaration of Independence is one of the most famous texts in the English language. Its assertion that all people hold the right to "Life, Liberty, and the pursuit of Happiness" still helps to define how we think about a good life and the conditions that make it possible.

The Declaration was drafted during the Revolutionary War, a revolt of the 13 American colonies against rule by the British. By 1763, Britain had won a series of wars against France for possession of these colonies and was now taxing them to offset the huge cost of the wars. Parliament did not have a single representative from the American colonies, yet it was making decisions on their behalf. Protests in Boston against taxation without representation led to British military intervention, which spiraled into war. At the First Continental Congress of 1774, the colonists demanded their own parliament. A year later, at the Second Congress, with King George III spurning their demands, they pushed for total independence.

From Old World to New

Thomas Jefferson, a delegate to the Second Continental Congress, was appointed to draft a declaration of independence. He was a key figure in the American Enlightenment, the intellectual movement that was a prelude to the revolution.

Colonists from Europe could look back to the Old World and see absolute monarchies and corrupt oligarchies presiding over squalid, unequal societies, which were often at war, with religious tolerance and minimal freedoms thrown aside. Jefferson and other intellectuals in the New World looked to thinkers such as English liberal philosopher John Locke, who stressed the "natural rights" of humanity, and the need for government to hold to a "social contract" with the governed.

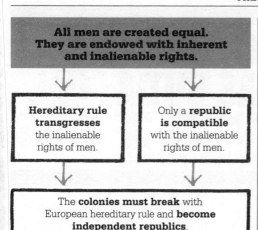

All men are created equal. They are endowed with inherent and inalienable rights.

Hereditary rule transgresses the inalienable rights of men.

Only a **republic is compatible** with the inalienable rights of men.

The **colonies must break** with European hereditary rule and **become independent republics**.

Thomas Jefferson

Thomas Jefferson was born in Shadwell, Virginia. He was a plantation owner, and later a lawyer, who became the third president of the United States in 1801. A key figure in the Enlightenment, he was appointed as the principal author of the Declaration of Independence in June 1776 while serving as a delegate from Virginia to the Second Continental Congress.

As a planter, Jefferson owned well over 100 slaves, and he struggled to reconcile this position with his beliefs in equality. His text denouncing slavery in the original draft of the Declaration was excised by the Congress. Following victory over Britain in 1783, Jefferson's subsequent move to ban slavery in the new republic was defeated by a single vote in Congress.

After losing the presidency in 1808, Jefferson remained active in public life, founding the University of Virginia in 1819. He died on July 4, 1826.

Key works

1776 *Declaration of Independence*
1785 *Notes on the State of Virginia*

While Locke had defended Britain's constitutional monarchy, Jefferson and others took a far more radical message from his writings. To Locke's support for private property and freedom of thought, Jefferson added republicanism. In this, he was highly influenced by Thomas Paine, whose pamphlet *Common Sense* early in 1776 popularized the arguments for a republic. The Declaration of Independence marked a break not only with colonialism, but with all hereditary rule, which was held to be incompatible with the notion that "all men are created equal" and to transgress their "inalienable rights."

Signed on July 4, 1776, by representatives of 13 states, the full text still retains its original force in its denunciation of the arbitrary rule of monarchs. It helped shape the French Revolution and, from Gandhi to Ho Chi Minh, inspired leaders of future independence movements. ∎

Jefferson presented the first draft of the Declaration of Independence to the Congress. The final version was read aloud in the streets in the hope that it would inspire men to sign up to fight.

GOVERNMENT HAS BUT A CHOICE OF EVILS
JEREMY BENTHAM (1748–1832)

IN CONTEXT

IDEOLOGY
Utilitarianism

FOCUS
Public policy

BEFORE
1748 Montesquieu asserts in *The Spirit of the Laws* that liberty in England is maintained by the balance between the power of different parts of society.

1748 David Hume suggests that good and bad can be seen in terms of usefulness.

1762 Jean-Jacques Rousseau argues in *The Social Contract* that every law the people have not ratified in person is not a law.

AFTER
1861 John Stuart Mill warns of the "tyranny of the majority" and states that government should only interfere with individual liberties if they cause harm to others.

The idea that government has but a choice of evils runs right through the work of English philosopher Jeremy Bentham from as early as 1769, when he was a young trainee lawyer, to the end of his life 50 years later, when he had become a hugely influential figure in British and European political thought.

The year 1769, Bentham wrote half a century later, was "a most interesting year." At the time, he was reading the works of philosophers such as Montesquieu, Beccaria, and Voltaire—all forward-thinking leaders of the continental Enlightenment. But it was the work of two British writers—David Hume and Joseph Priestley—that set off great sparks of revelation in young Bentham's mind.

Morality and happiness
In *An Enquiry Concerning Human Understanding* (1748), Hume says that one way to distinguish good and bad is by usefulness. A good quality is only really good if it is put to good use. But for the sharp, no-nonsense lawyer Bentham, this was still too vague. What if you consider usefulness, or "utility," to be the only moral quality? What if you decide whether an action is good or not entirely by its usefulness, by whether it produces a good effect—crucially, whether it makes people happier or not?

Looked at in this way, all morality is at its core about creating happiness and avoiding misery. Any other description is an unnecessary elaboration or, worse, a deliberate veiling of the truth. Religions are often guilty of this obfuscation, Bentham says, but so, too, are those high-flown political idealists who assert people's rights and so miss the point that it is all really about making people happy.

This is true, Bentham argues, not just on a personal and moral level, but on a public and political level, too. And if both private morality and public policy are reduced to this simple aim, everyone can agree—and men and women of good will can work together to achieve the same end.

So what, then, is a happy, useful outcome? Bentham is a realist and accepts that even the best action produces some bad along with the good. If one child has two candies, another has one, and a third has none, the fairest action for the children's parents would be to take a candy from the child with two and give it to the one with none. This still leads to one of the children losing a candy. Similarly, any government action will work to the advantage of some but the disadvantage of others. For Bentham, such actions should be judged according to the following criterion: an action is good if it produces more pleasure than pain.

The greatest good

Reading Priestley's *An Essay on the First Principles of Government* (1768) sparked the second great revelation of 1769 for Bentham. He draws from Priestley the idea that a good act is one that produces the greatest happiness for the greatest number. In other words, it's all about arithmetic. Politics can be simplified to one question: Does it make more people happy than it makes sad? Bentham developed a mathematical method, which he called "felicific calculus," to work out whether a given government act produced more happiness or less.

This is where the idea that "government has but a choice of evils" comes in. Any law is a restriction on human liberty, argues Bentham—an interference with

Any law is a **restriction** on human freedom and human happiness.

↓

So any law is an **evil**.

↓

Government has but a choice of evils.

↓

But a law may produce **more good** than harm.

↓

This means that a **good law** is a **necessary evil**.

the individual's freedom to act completely as he or she wants. Therefore, every law is necessarily an evil. But doing nothing may also be an evil. The decision rests on the arithmetic. A new law can be justified if and only if it does more good than harm. He likens government to a doctor who should only intervene if he is sure the treatment will do more good than »

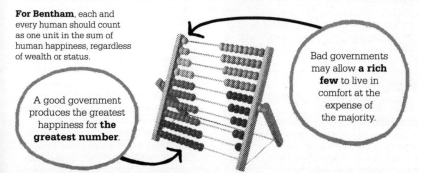

For Bentham, each and every human should count as one unit in the sum of human happiness, regardless of wealth or status.

A good government produces the greatest happiness for **the greatest number**.

Bad governments may allow **a rich few** to live in comfort at the expense of the majority.

harm—an apt analogy for Bentham's time, when doctors frequently made patients more ill by bleeding them, draining some of their blood in an attempt to clear out disease. When deciding the punishment for a criminal, for instance, the lawmaker must take into account not just the direct effects of the mischief, but the secondary effects, too—a robbery does not just harm the victim but creates alarm in the community. The punishment must also make the robber worse off so that it outweighs any profit he gained by committing the crime.

Hands-off government

Bentham extended his idea into the field of economics, endorsing the view of Scottish economist Adam Smith, who argued that markets work best without government restrictions. Since Bentham's time, many people have used his warning to lawmakers as a justification for "hands-off" government—for scaling back bureaucracy and for deregulation. His views have even been used as an argument in favor of a conservative government that avoids introducing new laws, especially new laws that try to change people's behavior.

However, Bentham's arguments also have far more radical implications.

Inequalities in society mean that a rich minority exists alongside the poor. For Bentham, this is morally unacceptable, and a government's role is to ensure that a balance is reached.

Governments cannot stand still until everyone is infinitely happy, which will never happen. This means there is always work to do. Just as most people continue to search for happiness throughout their lives, governments must constantly strive to make ever more people happy.

Bentham's moral arithmetic highlights not just the benefits of happiness, but its cost. It makes it clear that for someone to be happy, someone else may have to pay a price. For a very rich few to live in comfort, for instance, many others must live in discomfort. Each person only counts as one unit in Bentham's sum of human happiness. This means that this imbalance is immoral, and it is every government's duty to continually work to address the situation.

Pragmatic democracy

So how can rulers be persuaded to spread the wealth when that would seem to make them less happy? The answer, Bentham argues, is more democracy, meaning the extension of the franchise. If rulers fail to increase human happiness for the greatest number, they get voted out at the next election. In a democracy, politicians have a vested interest in increasing happiness for the majority to ensure they are reelected. While other thinkers, from Rousseau to Paine, were pushing for democracy as a natural right—without which a man is denied his humanity—Bentham argued for it entirely pragmatically: as a means to an end. The idea of natural laws and rights is, to Bentham, nothing more than "nonsense on stilts."

With their costs and benefits, profit and loss, Bentham's arguments for extending voting rights appealed to hard-nosed British industrialists and businessmen— the rising new power base in the Industrial Revolution—in a way that no amount of idealism and talk of man's natural rights could. Bentham's down-to-earth, "utilitarian" arguments helped shift Britain toward parliamentary reform and liberalism in the 1830s. Today, a Benthamite approach is a useful everyday benchmark for public policy decisions, encouraging governments to consider whether each policy is, on balance, good for the majority of people.

Jeremy Bentham

Jeremy Bentham was born in Houndsditch, London, in 1748, to a family who were financially comfortable. He was expected to become a lawyer, and he went to Oxford University when just 12, graduating to train as an attorney in London at 15. But the chicanery of the legal profession depressed him, and he became more interested in legal science and philosophy.

Bentham retired to London's Westminster to write, and for the next 40 years, he turned out works of commentary and ideas on legal and moral matters. He began by criticizing the leading legal authority William Blackstone for his assumption that there was nothing essentially wrong with Britain's laws, then he went on to develop a complete theory of morals and policy. This was the basis of the utilitarian ethic that had already come to dominate British political life by the time of his death in 1832.

Key works

1776 *Fragment on Government*
1780 *Introduction to Principles of Morals and Legislation*
1787 *Panopticon*

Hard facts

However, there are some real problems with Bentham's ideal-free recipe of utilitarianism. The English author Charles Dickens hated the new breed of utilitarians that followed Bentham and satirized them mercilessly in his novel *Hard Times* (1854), depicting them as killjoys stomping on the imagination and sapping the human spirit with their insistence on reducing life to hard facts. It is not a picture that Bentham, a deeply empathetic man, would necessarily recognize, but it was a clear reference to his reduction of every issue to arithmetic.

One recurring criticism of Bentham's idea is that it encourages scapegoating. The greatest happiness principle can permit huge injustices if the overall effect is general happiness. After a terrible terrorist bombing, for instance, the police are under great pressure to find the perpetrators. The general population will be much happier and the alarm will subside if the police arrest anyone who appears to fit the bill, even if they are not actually the guilty party (provided there are no further attacks).

Following Bentham's argument, some critics claim, it is morally acceptable to punish the innocent if their suffering is outweighed by an increase in the happiness of the general population. Supporters of Bentham can get around this problem by saying that the general population would be unhappy to live in a society in which innocent people are made into scapegoats. But that issue only arises if the population finds out the truth; if the targeting of scapegoats is kept secret, it would appear justified according to Bentham's logic. ∎

Utilitarian arguments have been used to justify the prosecution of innocent people—such as Gerry Conlon, accused of IRA bombings—on the basis that the majority is made happier.

THE PEOPLE HAVE A RIGHT TO KEEP AND BEAR ARMS
JAMES MADISON (1751–1836)

IN CONTEXT

IDEOLOGY
Federalism

FOCUS
Armed citizenry

BEFORE
44–43 BCE Cicero argues in his *Philippics* that people must be able to defend themselves, just as wild beasts do in nature.

1651 Thomas Hobbes argues in *Leviathan* that by nature, men have a right to defend themselves forcefully.

AFTER
1968 After the assassinations of Robert Kennedy and Martin Luther King, federal restrictions on gun ownership are introduced.

2008 The Supreme Court decides that the Second Amendment protects an individual's right to keep a gun at home for self-defense.

Even as the Founding Fathers were putting the finishing touches on the US Constitution in 1788, demands came for the addition of a Bill of Rights. The idea that the people have a right to keep and bear arms appears as the Second Amendment in this bill with the words, "the right of the people to keep and bear Arms, shall not be infringed." The exact wording is crucial, since it has become the focus of modern debate over gun control and how much freedom US citizens have by law to own and carry guns.

The architect of the Bill of Rights was Virginia-born James Madison, who was also one of the main creators of the Constitution itself. This makes him possibly unique among political thinkers in that he was able to put his ideas directly into practice—ideas that are still, two centuries later, the basis of the political way of life of the world's most powerful nation. Indeed, in later becoming president, Madison climbed to the very peak of the political edifice that he had himself created.

The Bill of Rights is considered by some as the very embodiment of the Enlightenment thinking on natural rights, which began with John Locke and culminated in Thomas Paine's inspirational call for the Rights of Man. Though the latter stressed the importance of democracy (the universal right to vote) as a principle in his treatise, Madison's intentions were more pragmatic. They were rooted in the tradition of English politics—where parliament sought to prevent the sovereign from overreaching his power rather than striving to protect basic universal freedoms.

Defense from the majority
As he admitted in a letter to Thomas Jefferson, the only reason Madison put forward the Bill of Rights was to satisfy the demands of others. He personally believed that the establishment of the Constitution

Shay's Rebellion in 1786–1787 saw a rebel militia seize Massachusetts's courthouse. Quashed by government forces, it encouraged the principle of strong government in the Constitution.

by itself—and therefore the creation of proper government—should have been enough to guarantee that fundamental rights are protected. In fact, he admitted that the addition of a Bill of Rights implied that the Constitution was flawed and could not protect these rights in itself. There was also a risk that defining specific rights would impair protection of rights that were not specified. Moreover, Madison acknowledged that bills of rights had not had a happy history in the United States.

But there were also strong reasons why a bill of rights might be a good idea. Like most of the Founding Fathers, Madison was nervous of the power of the majority. "A democracy," wrote Thomas Jefferson, "is nothing more than mob rule, where fifty-one percent of the people may take away the rights of the other forty-nine." A bill of rights might help protect the minority against the mass of the people.

"In our Governments," Madison wrote, "the real power lies in the majority of the Community, and the invasion of private rights is chiefly to be apprehended, not from acts of Government contrary to the sense of its constituents, but from acts in which the Government is the mere instrument of the major number of the constituents." In other words, the Bill of Rights was actually intended to protect property owners against the democratic instincts of the majority.

Militias legitimized

Madison also had a simple political reason for creating the Bill of Rights. He knew he would not gain support for the Constitution from the delegates of some individual states if he did not. After all, the Revolutionary War had been fought to challenge the tyranny of centralized power, so these delegates were wary of a new central government. They would only ratify the Constitution if they had some guarantee of protection against it. So rights were not natural laws, but the states' (and property owners') protection against the federal government. »

> The central, federal government may be swayed by the **power of the majority**.

> Driven by the majority, the federal government may use a standing army to **enforce its will** on states.

> People in each state must be able to form militias to **defend themselves** against an oppressive federal army.

> **The right of the people to keep and bear arms shall not be infringed.**

Though Madison believed that the existence of the Constitution would ensure that basic rights were protected under a federal government, he formulated the Bill of Rights as an extra measure to counteract the power of the majority in a democracy.

> The Bill of Rights acts as a **protective barrier** against these incursions …

> The majority can **trample** on the rights and property of the minority in a democracy.

> … so that the **rights and property** of the minority are protected.

This is where the Second Amendment came in. Madison ensured that states or citizens would not be deprived of the ability to protect themselves by forming a militia against an overbearing national government, just as they had done against the British crown. Such a situation envisioned a community banding together to resist an army of oppression. The Second Amendment actually says in its final version, "A well regulated Militia, being necessary to the security of a free State, the right of the people to keep and bear Arms, shall not be infringed." The amendment, then, was about a militia and "the people" (in other words, the community) protecting the state, not people as individuals.

Individual self-defense

Madison was not talking about individuals carrying arms to defend themselves against individual criminal acts. Yet that is how his words in the Second Amendment have come to be used, and many Americans now claim that the right to carry guns is enshrined in the Constitution—challenging any move to institute gun controls as unconstitutional.

Attempts to overturn this interpretation in the courts have repeatedly met with failure, with the insistence that the Constitution upholds citizens' rights to

bear arms in defense of themselves, as well as the state. Many argue even further that, regardless of Madison's intentions, owning and carrying a gun should be considered a basic freedom.

A century before Madison's bill, English philosopher John Locke, in identifying the right to self-defense as a natural right, took his cue from an imagined "natural" time before civilization. Just as a wild animal will defend itself with violence if cornered, so, Locke argues, may humans. The implication is that government is in some way an unnatural imposition from which people need protection. In retrospect, some commentators have put a Lockean gloss on the Bill of Rights and assume that it is confirming self-defense by violent means as a natural, inalienable right.

However, it seems possible that Madison and his fellow Founding Fathers were more in tune with Scottish philosopher David Hume's view of government than with

 The ultimate authority… resides in the people alone.
James Madison

Locke's. Hume is too pragmatic to pay much attention to the idea of a natural time of freedom before rights were curtailed by civilization. For Hume, people want government because it makes sense, and rights are something negotiated and agreed upon, like every other aspect of law. So there is nothing fundamental about the right to bear arms—it is simply a matter that people generally agree about or not. According to Hume, freedoms and rights are just examples of tenets on which people concur—and perhaps decide mutually to enshrine in law to ensure that they are adhered to. Taking this view, there is no fundamental principle at stake in the right to bear arms—rather, it is a consensus. And consensus does not necessarily require a democratic majority.

Lasting controversy

Gun control remains a hot issue in the US, with powerful lobbies—such as the National Rifle Association (NRA)—campaigning against any restrictions on gun ownership at all. Those against gun control appear to have the upper hand, with most states allowing people to own firearms. Still, there are very few states where gun ownership is entirely unregulated, and there are arguments over whether, for instance, people should be allowed to carry concealed guns. The high level of gun crime in the

Natural self-defense as used by wild animals against attack is cited by proponents of natural law to justify the right of an individual to defend themselves by any means.

US, and the increasing frequency of mass murders—such as the shooting in a movie theater in Aurora, Colorado, on July 2012—have led many to question if unrestricted ownership of firearms is appropriate in a nation that is no longer a frontier state.

It is remarkable that Madison's Bill of Rights is still, with only a few changes, at the heart of the US political system. Some, maybe even Madison himself, would argue that a good government would have protected these rights without need of a bill. Yet the Bill of Rights remains perhaps the most powerful meld of political theory and practice ever devised. ∎

James Madison

James Madison Jr. was born in Port Conway, Virginia. His father owned Montpelier, the largest tobacco plantation in Orange County, worked by 100 or more slaves. In 1769, Madison enrolled at the College of New Jersey, now Princeton University. During the Revolutionary War, he served in the Virginia legislature and was the protégé of Thomas Jefferson. At 29, he became the youngest delegate to the Continental Congress in 1780, and gained respect for his ability to draft laws and build coalitions. Madison's draft—the Virginia Plan—formed the basis of the US Constitution. He cowrote the 85 *Federalist* *Papers* to explain the theory of the Constitution and ensure its ratification. Madison was one of the leaders of the emerging Democratic-Republican party. He followed Jefferson to become the fourth US president in 1809, and held the office for two terms.

Key works

1787 *United States Constitution*
1788 *Federalist Papers*
1789 *The Bill of Rights*

THE MOST RESPECTABLE WOMEN ARE THE MOST OPPRESSED
MARY WOLLSTONECRAFT (1759–1797)

IN CONTEXT

IDEOLOGY
Feminism

FOCUS
Women's emancipation

BEFORE
1589 *Her Protection for Women*
by English novelist Jane Anger
castigates men for seeing women
merely as objects of sexual desire.

1791 In *Declaration of the Rights of
Woman*, French playwright Olympe
de Gouges writes, "Woman is born
free and remains equal to man."

AFTER
1840s In the US and the UK, women's
property is legally protected from
their husbands.

1869 In *The Subjection of Women*,
John Stuart Mill argues that women
should be given the right to vote.

1893 In New Zealand, women
are given the vote—one of the
first countries to do so.

P ublished in 1792, British writer Mary
Wollstonecraft's *A Vindication of
the Rights of Woman* is seen as
one of the first great feminist tracts. It was
written at a time of intellectual and political
ferment. The Enlightenment had established
the rights of men at the center of political
debate, which culminated in France in
the Revolution against the monarchy
in the very year that Wollstonecraft wrote
A Vindication. Yet few talked about the
position of women in society. In fact,
French philosopher Jean-Jacques Rousseau,
an ardent advocate of political freedom,
argued in his work *Émile* that women
should only be educated to make them
good wives able to give pleasure to men.

Freedom to work
Wollstonecraft wrote *A Vindication* to show
how wrong Rousseau was about women.
The rejuvenation of the world could only
happen, she argued, if women were happy,
as well as men. Yet women were trapped by a
web of expectations due to their dependence
on men. They were forced to trade on their
looks and to connive to win the affections of
a man. Respectable women—women who
did not indulge in this game of seduction—
were put at a huge disadvantage.
  Wollstonecraft argued that women
needed the freedom to earn a living,
granting them autonomy from men. To
achieve this freedom required education.
To those who argued that women were

 How much more respectable is
the woman who earns her own
bread by fulfilling any duty, than
the most accomplished beauty.
Mary Wollstonecraft

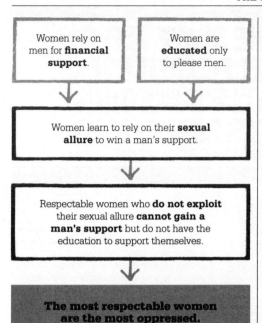

Women rely on men for **financial support**.

Women are **educated** only to please men.

Women learn to rely on their **sexual allure** to win a man's support.

Respectable women who **do not exploit** their sexual allure **cannot gain a man's support** but do not have the education to support themselves.

The most respectable women are the most oppressed.

Mary Wollstonecraft

Wollstonecraft was born in 1759 to a family whose fortunes were in decline. In her early 20s, she set up a progressive school in London, then became a governess in Ireland to the children of Lady Kingsborough, whose vanity and disdain did much to foster Mary's views on women.

In 1787, she returned to London to write for the radical magazine *Analytical Review*. In 1792, she went to France to celebrate the Revolution and fell in love with American author Gilbert Imlay. They had a child but did not marry, and the relationship ended. After failed suicide attempts and a move to Sweden, she moved back to London and married William Godwin. She died in 1797 giving birth to their only child, Mary, who wrote the novel *Frankenstein* under her married name of Shelley.

Key works

1787 *Thoughts on the Education of Daughters*
1790 *A Vindication of the Rights of Men*
1792 *A Vindication of the Rights of Woman*
1796 *The Wrongs of Woman, or Maria*

inferior to men intellectually, she insisted that this misapprehension was simply due to a woman's lack of education. She argued that there were many occupations women could pursue with the right education and opportunities: "How many women thus waste life away the prey of discontent, who might have practiced as physicians, regulated a farm, managed a shop, and stood erect, supported by their own industry?" Independence and education for women would also be good for men, because marriages might be based on mutual affection and respect. Wollstonecraft proposed reforms to education, such as combining private and public education and a more democratic, participatory approach to schooling.

Wollstonecraft's proposals for the education and emancipation of women were largely overlooked in her lifetime, and for a time after her death, she was better known for her unconventional lifestyle than her ideas. However, later campaigners—such as Emily Davies, who set up Girton College for women at the University of Cambridge in 1869—were strongly influenced by her ideas. Change was nonetheless slow to come; it was more than 150 years after the publication of *A Vindication* that the University of Cambridge finally offered full degrees to women. ∎

THE SLAVE FEELS SELF-EXISTENCE TO BE SOMETHING EXTERNAL
GEORG HEGEL (1770–1831)

The German philosopher Georg Hegel's great work *The Phenomenology of Mind* (or *"Spirit"*) appears at first to have little to do with politics, since it deals with difficult and abstract arguments about the nature of human consciousness. However, his conclusions regarding the way we reach a state of self-awareness have profound implications for the way society is organized and pose difficult questions concerning the nature of human relations.

Hegel's philosophy is focused on how the thinking mind views the world. He wants to understand how each human consciousness creates its own worldview. Crucial to his argument is his emphasis on self-consciousness. For Hegel, the human mind, or spirit, desires recognition and in fact needs that recognition in order to achieve self-awareness. This is why human consciousness, for Hegel, is a social, interactive process. It is possible to live in isolation without being fully aware, Hegel believes. But for the mind to fully exist—to be free—it must be self-conscious, and it can only become self-conscious by seeing another consciousness react to it.

Master–Slave
According to Hegel, when two minds meet, what matters to both is being recognized: receiving from the other the confirmation of their own existence. However, there is only room for one worldview in the mind of each individual, so a struggle ensues about who is going to acknowledge whom—whose worldview is to triumph. Hegel describes how each mind must try to kill the other. The problem is, though, that if one destroys the other, the loser will no longer be able to give the affirmation the winner needs. The way out of this dilemma is a Master–Slave relationship, in which one person "gives in" to the other. The one who values liberty more than life becomes Master; the one who values

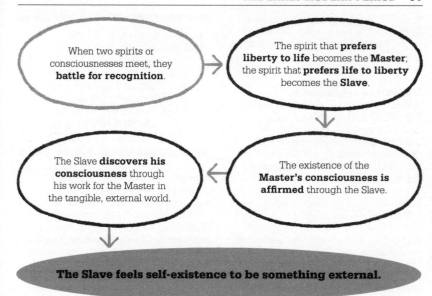

When two spirits or consciousnesses meet, they **battle for recognition**.

The spirit that **prefers liberty to life** becomes the **Master**; the spirit that **prefers life to liberty** becomes the **Slave**.

The Slave **discovers his consciousness** through his work for the Master in the tangible, external world.

The existence of the **Master's consciousness is affirmed** through the Slave.

The Slave feels self-existence to be something external.

life more than liberty becomes Slave. This relationship evolves not only in literal master and slave situations, but in any situation where two minds meet.

Hegel appears to be implying that slaves are only slaves because they prefer to submit rather than die, and they collude with their masters. He wrote, "It is solely by risking life that freedom is obtained." He asserts that terror of death is the cause of oppression throughout history and is at the root of slavery and class distinction. He admired Napoleon for this reason and praised his willingness to risk his own life in order to achieve his aims. Hegel is suggesting that slavery is primarily a state of mind, which finds echoes in the later case of escaped American slave Frederick Douglass (1818–1890). Dragged back to his master, »

Napoleon Bonaparte's vision for a new order and courage in battle made him a man "whom it is impossible not to admire," said Hegel, who respected Napoleon's qualities as a "Master."

Douglass decided to stand up and fight, even if it might mean death, and afterward wrote, "However long I might remain a slave in form, the day had passed forever when I could be a slave in fact."

Dialectical relationship
Today, the choice between death and slavery seems an unacceptable one to have to make. But it may be that Hegel's arguments about the Master–Slave relationship are much less literal and far more subtle and complex. He suggests ways in which the Slave might in fact benefit more from the relationship than the Master. He describes the development of their relationship as a dialectic. By this, he means a particular kind of argument that begins with a thesis (the minds) and its antithesis (the result of the encounter between minds), which together produce a synthesis (the resolution into Master and Slave). This dialectic is not necessarily a description of a real struggle between a slaveholder and slave. Hegel is talking about a struggle for domination between minds—and there is no room in his conception for cooperation. There must be a resolution into Master and Slave.

He goes on to show how the relationship develops further. The synthesis seems to confirm the existence of the Master's

 If a man is a slave, his own will is responsible for his slavery ... the wrong of slavery lies at the door not of enslavers or conquerors but of the slaves and conquered themselves.
Georg Hegel

mind. At first, everything appears to revolve around him, and his ability to get the Slave to serve his needs confirms his own freedom and self-consciousness. The Slave's independent self-consciousness, meanwhile, is totally dissolved. However, at this point, another dialectic relationship develops.

Because the Master does nothing, he relies on the Slave to affirm his existence and freedom. He is, in fact, in a dependent relationship with the Slave, which means that he is anything but free. The Slave, however, is working with real things—with nature—even if only for his Master. This reaffirms his existence in a tangible, external way that the idle Master cannot hope to emulate: "In [his work for] the Master, the Slave feels self-existence

Georg Hegel

Georg Hegel was born in Stuttgart in the German Duchy of Württemberg. Much of his life was lived in the calm of Protestant southern Germany, but against the backdrop of the French Revolution. He was a student at Tübingen University at the height of the Revolution, and he encountered Napoleon at Jena, where he completed *The Phenomenology of Mind*.

After 8 years as rector at the Gymnasium in Nuremberg, he married Marie von Tucher and worked on his great book on logic. In 1816, after the early death of his wife, he moved to Heidelberg, and many of his ideas are contained in notes from the lectures he gave to philosophy students there. He died in 1831, after returning to Berlin during a cholera epidemic. Perhaps appropriately for such a complex thinker, it is said that his last words were "and he didn't understand me."

Key works

1807 *The Phenomenology of Mind*
1812–1816 *The Science of Logic*
1821 *The Philosophy of Right*

Hegel asserted that a Slave, while engaged in tangible work, would come to experience a realization of his own existence (and therefore become "free") in a way that his Master would not.

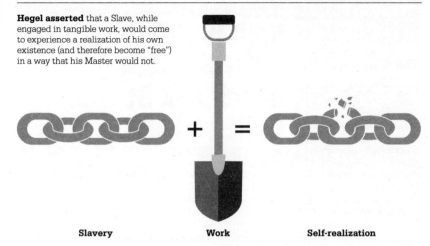

Slavery   Work   Self-realization

to be something external, an objective fact." In making things, and making things happen, "self-existence comes to be felt explicitly, as his own proper being, and [the Slave] attains the consciousness that he himself exists in his own right." So now their situations become inverted— the Master disappears as an independent mind, while the Slave emerges as one. Ultimately, for Hegel, the Master–Slave dialectic may be more harmful to the Master than it is to the Slave.

Slave ideologies
So what happens when the Slave reaches this new kind of self-realization yet is not ready for a fight to the death? At this point, Hegel argues, the Slave finds "slave ideologies" that justify his position, including stoicism (in which he rejects external freedom for mental freedom), skepticism (in which he doubts the value of external freedom), and unhappy consciousness (in which he finds religion and escape, but only in another world).

Hegel finds these Master–Slave relationships in many places—in the wars between stronger states and weaker states and conflicts between social classes and other groupings. For Hegel, human existence is an endless fight to the death for recognition, and this fight can never properly be resolved.

Hegel's influence
Karl Marx was strongly influenced by Hegel's ideas and adopted his idea of the dialectic, but found Hegel too abstract and mystical in his concentration on consciousness. Instead, Marx chose a materialist approach. Some find Hegel's argument that only fear keeps people enslaved inspirational; others consider his insistence that submission is a choice is a case of blaming the victim and does not relate well to the real world, in which power relations are complex. Hegel remains one of the hardest political philosophers to understand, and one of the most controversial. ■

A slave about to be whipped by his master could be to blame for his position, following Hegel's logic. Critics of Hegel argue that this position is clearly unjust.

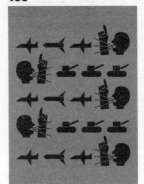

WAR IS THE CONTINUATION OF POLITIK BY OTHER MEANS
CARL VON CLAUSEWITZ (1780–1831)

IN CONTEXT

IDEOLOGY
Realism

THEME
Diplomacy and war

BEFORE
5th century BCE Sun Tzu states that the art of war is vital to the state.

1513 Niccolò Machiavelli argues that even in peacetime, a prince must be ready for war.

AFTER
1935 German general Erich Friedrich Wilhelm Ludendorff develops his notion of a "Total War" that mobilizes the entire physical and moral forces of a nation.

1945 Adolf Hitler cites "the great Clausewitz" in his last testament in the bunker.

Few phrases from military theory have been as influential as Prussian soldier Carl von Clausewitz's statement that "war is the continuation of *Politik* by other means," taken from his book *On War*, published after his death in 1832. The phrase is one of a series of truisms Clausewitz coins as he attempts to put war in context by examining its philosophical basis, much as philosophers would explore the role of the state. The German word *Politik* translates as both politics and policy, covering both the principles of governance and its practicalities.

War leads to politics

For Clausewitz, war is a clash of opposing wills. "War is nothing but a duel on an extensive scale," he writes, "an act of violence intended to compel our opponent to fulfill our will." The aim is to disarm your enemy so that you become the master. But there is no single, decisive blow in war—a defeated state seeks to repair the damage of defeat by using politics. Clausewitz is keen to emphasize that the business of war is serious in intent, and no mere adventure. It is always, he says, a political act, because one state wishes to impose its will on another—or risk submission.

War is simply the means to a political end that might well be achieved through other means. His point is not to highlight the cynicism of politicians who go to war, but to ensure that those who wage war are always aware of its overriding political goal. ∎

Otto von Bismarck declared Wilhelm I of Prussia Emperor of Germany in 1871. Bismarck had provoked war with France to achieve this political end.

THE TENDENCY TO ATTACK "THE FAMILY" IS A SYMPTOM OF SOCIAL CHAOS
AUGUSTE COMTE (1798–1857)

IN CONTEXT

IDEOLOGY
Positivism

FOCUS
The family

BEFORE
14th century Ibn Khaldun's
Muqaddimah uses scientific reasoning
to examine social cohesion and conflict.

1821 In France, early socialist Henri
de Saint-Simon argues that the new
industrial society will bring forth
a new Utopia, with a new kind of
politics led by men of science.

1835 Belgian philosopher Adolphe
Quetelet puts forward the idea
of a social science to study the
average man.

AFTER
1848 Karl Marx argues for the
abolition of the family in
the *Communist Manifesto*.

1962 Michael Oakeshott argues that
society cannot be understood rationally.

 Families become tribes
and tribes become nations.
Auguste Comte

French philosopher Auguste
Comte's defense of the family in
his *Course in Positive Philosophy*
(1830–1848) is based on more than mere
sentimental attachment. Comte's "positivist"
philosophy takes the view that in any true
understanding of society, the only valid
data comes from the senses and from the
logical analysis of this data. Society, he
argues, operates according to laws, just
like the physical world of natural science.
It is the task of the scientist of society
to study it and tease out these laws.

Family is the social unit
It is crucial, believes Comte, to look at
general laws and not become obsessed
with idiosyncratic individual views. "The
scientific spirit forbids us to regard society
as composed of individuals. The true social
unit is the family." It is on the basis of
families that society is constructed—a
social science that starts with the demands
of individuals is doomed to failure. It is also
within the family that individual whims
are harnessed for the good of society.
Humans are driven by both personal
instinct and social instincts. "In a family,
the social and the personal instincts are
blended and reconciled; in a family, too,
the principle of subordination and mutual
cooperation is exemplified." Comte's
position stresses social bonds but is in
conflict with socialism—Marxists who
argue for the abolition of the family are,
in Comte's view, arguing for the very
destruction of human society. ∎

A STATE TOO EXTENSIVE IN ITSELF ULTIMATELY FALLS INTO DECAY

SIMÓN BOLÍVAR (1783–1830)

IN CONTEXT

IDEOLOGY
Liberal republicanism

FOCUS
Revolutionary warfare

BEFORE
1494 In the Treaty of Tordesillas, the territories of the Americas are divided between Spain and Portugal.

1762 Jean-Jacques Rousseau argues against the divine right of kings to rule.

AFTER
1918 Following World War I, President Woodrow Wilson lays out a reconstruction plan for Europe based on liberal nationalist principles.

1964 Che Guevara addresses the United Nations, arguing that Latin America has yet to gain true independence.

1999 Hugo Chávez becomes president of Venezuela with a political ideology he describes as Bolívarian.

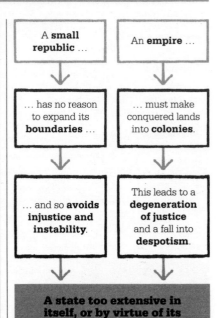

A **small republic** …

→

… has no reason to expand its **boundaries** …

→

… and so **avoids injustice and instability**.

An **empire** …

→

… must make conquered lands into **colonies**.

→

This leads to a **degeneration of justice** and a fall into **despotism**.

A state too extensive in itself, or by virtue of its dependencies, ultimately falls into decay.

Christopher Columbus claimed America for Spain in 1492, paving the way for an empire that would extend over five continents. The Spanish would rely on the collaboration of local elites to manage their lands. Venezuelan revolutionary Simón Bolívar saw this aspect of their empire as a source of dynamism, but also as a potential weakness.

Small but strong republics
Spain's power began to crumble in 1808, when Napoleon invaded and placed his brother on the throne. Bolívar recognized this as an opportunity for the Spanish

THE EARLY MODERN PERIOD

American countries to throw off the yoke of colonialism. During an 18-year fight for freedom, Bolívar was exiled for a year in Jamaica. As he planned for the future, he pondered how he could ensure a state large enough to govern but small enough to foster the greatest happiness for its people.

Bolívar considered the question in *The Jamaica Letter*. In this letter, he explained his reason for rejecting monarchies: kingdoms were inherently expansionist, driven by a king's "constant desire to increase his possessions." A republic, on the other hand, was "limited to the matter of its preservation, prosperity, and glory."

Bolívar believed that Spanish America should become 17 independent republics, and the ambition of these must be to educate, to help people in their fair ambitions, and to protect the rights of all citizens. Each would have no reason to expand its boundaries, because this used up valuable resources while bringing no advantages. In addition, "a state too extensive in itself, or by virtue of its dependencies, ultimately falls into decay." Worse still, "its free government becomes a tyranny," its founding principles are disregarded, and it "degenerates into despotism." Small republics, he said, enjoyed permanence; large ones veered toward empire and instability.

American republics

The independent republics that emerged in Spanish America after the wars of liberation reflected Bolívar's vision in their size, if not in their freedoms, since political power came to be monopolized by small elites. In this, they perhaps reflected Bolívar's own elitist instincts and ambivalence toward full

democracy. The revolutionary vision of "El Libertador" is still revered in Latin America, though Bolívar's name has been misappropriated by politicians to sanction actions he would have deplored. ∎

Bolívar's portrait is held aloft during a pro-Hugo Chávez rally in Venezuela. Chávez described his political movement as a Bolívarian revolution, stressing its anti-imperialist stance.

Simón Bolívar

Born to aristocratic parents in Venezuela, Simón Bolívar was tutored by renowned scholar Simón Rodríguez, who introduced him to the ideals of the European Enlightenment. At age 16, after completing his military training, Bolívar traveled through Mexico and France, then on to Spain, where he married, though his wife died 8 months later.

In 1804, Bolívar witnessed Napoleon Bonaparte become emperor of France. He was inspired by the nationalist ideas he encountered in Europe and vowed not to rest until South America gained independence from Spain. Bolívar led the liberation of modern-day Ecuador, Colombia, Venezuela, Panama, northern Peru, and northwest Brazil from Spain. Retreating from his earlier idealism, Bolívar felt forced to declare himself dictator of the new state of Gran Colombia in 1828. He died 2 years later, disillusioned with the results of the revolutions he had inspired.

Key works

1812 *The Cartagena Manifesto*
1815 *The Jamaica Letter*

THE RISE O MASSES

1848–1910

The revolutions and wars of the late 18th and early 19th centuries left an uncertain legacy in Europe. The Treaty of Paris in 1815 ended the Napoleonic Wars, and for almost a century, there were few conflicts between the European powers. The world economy continued to grow, driven by industrialization and the rapid growth of railways and telecommunications. It was just about possible to believe that the political settlements enacted in the first part of the 19th century would provide a stable institutional framework for humanity. German philosopher Georg Hegel thought the most perfect form of the state had been achieved in Prussia in the 1830s, while European colonialism was presented by many as a civilizing mission for the rest of the world. Once political and civil rights had been secured, a just society would emerge.

Communist thoughts

Two young scholars of Hegel, Friedrich Engels and Karl Marx, violently disagreed with his conclusions. They pointed to the creation—through industrialization—of a new class of propertyless workers who enjoyed increased political freedom but suffered a form of economic slavery. Using the tools of analysis developed by Hegel, they believed they could show how this class had the potential to push civil and political rights into the realm of economics.

Marx and Engels wrote their *Communist Manifesto* as revolutionary movements were gathering momentum across Europe. They attempted to provide a radical template through which a new kind of mass politics would come into existence. New workers' parties, such as Germany's SPD, adopted the manifesto as their guiding light and looked with confidence to a future in which the great mass of the people would exercise political and economic power. Politics was shifted from the concern of the elites to a mass activity, with millions joining political organizations and—as the right to vote spread—millions more participating in elections.

The old order in retreat

In the US, differences over the place of slavery in the new territories led to civil war. Victory for the Union saw an end to slavery across the country and provided new vigor to the nation, marking the start of its rise in economic and political power. To the south, the new republics of Latin America struggled to achieve the political stability that their constitutions had promised, and power passed back and forth between sections of a narrow elite. Much of the region stagnated, but demands for reform would lead to the outbreak of revolution in Mexico in 1910.

In Asia, the first anticolonial organizations were set up to fight for political rights, and a section of Japan's traditional rulers instituted a thorough modernization that swept away the old feudal order. Across the world, the old regimes appeared to be in retreat.

However, whatever some Marxists may have believed, progress toward political power for the masses was not guaranteed. Friedrich Nietzsche was prominent among those who expressed a profound cynicism about the ability of society to be reformed by the masses. His ideas were adapted later by Max Weber, who attempted to reimagine society not as a place of class struggle, as in Marxist thinking, but as a battle for power between competing belief systems.

Reform movements

Liberals and conservatives adapted themselves to a changed world by forming mass membership parties of their own, and sought to manage the growing demands for welfare and economic justice from the left. Liberal philosophy had been given a firm theoretical base by thinkers such as Britain's John Stuart Mill, who held that the rights of the individual should be the basis for a just society rather than the class struggle of the Marxists.

In order to achieve radical reform, some campaigners advocated radical tactics, such as civil disobedience, direct action, and resistance to authority. Russian revolutionary Peter Kropotkin set out the principles of what would become anarcho-communism, urging his adherents to act against all oppression. In Britain, suffragettes, including Emmeline Pankhurst, took militant action to demand that women be given the right to vote.

Meanwhile, in Russia, Vladimir Lenin and others agitated tirelessly for a socialist revolution. Tensions between Europe's old elites were also starting to grow. The stage was set for the tumultuous changes that were about to sweep the world. ■

SOCIALISM IS A NEW SYSTEM OF SERFDOM

ALEXIS DE TOCQUEVILLE (1805–1859)

I n September 1848, Alexis de Tocqueville made an impassioned speech in France's Constituent Assembly, which had been elected after the overthrow of King Louis-Philippe that February. He argued that the ideals of the French Revolution of 1789 implied a democratic future for France and a rejection of socialism.

De Tocqueville attacked socialism on three counts. First, he argued that socialism plays on "men's material passions"—its aim is the generation of wealth. It ignores the loftiest human ideals of generosity and virtue, which were the seeds of the revolution. Second, socialism undermines the principle of private property, which he saw as vital to liberty. Even if socialist states do not seize property, they weaken it. Finally, his strongest criticism was that socialism is contemptuous of the individual.

Under socialism, de Tocqueville believed, individual initiative is snuffed out by an overbearing state. The state directs society as a whole but increasingly becomes the "master of each man." While democracy enhances personal autonomy, socialism reduces it. Socialism and democracy can never go together—they are opposites.

A classless society

De Tocqueville believed that the ideals of the French Revolution had been betrayed. The revolution of 1789 was about liberty for all, which meant the abolition of class divisions. But since then, the upper classes had become more privileged and corrupt. The lower classes burned with anger and disaffection and were therefore more easily seduced by socialist ideas.

The solution, de Tocqueville claimed, was not to be found in socialism, but in a reassertion of the original revolutionary ideal of a free, classless society. Socialism,

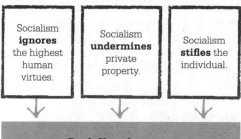

Socialism **ignores** the highest human virtues.	Socialism **undermines** private property.	Socialism **stifles** the individual.

↓   ↓   ↓

Socialism is a new system of serfdom.

Alexis de Tocqueville

by pitting property owners against the proletariat, would reinstate social divisions, betraying this vision. The establishment of a socialist system would be like reverting to the prerevolutionary monarchy. The domineering socialist state was, for de Tocqueville, incompatible with freedom and competition.

De Tocqueville espoused a democratic society in which individual enterprise could flourish, but the poor and vulnerable would be protected through the Christian ideal of charity. As a model for this, he pointed to the US, which he believed had achieved the most advanced version of democracy.

De Tocqueville's contrast between democracy-as-freedom and socialism-as-confinement became a recurring motif in 19th- and 20th-century debates. His speech was made in a year in which revolutions and uprisings spread across Europe, fomented in part by socialist ideas. However, after 1848, the uprisings fizzled out, and for a time, socialism failed to take root in the way he had feared. ■

De Tocqueville was born in Paris to aristocratic parents. When Louis-Philippe d'Orléans came to the throne in 1830, de Tocqueville took up a post in the new government, but political changes made his position precarious, so he left France for the US. The result was his most famous work, *Democracy in America*, in which he argued that democracy and equality had progressed furthest in the US. He also warned of the dangers of democracy—materialism and excessive individualism.

After the 1848 revolution, de Tocqueville became a member of the Constituent Assembly in France, which was responsible for devising the constitution of the Second Republic. He withdrew from politics after his opposition to Louis-Napoléon Bonaparte's coup of 1851 led to a night in prison. Dogged by ill health for much of his life, he died of tuberculosis 8 years later aged 53.

Key works

1835, 1840 *Democracy in America*
1856 *The Old Regime and the Revolution*

Under socialism, de Tocqueville argued, workers would be mere cogs in the overbearing machinery of the state.

THAT SO FEW DARE TO BE ECCENTRIC MARKS THE CHIEF DANGER OF THE TIME

JOHN STUART MILL (1806–1873)

IN CONTEXT

IDEOLOGY
Liberalism

FOCUS
Individual liberty

BEFORE
1690 John Locke, an opposer of authoritarian governments, pioneers liberal thought.

1776 The Declaration of Independence states that all men are created equal, with rights to liberty, life, and happiness.

AFTER
1940s Liberals lose faith in free markets after the Great Depression and argue for a welfare state.

1958 British scholar Isaiah Berlin distinguishes "negative" from "positive" liberty.

1974 US philosopher Robert Nozick argues that personal liberties are sacrosanct.

In *On Liberty*, John Stuart Mill made a famous defense of an important tenet of liberalism: that individuality is the foundation of a healthy society. His investigations were motivated by a basic question of political theory—that of the appropriate balance between individual freedom and social control.

Mill argued that the transformations of the political conditions of the mid-19th century necessitated a fresh look at this matter. In earlier times, when absolutist monarchies wielded power, rulers' rapacity could not be kept in check by the ballot box. Because of this, the interests of the state were considered to be opposed to those of the individual, and government interference was viewed with suspicion.

The expansion of democratic systems of government in the 19th century was assumed to have resolved this tension. Regular elections made the masses the ultimate rulers, bringing into alignment the interests of the state with those of the people. In this setting, it was thought that interference by the government could not be to the detriment of the individuals who had elected it.

Tyranny of the majority
Mill warned about the complacency of this view. He said that the elected government distills the views of the majority, and this majority might end up wanting to oppress the minority. This "tyranny of the majority" meant that there was a risk that interference by even elected governments would have harmful effects. At least as serious as political tyranny was the risk of the social tyranny of public opinion, which tends to lead to conformity of belief and action. These forms of tyranny were all the more serious, argued Mill, because people's opinions were often unthinking, rooted in little more than self-interest and personal preference. Ultimately, the received wisdom

> For a healthy society, **individuals** should be **free to think and act**, as long as they don't harm others.

⬇

> Often this doesn't happen because of the **tyranny of the majority**.

⬇

> This brings **conformity** and hampers the testing out of new ideas and ways of life.

⬇

> **That so few dare to be eccentric marks the chief danger of the time.**

is then nothing more than the interests of a society's most dominant groups.

Britain at the time was still going through the transition toward a modern democracy, and Mill said that people did not yet appreciate the dangers. The prevailing mistrust of government was a relic from the era in which the state was viewed as a threat to individuals, and the potential for tyranny by a democratic majority was not yet widely understood. This confusion meant that the government's actions were both unnecessarily called for and unjustifiably condemned. Also, the tyranny of public opinion was on the rise, and Mill feared a general tendency for society to increase its control over the individual.

Justifiable interference
A moral dam was needed to stop this trend, so Mill attempted to set out a clear principle to define the right balance between individual autonomy and government interference. He argued that society could only justifiably interfere with individuals'

liberties in order to prevent harm to others. Concern for the individual's own good might justify an attempt to persuade him to take a different course of action, but not to compel him to do so. "Over himself, over his own body and mind, the individual is sovereign," Mill said. This principle of individual liberty applied to thought, to the expression of opinions, and to actions.

Mill argued that if this principle is undermined, the whole of society suffers. Without freedom of thought, for example, human knowledge and innovation would be restricted. To demonstrate this, Mill put forward an account of how humans arrive at truth. Because human minds are fallible, the truth or falsity of an idea only becomes known by testing it in the bubbling cauldron of opposing ideas. By stifling ideas, society might lose a true idea. It might also suppress a false idea that would have been useful to test and potentially reveal the truth of another idea. Mill rejected the argument that some ideas are more socially useful than others irrespective of their truth. He believed that this argument assumes infallibility in deciding which beliefs are useful. Although heretics were no longer burned at the stake, Mill believed »

Freedom of action—such as the right of assembly at this gay pride parade in Paris— was central to Mill's idea of individual liberty, alongside freedom of thought and freedom of opinion.

that the social intolerance of unorthodox opinions threatened to dull minds and cramp the development of society.

A profusion of ideas

Even when society's received wisdoms were true, Mill argued that it was important to maintain a profusion of ideas. For a true idea to keep its vitality and power, it needs to be constantly challenged and probed. This was particularly the case with ideas about society and politics, which can never attain the certainty of mathematical truths. Testing ideas is best done by hearing the views of those who hold conflicting opinions. Where there are no dissenters, their views must be imagined. Without this discussion and argument, people will not appreciate the basis of even true ideas, which then become dead dogmas, parroted without any real understanding. Correct principles of behavior and morality, when they have been converted into barren slogans, can no longer motivate authentic action.

Mill used his principle of liberty to defend the individual's freedom to act. However, he acknowledged that freedom of action would necessarily be more limited than freedom of thought, because an action is more capable of hurting others than a thought. Like freedom of ideas, individuality—the freedom to live an unorthodox life—promotes social innovation: "the worth of different modes of life should be proved practically," he said. Although people might usefully draw on traditions as a guide to their own lives, they should do so creatively in ways that are especially relevant to their particular circumstances and preferences. Mill believed that when people automatically follow customs—in a similar way to the impact of unthinkingly held opinions— ways of living become sterile, and the individual's moral faculties are weakened.

Experimenting for all

As with the free expression of ideas, those who act in new ways provide a benefit to society as a whole, even to conventional people. Nonconformists discover new ways of doing things, some of which can then be adopted by others. But social innovators need to be free to experiment for these benefits to be realized.

Given the power of the majority view, free spirits and eccentrics help inspire people toward new ways of doing things. When Mill wrote *On Liberty*, the Industrial Revolution had made Britain the most economically advanced country in the world. Mill believed that this success had come from the relative plurality of thought

Ideas and policies **need to be tested** against each other.

Those that do not stand the test are **discarded**.

In Mill's bubbling cauldron of ideas, each idea must constantly be tested against other ideas. The cauldron acts like a still. False, or broken, ideas evaporate away as they are rejected, while true ideas are left in the mix and grow stronger.

and freedom of action that existed in Europe. He contrasted the dynamism of Europe with the stagnation of China, which he believed had declined because customs and traditions had hardened and suppressed individuality. In Britain, economic development had brought mass education, faster communications, and greater opportunities for previously excluded social classes. But this progress also brought a greater homogeneity of tastes and, with it, a decline in individuality. He believed that if this trend continued, England would suffer the same fate as China. Mill thought that English society had already become too conformist and unappreciative of the value of individuality and originality. People acted in accordance with social rank, not their consciences. This is why he believed that a lack of eccentricity was such a danger.

The harm principle

Mill's criterion of harm was a useful and easily stated principle to define the appropriate boundary between state and individual, expressed at a time when the relationship between the government and the people was going through rapid change.

Policies on smoking during the 20th century illustrate how the principle can be used as a way of thinking about government restrictions on individual behavior. Although it had long been understood that tobacco did people harm, society had never prevented individuals from smoking. Instead, health information was supplied to persuade people to stop smoking and, by the late 20th century, smoking was declining in the US and many European countries.

This was in line with Mill's principle of liberty: people could freely smoke even though it harmed them, because it did not harm others. Then new medical information came to light showing that passive smoking was harmful. This meant that smoking in public places now violated the harm principle. The principle was reapplied, and smoking bans in public places were initiated to reflect this new knowledge. With its rapid decline in popularity, smoking has in

Demonstrators protest at a neo-Nazi rally. Mill held that individual liberty—such as the neo-Nazis' right to gather—could be opposed if it led to more unhappiness than happiness.

a sense become a habit of eccentrics, but despite the increasing evidence about the health dangers, few would advocate an outright ban.

Harm vs. happiness

The harm principle may not always deliver the results imagined by liberals, however. For example, if people found homosexuality immoral and repugnant, they might argue that the mere knowledge that homosexuality was being practiced would harm them. They might argue that the state should intervene to uphold sexual morals. This raises the issue of the underlying ethical basis for Mill's defense of the individual. *On Liberty* was written in the context of the philosophical system of utilitarianism, which Mill espoused. Mill was a follower of the English philosopher Jeremy Bentham, who argued that the morality of actions should be judged according to the extent to which they contribute to the sum total of human happiness. For instance, instead of judging lying as wrong in itself, one would need to condemn it because its various consequences—when reckoned together— cause more unhappiness than happiness. Mill refined and developed Bentham's theory, for example, by making a distinction between "higher" and "lower" pleasures, meaning that it would be better to be born an unhappy Socrates than a happy pig, because only a Socrates has the possibility of experiencing higher pleasures. »

One might perceive a conflict between utilitarianism and the approach taken in *On Liberty*, because the defense of individual liberty sounds like a separate principle, which might conflict with the happiness principle that takes precedence in a utilitarian approach. If homosexuality made the majority unhappy, for instance, utilitarianism would recommend that it should be banned, which would be a clear infringement of individual liberty. Despite this apparent conflict, Mill maintains that utility is still the ultimate, overarching principle in his system.

Mill is not making an absolutist argument for individual autonomy. One way of viewing his argument is as concrete application of the happiness principle in the area of state versus individual action. Mill argues that liberty leads to social innovation and the growth of knowledge, which then contribute to happiness. This leaves open the possibility that Mill may have been too optimistic in thinking that the happiness principle always points toward liberty. He may even have been too optimistic with respect to the expression of opinions, not just to behavioral norms. For example, some might argue that the banning of the expression of certain opinions—the

 The liberty of the individual must be thus far limited; he must not make himself a nuisance to other people.
John Stuart Mill

declaration of support for Adolf Hitler in today's Germany, for example—reduces unhappiness and is therefore justifiable on utilitarian grounds.

Negative liberty

Another criticism that could be leveled at Mill's arguments concerns the way in which he believes that truth bubbles up from the cauldron of opposing ideas. He believes that this cauldron bubbles most vigorously when society completely avoids any interference with individual thought or action. This is a notion of liberty that the British political theorist and philosopher Isaiah Berlin later called "negative liberty," which he defines as the absence of constraints on actions.

Leftist critics consider negative liberty alone to be insufficient. They point out that oppressed groups—such as the poorest in society, or women without rights—might have no way of expressing their unorthodox views: they are marginalized, which means that they have little access to the media and institutions in which opinions are expressed and publicized. For this reason, those on the left often argue that negative liberties are meaningless without "positive liberties," which actively help give marginalized people the power to express their opinions and influence policy. If he had witnessed the achievements of feminism over the 20th century, Mill might well have argued that women did manage to obtain political equality through the vigorous expression of their views. However, leftists would counter once more that formal political rights mean little without positive liberties, such as the provision of equal pay and guaranteed employment rights.

A religious preacher addresses onlookers at Speaker's Corner in Hyde Park, London. Mill argued against censorship and for freedom of speech, whatever the opinion being expressed.

Pragmatic liberalism

Mill's political philosophies—utilitarianism and his defense of liberty—have had a profound influence on the development of liberal democracies throughout the world. His is perhaps the most famous and frequently cited argument for a pragmatic form of liberalism, which is tied to a principle of collective well-being rather than arguing for abstract, inalienable rights.

In modern liberal democracies, particularly in the US and the UK, many debates—such as those on sexual morality, smoking, and even the role of free markets in the economy—have been structured around the considerations that Mill put forward nearly two centuries ago. But even in these countries, many social constraints on individual actions are justified by more than just the minimal criterion of negative liberty. Bans on recreational drugs, for example, depend on a paternalistic principle, and even in free market countries, the government regulates commerce and attempts to make economic outcomes more equal. These are all actions that may be considered to go beyond Mill's condition for intervention, but as the debates about the appropriate scope of social control continue unabated, those arguing for more liberal stances often invoke the arguments made by Mill. ∎

John Stuart Mill

Born in London in 1806, John Stuart Mill became one of the most influential philosophers of the 19th century. His father, James Mill, was part of the circle of thinkers of the leader of utilitarian philosophy, Jeremy Bentham. The elder Mill set out to ensure that his precocious son became a great thinker. As a young boy, Mill studied Latin, Greek, history, mathematics, and economics. But at the age of 20, Mill realized that these intellectual exertions had stunted his emotional life, and he suffered from a bout of deep depression.

In 1830, Mill developed a close friendship with Harriet Taylor, marrying her in 1851 after the death of her husband. Harriet was influential to Mill's development, helping him broaden his conception of human life from the ascetic ethic of his father to one that valued emotion and individuality. This is said to have influenced his thinking on utilitarianism and liberty.

Key works

1859 *On Liberty*
1865 *Utilitarianism*
1869 *The Subjection of Women*

Mill's Three Basic Liberties

The liberty of **thought and ideas**: absolute freedom of opinion of sentiment and the freedom to express them in speech or writing.

The liberty to pursue one's own **tastes and pursuits**: to live our lives exactly how we see fit, as long as this does no harm to others in society.

The liberty of **combination among individuals**: the right to unite with others for any nonharmful purpose, as long as members are not coerced.

NO MAN IS GOOD ENOUGH TO GOVERN ANOTHER MAN WITHOUT THAT OTHER'S CONSENT
ABRAHAM LINCOLN (1809–1865)

IN CONTEXT

IDEOLOGY
Abolitionism

FOCUS
Equal rights

BEFORE
1776 The Constitution of the United States establishes the new republic.

1789 In the French Revolution, the Declaration of Rights states that "men are born and remain free and equal in rights."

AFTER
1860 Lincoln's election as the 16th US president provokes the secession of Southern states in defense of their right to maintain slavery.

1865 With the surrender of General Robert E. Lee of the Confederacy, the Civil War ends in victory for the Union.

1964 The US Civil Rights Act bans job discrimination on the basis of "race, color, religion, or national origin."

T he foundation of the United States of America after the Revolutionary War against Britain left the nature of the new republic unresolved. Although the country was formally committed to the equality of "all men" through the Declaration of Independence of 1776, slavery saw millions of Africans transported across the Atlantic to plantations throughout the Southern states. The 1820 Missouri Compromise outlawed slavery in the Northern states, but not in the South.

Abraham Lincoln's statement that "no man is good enough to govern another man without that other's consent" comes from a speech of 1854. He argued against the right of states to maintain their own laws by contesting that the foundation of the United States on the right to individual liberty overrode the right to "self-government." The republic was built on liberty and equality, not on political convenience or as a compromise among states that retained their own authority.

Considered a moderate opponent of slavery, Lincoln had previously argued against extending slavery, but not for abolishing it. Yet this speech heralds the defense of republican virtues that became the rallying cry for Northern states when the Civil War erupted in 1861. Lincoln's message became more radical and led to the Emancipation Proclamation of 1863 and the outlawing of slavery across the United States in 1865. ∎

> One section of our country believes slavery is right and ought to be extended, while the other believes it is wrong and ought not to be extended.
> **Abraham Lincoln**

PROPERTY IS THEFT

PIERRE-JOSEPH PROUDHON (1809–1865)

IN CONTEXT

IDEOLOGY
Socialism, mutualism

FOCUS
Private property

BEFORE
462 BCE Plato advocates collective ownership, arguing that it promotes the pursuit of common goals.

1689 John Locke argues that human beings have a natural right to property.

AFTER
1848 In the *Communist Manifesto*, Karl Marx and Friedrich Engels outline their vision of a society with no property.

1974 US philosopher Robert Nozick argues for the moral primacy of private property.

2000 Peruvian economist Hernando de Soto claims that secure property rights are essential for lifting developing countries out of poverty.

 The downfall and death of societies are due to the power of accumulation possessed by property.
Pierre-Joseph Proudhon

Pierre-Joseph Proudhon, the French politician and thinker, made his famous assertion that property is theft at a time when many in France felt frustrated by the outcomes of the revolutions of the previous few decades. When Proudhon published *What Is Property?*, 10 years had passed since the 1830 revolution that had ended the Bourbon monarchy. It was hoped that the new July monarchy would finally bring about the vision of freedom and equality embodied by the 1789 French Revolution. But by 1840, class conflict was rife, and the elite had grown rich while the masses remained in poverty. Many saw the result of the political struggles not as liberty and equality, but as corruption and rising inequality.

Proudhon said that the rights to liberty, equality, and security were natural, absolute, and inviolable and were the very basis of society. However, he claimed that the apparent right to property was not the same as these. In fact, he maintained that property undermined these fundamental rights. While the liberty of the rich and the poor can coexist, the property of the wealthy sets alongside the poverty of the many. Thus, property was inherently antisocial. Property was a primary issue of the working-class and socialist movements that were emerging in Europe in the 19th century, and Proudhon's fiery declaration encapsulates the revolutionary ferment of the time. ■

THE PRIVILEGED MAN IS A MAN DEPRAVED IN INTELLECT AND HEART
MIKHAIL BAKUNIN (1814–1876)

IN CONTEXT

IDEOLOGY
Anarchism

FOCUS
Corruption of power

BEFORE
1793 English political philosopher William Godwin outlines an anarchist philosophy, arguing that government corrupts society.

1840 Pierre-Joseph Proudhon imagines a just form of society devoid of political authority.

AFTER
1892 Peter Kropotkin proposes "anarchist communism," arguing for a form of cooperative distribution, as well as production.

1936 Spain's anarchist union, the CNT, boasts more than 1 million members.

1999 Anarchist ideas reemerge around anticapitalist demonstrations in Seattle.

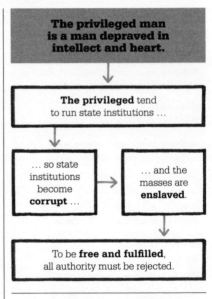

The privileged man is a man depraved in intellect and heart.

↓

The privileged tend to run state institutions …

↓

… so state institutions become **corrupt** …

→

… and the masses are **enslaved**.

↓

To be **free and fulfilled**, all authority must be rejected.

I n Europe in the 19th century, modern nation-states emerged, democracy spread, and the relationship between individuals and authority was recast. In *God and the State*, Russian revolutionary Mikhail Bakunin investigated the requirements for the moral and political fulfillment of human society.

At the time, society was seen as an association of individuals under the authority of a government or the Church. Bakunin argued that humans become truly fulfilled by exercising their capacity to think and by rebelling against authority, whether of gods or of man. He made a searing attack on "religious hallucination," arguing that it is a tool of oppression to keep people servile and that it helps the powerful to maintain their position. Life for the masses is wretched, and solace can come from belief in God. But living in accordance with religion dulls the intellect, so it cannot allow human liberation. Bakunin argued that the oppressors of the people—priests, monarchs, bankers, police, and politicians—would agree with Voltaire's dictum that if there was no God, it would be necessary to invent him. Bakunin insisted instead that freedom required the abolition of God.

Acquiescence to the man-made institution of the state would also enslave people. The laws of nature unavoidably constrain what men can do, but Bakunin claimed that once these laws were discovered and known to all, no political organizations would be required to regulate society. Everyone could consciously obey natural laws because every individual would know them to be true. But as soon as an external authority, such as the state, imposes laws—even true ones—people are no longer free.

Power corrupts

Bakunin argued that, when acting as society's guardians, even learned, well-informed people inevitably become corrupt. They abandon the pursuit of truth, seeking instead the protection of their own power. The masses, kept in ignorance, need their protection. Bakunin believed that accordingly, privilege kills the heart and mind.

The implication was, for Bakunin, that all authority must be rejected, even that based on universal suffrage. This was the basis of his philosophy of anarchism, which he said would light the path to human freedom. Bakunin's writings and activism helped inspire the emergence of anarchist movements in the 19th century. His ideas propelled the rise of a distinct strand of revolutionary thought, which sat alongside Marxist beliefs. ∎

St. Basil's Cathedral in Moscow represents the authorities that Bakunin called on people to rebel against and instead exercise their own freedoms.

Mikhail Bakunin

Bakunin's rebelliousness was first in evidence when he deserted the Russian army as a young man. He spent time in Moscow and Berlin, immersing himself in German philosophy and Hegelian thought. He began writing revolutionary material, which drew attention from the Russian authorities. He was arrested in 1849 when, inspired by the 1848 uprising in Paris, he tried to incite insurrection.

After 8 years in prison in Russia, Bakunin traveled to London and then Italy, where he recommended his revolutionary activities. In 1868, he joined the First International, an association of left-wing revolutionary groups, but a disagreement with Karl Marx led to his expulsion. Although both men believed in revolution, Bakunin rejected what he saw as the authoritarianism of the socialist state. Bakunin died in Switzerland, agitating for revolution until the end.

Key works

1865–1866 *The Revolutionary Catechism*
1871 *God and the State*
1873 *Statism and Anarchy*

COMMUNISM IS THE RIDDLE OF HISTORY SOLVED
KARL MARX (1818–1883)

IN CONTEXT

IDEOLOGY
Communism

FOCUS
Alienation of labor

BEFORE
380 BCE Plato argues that the ideal society has strong limitations on private property.

1807 Georg Hegel puts forward a philosophy of history that inspires Marx's theories.

1819 French writer Henri de Saint-Simon advocates a form of socialism.

AFTER
1917 Vladimir Lenin leads the Bolshevik Revolution in Russia, inspired by Marx's ideas.

1940s Communism spreads across the world and the Cold War begins.

1991 The Soviet Union breaks up, and nations in Eastern Europe adopt capitalist economic systems.

O ver the middle decades of the 19th century, Karl Marx—philosopher, historian, and iconic revolutionary—made one of the most ambitious analyses of capitalism ever attempted. He sought to uncover laws governing the transition of societies between different economic systems as part of his investigations into the changing nature of work and its implications for human fulfillment. Marx's work addressed central concerns of the time: how the rise of industrial capitalism affected living conditions and society's moral health, and whether better economic and political arrangements might be worked out and put into practice.

Marx was active in a period that saw new revolutionary ideas emerging in Europe that led to the uprisings of 1848. In the *Economic and Philosophic Manuscripts* of 1844, he sketched out important elements of his economic thought, considering how capitalist organization blights the lives of workers. He argued that communism solves a problem that bedevils capitalism—the organization of work. In the *Manuscripts*, Marx developed the notion of "alienated labor," the separation of human beings from their true nature and potential for fulfillment. Marx saw various kinds of alienation as inevitable in capitalist labor markets.

The fulfillment of work
Marx believed that work has the potential to be one of the most fulfilling of all human activities. The worker puts his effort and ingenuity into the transformation of the objects of nature into products. The goods that he creates then embody his effort and creativity. Under capitalism, the existence of private property separates society into capitalists—who own productive resources, such as factories and machines—and workers—who possess nothing except for their labor. Labor becomes a commodity

Private property is thus the product ... of alienated labor.
Karl Marx

to be bought and sold, and workers are hired by capitalists to produce goods that are then sold for profit. Marx argued that this removes the fulfilling quality of work, leading to alienation and dissatisfaction.

One form of this alienation arises from the fact that goods made by a worker who is employed by a capitalist do not belong to the worker and cannot be kept by him. A suit cut by a tailor in a clothing factory is the property of the capitalist who owns the factory—the worker makes the suit and then hands it over to his employer. To the worker, the goods that he makes become "alien" objects with which he has little real connection. As he creates more goods that contribute to a world that he stands outside of, his inner life shrinks and his fulfillment is stunted. The worker may produce beautiful objects for other people to use and enjoy, but he creates only dullness and limitation for himself.

Workers disconnected

Marx said that workers also suffer from alienation through the very act of working. Under capitalism, workers' activity does not arise out of their inherent creativity, but from the practical necessity of working for someone else. The worker does not like work, since it crushes his body and mind and makes him unhappy—it becomes a kind of forced activity that, given the choice, he would not do. Like the goods that he eventually produces, the activity of work becomes something that is external to the worker and with which he has little real connection: "The worker therefore only feels himself outside his work, and in his work, he feels outside himself." The worker becomes someone else's subject. His labor is no longer his own, and his activity is no longer spontaneous and creative, but directed by another who treats him as a mere tool of production.

The worker's alienation from the fruits of his labor and from the activity of working estranges him from his human identity— what Marx calls his "species-being." This is because human identity is rooted in people's ability to transform the raw material of nature into objects. Workers in capitalist systems lose the connection with this »

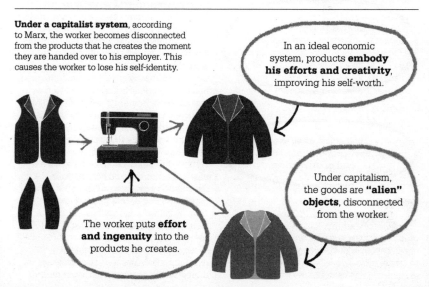

Under a capitalist system, according to Marx, the worker becomes disconnected from the products that he creates the moment they are handed over to his employer. This causes the worker to lose his self-identity.

In an ideal economic system, products **embody his efforts and creativity**, improving his self-worth.

Under capitalism, the goods are **"alien" objects**, disconnected from the worker.

The worker puts **effort and ingenuity** into the products he creates.

basic identity—economic necessity makes productive activity a means to an end rather than the way in which an individual's fundamental identity is embodied and played out. Activity is what makes up life, and once this becomes alien to the worker, the worker loses the sense of his human self.

Private property to blame

These forms of alienation—from the goods produced, from the activity of work, and from human identity—cause people to become increasingly alienated from each other. Because the labor market estranges people from their own essential identity, they become estranged from each other's identity, too. The worker is placed into a relationship of confrontation with the capitalist, who owns the fruits of the work and who controls the worker's labor activity for his own enrichment.

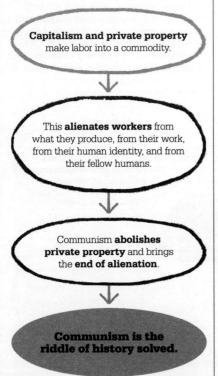

Capitalism and private property make labor into a commodity.

This **alienates workers** from what they produce, from their work, from their human identity, and from their fellow humans.

Communism **abolishes private property** and brings the **end of alienation**.

Communism is the riddle of history solved.

Marx believed that private property lay at the root of the alienation of the worker. The division of society into property-owning capitalists and propertyless workers is what leads to the alienation of workers. In turn, alienation itself reinforces this division and perpetuates private property. An aspect of the system of private property is exchange and the "division of labor." Labor becomes specialized: one worker makes the head of the pin, one worker makes the point, and another assembles the pin. Capitalists specialize in different kinds of goods and trade them with each other. In all of this, the worker becomes a mere cog, a small part of the larger economic machine.

Marx saw the process of the alienation of the worker and the strengthening of private property as a basic law of capitalism, which sets up a tension in human society as people become estranged from their essential nature. A solution is not to be found in higher wages, because workers would remain enslaved even if they were paid more. Alienated labor goes with private property, so "the downfall of one must therefore involve the downfall of the other."

Communism the solution

For Marx, communism resolves the tension caused by the alienation of the worker by abolishing private property, and finally solves the riddle thrown out by capitalism. It resolves the conflict between man and nature and between human beings, and in so doing reconnects man to his fundamental humanity. Alienation made work and interactions between people into a means of economic gain rather than ends in themselves. Under communism, these activities are restored to their rightful place as ends, the manifestation of true human values. For example, association between workers now arises out of a feeling of brotherhood rather than as something that has to be done. Communism brings the return of "man to himself as a social being."

Underlying the statement that communism solves history's riddle is a view of history that Marx went on to develop more fully in his later work. He believed that historical developments are determined by "material"—or economic—factors. Human beings have material needs and possess the ability to produce goods to satisfy them. Production of these goods can be organized in different ways, each of which gives rise to different kinds of social and political arrangements, which in turn lead to particular beliefs and ideologies. Marx believed that material economic factors were the fundamental determinant, and therefore the motor, of history.

Overturning capitalism

Capitalism—a particular way of organizing production—is a response to the material needs of human beings. Capitalism arose as older feudal forms of production died out. As the forces of production develop under capitalism, the suffering of workers becomes obvious, and history moves inevitably toward revolution and the ushering in of communism to replace it.

The legacy of Marx

It is hard to overstate Marx's influence. His work led to new schools of thought in the fields of economics, political theory, history, cultural studies, anthropology, and philosophy, to name just a few. The appeal of Marx's ideas comes from their broad interpretation of the world and their message of transformation and liberation. The prediction that he and Friedrich Engels made in their *Communist Manifesto* of 1848—that the end of capitalism would be brought about through communist revolution—profoundly influenced 20th-century politics. Communist systems emerged in Europe and in Asia, and communist ideas influenced many governments and revolutionary movements throughout the century.

One challenge in assessing Marx's legacy is separating what he really meant from what was done in his name, particularly because communist ideology was used to justify totalitarianism and oppression in many places and at different times. By the end of the 20th century, communism in Eastern Europe had all but collapsed, and the wealthiest nations were firmly capitalist. So even if aspects of Marx's analysis of capitalist society still had a ring of truth, many critics see history as having refuted him, particularly in his prediction of the collapse of capitalism. More recently, Marx's ideas echo once more in claims that the global economic crisis of the early 21st century is a sign of deep contradictions that are inherent in the capitalist system. ∎

Karl Marx

Marx was born in Prussia to liberal Jewish parents who converted to Protestantism in response to anti-Jewish laws. As a journalist, he increasingly turned to radical politics and economics. In 1843, he moved to Paris, where he met Friedrich Engels, with whom he cowrote the *Communist Manifesto* in 1848.

After the revolutions of that year, Marx was expelled from Prussia, Belgium, and Paris before ending up in London, where he studied economics and history intensively. This eventually led to his major work, *Capital*. Marx found it hard to support himself and lived in poverty in the slum district of Soho, sustained by the financial support of Engels. He and his wife suffered from poor health, and several of their children died. Marx himself died before the final two volumes of *Capital* could be published.

Key works

1844 *Economic and Philosophic Manuscripts*
1848 *Communist Manifesto*
1867 *Capital Volume I* (*Volumes II and III* published 1885 and 1894, posthumously)

THE WILL TO POWER
FRIEDRICH NIETZSCHE (1844–1900)

IN CONTEXT

IDEOLOGY
Nihilism

FOCUS
Morality

BEFORE
1781 Kant's *Critique of Pure Reason* describes the gap between our thought and the world it attempts to apprehend.

1818 Schopenhauer publishes *The World as Will and Representation*, taking Kant's insight and suggesting that the gap can never be closed.

AFTER
1937 Bataille dismisses any political interpretation of Nietzsche as inadequate.

1990 *The End of History and the Last Man* by Francis Fukuyama adopts Nietzsche's metaphor of the Last Man to describe the apparent triumph of free-market capitalism.

T he name of Friedrich Nietzsche still invites hostility. His elusive, wide-ranging writings and visceral critique of morality would spark controversy even without his largely unwarranted tainting with fascism. Like Marx and Freud, he was—in French philosopher Paul Ricoeur's words—a leading light in the "school of suspicion," intent on stripping away the veil from received notions and comforting beliefs. His philosophy was nihilist, which means that he thought it impossible to find meaning in existence.

Opposed to the systematic thought of traditional philosophy, he nonetheless left numerous hints toward a political philosophy. This has little to do with the popular perception of him as a prototypical Nazi. Nietzsche was not an anti-Semite, considering it—and its accompanying nationalism—a means by which failed individuals blamed others for their own failings. He broke with his friend Richard Wagner partly due to the latter's increasingly strident racism and nationalism. This did not prevent Nietzsche's works from being mauled by his sister, who edited his works when illness incapacitated him toward the end of his life. She attempted to present his many writings in a more favorable light to the German nationalist and anti-Semitic circles in which she moved.

Will to power
Nietzsche's famous phrase "will to power" first appears in a short book that he considered to be his masterpiece, *Thus Spake Zarathustra*. In this dense, literary text, the protagonist, Zarathustra—a Germanized name for Zoroaster, founder of the ancient Persian religion—surveys a fallen world and seeks to teach a new way of thinking and living to the people. It is not a standard work of philosophy or of

politics; stylistically, it is something closer to an epic poem, and its central arguments are rarely presented directly, favoring instead a figurative address. But the main themes are clear.

For Nietzsche, will to power is not merely a demand to dominate and control. He did not necessarily intend to describe a will to power over others. Rather, he intended it to denote the endless striving after goals and the highest achievements in life that he thought motivated human behavior—whatever these goals may be in practice. In developing the concept, he was heavily influenced by his reading of the German philosopher Arthur Schopenhauer. The latter's bleak depiction of a reality in which no values could become meaningful was brightened, if at all, only by the "will to live": a desperate striving of all life in the universe to avoid the finality of death. Nietzsche's development of the same concept is, by contrast, positive—not a struggle against, but a struggle for.

Nietzsche suggests that the will to power is stronger than the will to life itself. Even the most privileged humans strive after goals that mean risking their lives. There are higher values than crude survival, and what should mark out a good life is the willingness to reach after them.

Criticizing contentment

The will to power was a response to the utilitarian thinking that was coming to dominate social philosophy, in which people simply strive after their own happiness and the greatest goal in life »

Friedrich Nietzsche

Nietzsche was born in Prussia to strongly religious parents. After completing his studies in theology and philology, he rejected religion. At the tender age of 24, he was appointed Professor of Classical Philology at Basel, where he met and befriended Richard Wagner, who was a marked influence on his early writings. His academic concerns drifted away from philology and into questions of philosophy. Nietzsche took a nihilistic position that stressed the meaninglessness of existence, but argued that Greek tragedy overcame this nihilism by affirming its meaninglessness—a theme that would recur throughout his later writings.

Beset by illness, Nietzsche resigned his teaching post in 1879 after a bout of diphtheria and moved frequently around Europe, continually writing, but with limited reception. He suffered a severe mental breakdown in 1889, and died shortly after at the age of 56.

Key works

1872 *The Birth of Tragedy*
1883–1885 *Thus Spake Zarathustra*
1886 *Beyond Good and Evil*

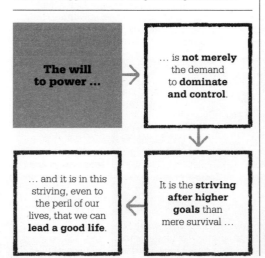

The will to power ... ... is **not merely** the demand to **dominate and control**.

It is the **striving after higher goals** than mere survival ...

... and it is in this striving, even to the peril of our lives, that we can **lead a good life**.

> The priests are the most evil enemies ... in them, hatred grows to monstrous and uncanny proportions, to the most spiritual and poisonous kind of hatred.
> **Friedrich Nietzsche**

is to be content. Nietzsche thought that utilitarianism, and the social philosophy it engendered, was the debased expression of the thinking of the English bourgeoisie—happy and entirely philistine.

Thus Spake Zarathustra contains an argument against this style of social thought. It describes the Last Man, a pitiable creature who is content, looks passively out on the world, "and blinks." The Last Man is a harbinger of the end of history itself, when all meaningful struggles have ceased.

But if we are not meant simply to be content with the world and instead must strive after higher goals, the question remains as to what those goals should be. Nietzsche was clear on what they should not be. Zarathustra, the first to found a system of morality, must now be the man to destroy it. The morality we have is debased and the god we worship little more than the expression of our own inadequacies. "God is dead," wrote Nietzsche. Likewise we, as people who

remain trapped by this morality, must overcome it. "Man is something to be surpassed. How have you overcome him?" demands Zarathustra of the crowd.

Rejecting the old morality

Nietzsche's later *Beyond Good and Evil* and the *Genealogy of Morals* clarify his argument that we should break with conventional morality. Both provide a history and a criticism of Western morality, in which "good" is necessarily paired with its opposite, "evil." Nietzsche believed that this form of moral thinking was at the root of all our current systems of morality and was itself based on little more than the preferences of ancient, aristocratic orders. Starting with ancient Greece, "master" morality arose as the primary system of moral thinking, dividing the world up into the "good" and the "bad," the "life-affirming" and the "life-denying." The aristocratic virtues of health, strength, and wealth all fell into the good; the contrasting "slave" virtues of illness, weakness, and poverty were the bad.

But in response to the morality of the masters, the slaves themselves developed their own moral system. This new slave morality took the antitheses of the master morality and presented them as good in themselves. The values of the master morality became inverted: where the master morality praised strength, the slave morality praised weakness, and so on. This allowed slaves to live

Nietzsche decried the social philosophy of the utilitarians as equivalent to pigs in a sty—passive, philistine, and ultimately concerned solely with their own contentment.

Nietzsche railed against the replacing of "life-affirming" virtues with "life-denying" virtues—a historical change that he blamed on the development of monotheistic religions.

In ancient times, the **qualities of the lion**—strength, vitality, and power—were the **most celebrated** virtues.

In modern times, the **qualities of the lamb**—meekness and harmlessness—have become **more honored** as virtues.

with their true position in life without being overwhelmed by self-hatred and resentment. By denying, for example, the natural inequality of people in favor of a spurious, ideal equality between slaves and masters, slave morality offered a means for slaves to think as if they were equal to their masters—when, in simple reality, they were not. Nietzsche associated this slave morality particularly with Christianity and Judaism, which he portrayed as offering illusory solutions to the problems of life.

Thus Spake Zarathustra offers, in place of the toppled deities of organized religion, the figure of the "overman" (*Übermensch* in German). Humanity is merely a bridge between animals and the overman to come. But the overman is not a finished being and still less the literal, biological evolution from humanity. An overman is a man who has mastered himself and can seek his own truths, remaining "faithful to the earth" and rejecting those who offer "otherworldly truths," of whatever kind.

Antipolitical thinking

Such intense individualism has led some to suggest that Nietzsche was an antipolitician. Although political in tone, Nietzsche's rejection of morality suggests a nihilism that had little to do with understanding how a public sphere operates. He wrote only of individuals, never of movements or organizations. He was, in this sense, "beyond right or left," as French philosopher Georges Bataille argued. Yet he has come to have a deep influence on political thinkers of the right and the left. French philosopher Gilles Deleuze, in *Nietzsche and Philosophy*, emphasized Nietzsche's concern with the will to power. Deleuze placed the will to power as the drive to differentiate, to make all things different, and the center of an "empirical" rejection of all transcendental or otherworldly claims about the existing world. Nietzsche became a philosopher of difference, in Deleuze's hands, and also of resistance to constraints. Conventional morality led only to "sad passions" that "disparage life." Nietzsche has since come to occupy a critical place among poststructuralist thinkers concerned to overhaul systems of domination—including those purporting to liberate, such as Marxism. ∎

IT IS NECESSARY TO DARE IN ORDER TO SUCCEED
PETER KROPOTKIN (1842–1921)

IN CONTEXT

IDEOLOGY
Anarcho-communism

FOCUS
Political action

BEFORE
1762 Jean-Jacques Rousseau writes *The Social Contract*, stating that "man is born free, and is everywhere in chains."

1840 In *What Is Property?*, Pierre-Joseph Proudhon calls himself an anarchist.

1881 Czar Alexander II is assassinated in St. Petersburg.

AFTER
1917 The Bolsheviks seize power in Russia.

1960s Counterculture movements in Europe and the US squat in empty buildings and form communities.

2011 The Occupy Movement protests against economic inequality by occupying Wall Street during the global economic crisis.

At the end of the 19th century, Czarist Russia was a hotbed for every new social movement from fascism to radical communism. Peter Kropotkin, who spurned his privileged life as the son of a prince, was a product of his times, advocating the destruction of authority. In *The Conquest of Bread* (1892), Kropotkin argued that the best aspect of humanity—its ability to cooperate—could allow it to do away with all oppressive structures. He saw in the developing labor movement the possibility to overthrow oppressors—from priests to capitalists—and establish a new society based on mutual respect and cooperation. He lay down the principles of what was to become anarcho-communism: belief in a collaborative, egalitarian society, free of the state.

Call to action

Anarchism is a theory of action, and Kropotkin urged those who would listen to always act. Sympathetic to the Bolshevik Revolution of 1917, he denounced its authoritarianism in the subsequent civil war. Establishing a new world did not require fresh rules, but anarchists able to act courageously against all oppression. Compromise and political calculation were alien to anarchism; instead, its adherents must act with moral fervor against a corrupt world. Kropotkin, like other anarchists, helped define the "politics of the deed"—a belief that would recur in radical ideologies over the next century. ∎

EITHER WOMEN ARE TO BE KILLED, OR WOMEN ARE TO HAVE THE VOTE

EMMELINE PANKHURST (1858–1928)

IN CONTEXT

IDEOLOGY
Feminism

FOCUS
Civil disobedience

BEFORE
1792 Mary Wollstonecraft publishes *A Vindication of the Rights of Woman*, an early defense of women's equality.

1865 Liberal philosopher John Stuart Mill campaigns successfully for parliament on a platform of women's suffrage.

1893 New Zealand is the first major country to grant women the vote.

AFTER
1990 The Swiss canton of Appenzell Innerhoden is forced to accept women's suffrage. (The other cantons had accepted it in 1971.)

2005 Women are granted the right to vote and stand for parliament in Kuwait.

Emmeline Pankhurst is arrested outside Buckingham Palace in May 1914. The WSPU strongly advocated direct action in pursuit of its goals.

By the early 1900s, the right to vote was gaining acceptance around the world, but the right for women to do so lagged behind. New Zealand had been the first major country to grant the vote to women, in 1893, but progress in Europe and North America was achingly slow, hindered by obstinate politicians, conservative public opinion, and often vicious press campaigns.

Activist Emmeline Pankhurst, with others, established the Women's Social and Political Union (WSPU) in Britain in 1903. Known as "suffragettes," their militant action and civil disobedience soon included window smashing, assaults, and arson. In 1913, campaigner Emily Davidson died after throwing herself under the king's horse at the Derby race, and a hunger strike of imprisoned suffragettes was met with force-feeding.

When Pankhurst, speaking later in 1913, said, "either women are to be killed or women are to have the vote," she was laying claim both to the suffragettes' moral authority to act as they saw fit in furthering a just cause and emphasizing their apparently implacable determination to win it. However, this determination lasted only until World War I in 1914, when the WSPU dropped their campaign in order to support the war effort. Women over the age of 30 were granted the right to vote in Britain at the war's end, with all adult women able to vote by 1928. ■

THE INDIVIDUAL IS A SINGLE COG IN AN EVER-MOVING MECHANISM
MAX WEBER (1864–1920)

IN CONTEXT

IDEOLOGY
Liberalism

FOCUS
Society

BEFORE
1705 Dutch philosopher Bernard Mandeville writes *The Fable of the Bees*, demonstrating collective institutions arising from individual behavior.

1884 The final volume of Marx's *Capital* is published, though it is unfinished.

AFTER
1937 American sociologist Talcott Parsons publishes *The Structure of Social Action*, introducing Weber's work to a new international audience.

1976 *Capitalism and Social Theory* by British sociologist Anthony Giddens criticizes Weber's sociology, arguing instead for the primacy of structures in social action.

An individual's actions are informed by their **view of the world**.

Individuals **operate collectively** in complex ways.

Individual viewpoints coalesce into **collective understandings**, such as religion.

But the **social structures** created by these collective understandings can **constrain individual freedoms**.

The individual is a single cog in an ever-moving mechanism.

---

apitalism's rise in the 19th century prompted new ways to think about the world. Relations between people were transformed, with traditional ways of life torn up. Scientific and technical knowledge appeared to be advancing relentlessly, and society was seen as an object that could be studied and understood. Max Weber provided a new approach to the study of society—in the new discipline of "sociology." His incomplete work *Economy and Society* is an attempt to describe the functioning of society, as well as a method by which such study can

Fire ants live in a complex community where the individual's role is key to the success of the nest. In a similar way, Weber saw the actions of individuals as part of a larger human society.

be taken further. One of Weber's methods of study was to use abstract notions such as "ideal-types." Like a caricature of a person, an ideal-type exaggerated key features and reduced the less important ones—but to draw out the underlying truth, rather than to amuse. This approach was key to Weber's method and allowed him to understand complex parts of society via a simplified version. The role of the sociologist was to construct and analyze ideal-types based on the observation of reality. This stood in contrast to Karl Marx and earlier writers on social issues, who attempted to deduce the operations of society based on its internal logic rather than through direct observation.

Collective understandings

Society, Weber argued, could only be understood on the basis of its constituent parts—in the first instance, individuals. These individuals operated collectively in ways that were complex but could be understood by the sociologist. Individuals possessed a capacity to act, and their actions would be informed by their view of the world. These views would emerge as collective understandings. Religion and political systems such as capitalism are examples of these understandings. Weber, in his earlier work *The Protestant Ethic and the Spirit of Capitalism*, claimed that it was the new "spirit" of individualist Protestantism that paved the way for capital accumulation and the creation of a market society. *Economy and Society* develops this idea, distinguishing between types of religious belief and analyzing the ways in which individuals may perform social action using a wide variety of belief structures.

Restraints to action

Once society's collective structures are in place, Weber notes, they may act not as enablers, expanding human freedom, but as constraints. This is why Weber speaks of people as "cogs" in a "machine." The structures people create also restrain their actions, producing further results: Protestants were instructed to work but also to avoid consuming, and their savings created capitalism. ∎

Max Weber

Max Weber was born in Erfurt, Germany, and initially studied law at the University of Heidelberg. Working in a time before the discipline of sociology existed, Weber's work covered legal theory, history, and economics. He eventually became an economics professor at Freiburg University. Politically engaged from early in his career, Weber made his name as a thinker in social policy, writing on Polish immigration in the 1890s and joining one of Germany's movements for social reform, the Evangelical Social Congress. After WWI, he cofounded the liberal German Democratic Party.

A tempestuous relationship with his father ended when his father died in 1897. Weber had a nervous breakdown and never fully recovered. He was unable to hold a permanent teaching post again and suffered from insomnia and bouts of depression.

Key works

1905 *The Protestant Ethic and the Spirit of Capitalism*
1922 *Economy and Society*
1927 *General Economic History*

THE CLASH OF IDEOLOG

1910–1945

The first half of the 20th century saw the erosion of the old imperial powers and the establishment of new republics. The result was widespread political instability, especially in Europe, which led to the two world wars that dominated the period. In the process of replacing the old European order, a wave of extreme nationalist, authoritarian parties emerged, and in Russia, the Bolshevik Revolution of 1917 paved the way for a totalitarian communist dictatorship. Meanwhile, the Great Depression of the early 1930s prompted a move to increased economic and social liberalism in the United States.

By the end of the 1930s, political thinking among the major powers was polarized between the ideologies of fascism, communism, and the social democracy of liberal, free-market capitalism.

World revolutions

The revolutions that sparked this shake-up in political thought did not begin in Europe. In 1910, a decade-long armed struggle known as the Mexican Revolution began, with the fall of the old regime of Porfirio Díaz. In China, the ruling Qing dynasty was overthrown in the Xinhai Revolution of 1911 and replaced with a republic founded by Sun Yat-Sen the following year. But the most influential revolutionary events of the period took place in Russia. Political unrest had led to an unsuccessful revolution in 1905, which was rekindled in 1917 and led to the violent overthrow of Czar Nicholas II by the Bolsheviks.

The optimism many felt at the end of World War I was short-lived. The formation of the League of Nations, with its hope of ensuring an enduring peace, did little to stem the rising tensions in Europe. Punitive war reparations and postwar economic collapse were a major factor in fostering the appeal of extremist movements.

Dictatorship and resistance

Out of small extremist parties in Italy and Germany arose the Fascist party of Benito Mussolini and the Nazi party of Adolf Hitler. In Spain, in reaction to the formation of a second Spanish Republic, nationalists fought for power under Francisco Franco. And in Russia after the death of Vladimir Lenin in 1924, Joseph Stalin became increasingly autocratic, eliminating

IES

opponents and establishing the Soviet Union as an industrial and military power.

While totalitarian regimes grew in strength on continental Europe, Britain faced the breakup of its empire. Independence movements in the colonies threatened British rule, especially in India, with the campaign of nonviolent civil disobedience led by Mahatma Gandhi, but also in Africa, where activists such as Jomo Kenyatta of Kenya were mobilizing resistance.

Entering the fray

In the United States, the massive crash on the New York stock market in 1929 ended the boom years of the 1920s and ushered in the Great Depression. In 1933, President Franklin D. Roosevelt introduced the New Deal, which brought a new liberalism to American politics. The United States preferred to remain neutral in Europe's unstable affairs, but Nazi Germany's anti-Semitic policies led to the migration of intellectuals from Europe to America, in particular from the Marxist-inspired Frankfurt School. These immigrants brought a fresh thinking that challenged some of Roosevelt's policies.

It was not only Europe that the United States tried to ignore. Asia was also experiencing political turmoil as Japanese militarism sparked the Sino-Japanese War of 1937. As the war turned against China, Mao Zedong rose to prominence as a communist leader.

Britain, too, was reluctant to become involved in any conflict, despite the threat of fascism. Even with the onset of the Spanish Civil War in 1936, with Germany and the Soviet Union supporting opposite sides, Britain kept its distance. But pressure was growing in Britain and the United States to stop appeasing Hitler's territorial demands. After war broke out in 1939, the alliance against Germany grew, with the United States joining after the attack on Pearl Harbor by the Japanese in 1941.

Although Britain, the United States, and the Soviet Union collaborated successfully during World War II, once fascism was defeated, the political lines were redrawn. A standoff soon emerged, with the communist East opposed to the capitalist West and the rest of Europe struggling to find its place in the middle. The scene was set for the Cold War, which would dominate postwar politics. ■

NONVIOLENCE IS THE FIRST ARTICLE OF MY FAITH
MAHATMA GANDHI (1869–1948)

IN CONTEXT

IDEOLOGY
Anticolonial nationalism

FOCUS
Nonviolent resistance

BEFORE
5th–6th centuries BCE Jainist teachings stressing nonviolence and self-discipline develop in India.

1849 Henry David Thoreau publishes *Civil Disobedience*, defending the morality of conscientious objection to unjust laws.

AFTER
1963 In his "I have a dream" speech in Washington, DC, civil rights leader Martin Luther King Jr. outlines his vision of black and white people living together in peace.

2011 Peaceful protests in Cairo's Tahrir Square lead to the overthrow of Egyptian president Hosni Mubarak.

In the worldwide empires that European powers built from the 16th century onward, it was the example of the imperialists themselves that ultimately gave rise to the nationalist movements that sprang up in opposition to colonial rule. Witnessing the colonizers' strong sense of national identity, based on European ideas about nations and the importance of sovereignty within geographical borders, eventually ignited a desire for nationhood and self-determination in the colonized peoples. However, the lack of economic or military strength led many anticolonial movements to develop distinctly non-European modes of resistance.

A spiritual weapon
In India, the fight for independence from the UK in the first half of the 20th century was characterized by the political and moral philosophy of its spiritual leader, Mohandas Gandhi, more commonly known by the honorific title "Mahatma," meaning "Great Soul." Although he believed in a strong democratic state, Gandhi held that such a state could never be won, forged, or held by any form of violence. His ethic of radical nonviolent resistance and civil disobedience, which he named *satyagraha* ("adherence to truth"), focused a lens of morality and conscience on the tide of anticolonial nationalism that was transforming the political landscape of the 20th century. He described this method as a "purely spiritual weapon."

Gandhi believed that the universe was governed by a Supreme Principle, which he called *satya* ("Truth"). For him, this was another name for God, the one God of Love that he believed to be the basis of all the great world religions. Because all human beings were emanations of this divine Being, Gandhi believed that love was the only true principle of relations between humans. Love meant care and respect for others and selfless, lifelong devotion to the cause of "wiping away every tear from every eye." This enjoined *ahimsa*, or the rule of harmlessness, on Gandhi's adherents. Although a Hindu himself, Gandhi drew on many different religious traditions as he developed his moral philosophy, including Jainism and the pacifist Christian teachings of Russian novelist Leo Tolstoy, both of which stressed the importance of not causing hurt to any living creature.

Political ends

Gandhi's ideology was an attempt to work out the rule of love in every area of life. However, he believed that the endurance of suffering, or "turning the other cheek" to abusive treatment at the hands of an individual or a state—as opposed to violent resistance or reprisal—was a means to a political end, as well as a spiritual one. This willing sacrifice of the self would operate as a law of truth on human nature to secure the reformation and cooperation of an opponent. It would act as an example to wider society—political friend and foe alike. Home rule for India would be, for Gandhi, the inevitable outcome of a mass revolution of behavior based on a rich brew of peaceful transcendental principles.

South African activist

Gandhi's first experience of opposing British rule came not in India, but in South Africa. After training as a lawyer in London, he worked for 21 years in South Africa—then

Gandhi was influenced by Jainism, a religion whose central principle is to avoid harming living things. Jain monks wear masks so that they do not inadvertently breathe in insects.

another British colony—defending the civil rights of migrant Indians. It was during these years that he developed his sense of "Indianness," which he saw as bridging every divide of race, religion, and caste, and which underpinned his later vision of a united Indian nation. In South Africa, he witnessed firsthand the social injustice, racial violence, and punitive government exploitation of colonial rule. His response was to develop his pacifist ideals into a practical form of opposition. He proved his gift for leadership in 1906, when he led thousands of poor Indian settlers in a campaign of disobedience against repressive new laws requiring them to register with the state. After 7 years of struggle and violent repression, the »

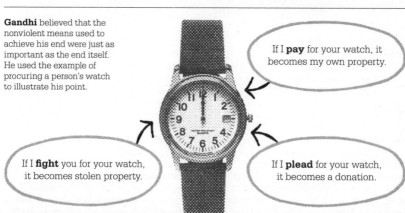

Gandhi believed that the nonviolent means used to achieve his end were just as important as the end itself. He used the example of procuring a person's watch to illustrate his point.

If I **pay** for your watch, it becomes my own property.

If I **fight** you for your watch, it becomes stolen property.

If I **plead** for your watch, it becomes a donation.

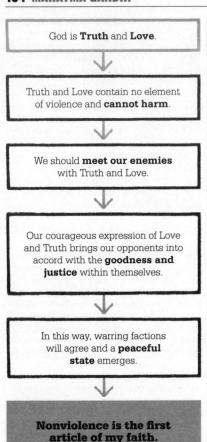

God is **Truth** and **Love**.

Truth and Love contain no element of violence and **cannot harm**.

We should **meet our enemies** with Truth and Love.

Our courageous expression of Love and Truth brings our opponents into accord with the **goodness and justice** within themselves.

In this way, warring factions will agree and a **peaceful state** emerges.

Nonviolence is the first article of my faith.

South African leader, Jan Christiaan Smuts, negotiated a compromise with the protestors, demonstrating the power of nonviolent resistance. It might take time, but it would win out in the end, shaming opponents into doing the right thing.

In the years that followed, Gandhi had considerable success in promoting his idea that nonviolent resistance was the most effective resistance. He returned to India in 1915 with an international reputation as an Indian nationalist and soon rose to a position of prominence in the Indian National Congress, the political movement for Indian nationalism. Gandhi advocated the boycott of British-made goods, especially textiles, encouraging all Indians to spin and wear *khadi*, or homespun cloth, in order to reduce dependence on foreign industry and strengthen their own economy. He saw such boycotts as a logical extension of peaceful noncooperation and urged people to refuse to use British schools and law courts, to resign from government employment, and to eschew British titles and honors. Amid increasing excitement and publicity, he learned to distinguish himself as an astute political showman, understanding the power of the media to influence public opinion.

Public defiance

In 1930, with the British government refusing to respond to Gandhi's congressional resolution calling for Indian dominion status, full independence was unilaterally declared by the Indian National Congress. Soon after, Gandhi launched a new *satyagraha* against the British tax on salt, calling on thousands to join him on the long march to the sea. As the world watched, Gandhi picked up a handful of the salt that lay in great white sheets along the beach and was promptly arrested. Gandhi was imprisoned, but his act of defiance had publicly demonstrated the unjust nature of British rule in India to commentators around the world. This carefully orchestrated act of nonviolent disobedience began to shake the hold of the British Empire on India.

Reports of Gandhi's campaigns and imprisonment appeared in newspapers all over the world. German physicist Albert Einstein said of him, "He has invented a completely new and humane means for the liberation war of an oppressed country. The moral influence he had on the consciously thinking human being of the entire civilized world will probably be much more lasting than it seems in our time, with its overestimation of brutal violent forces."

Strict pacifism

However, Gandhi's absolute confidence in his doctrine of nonviolence sometimes seemed unbalanced when he applied it

A religion that takes no account of practical affairs and does not help to solve them is no religion.
Mahatma Gandhi

to the conflicts unfolding in the wider world, and this earned him criticism from many quarters. "Self-suffering endurance" appeared sometimes to require mass suicide, as shown by his weeping plea to the British Viceroy of India that the British give up arms and oppose the Nazis with spiritual force only. Later, he criticized Jews who had tried to escape the Holocaust or had fought back against German repression, saying, "The Jews should have offered themselves to the butcher's knife. They should have thrown themselves into the sea from cliffs. It would have aroused the world and the people of Germany." Criticism also came his way from the left, and British Marxist journalist Rajani Palme Dutt accused him of "using the most religious principles of humanity and love to disguise his support of the property class." Meanwhile, British prime minister Winston Churchill attempted to dismiss him as a "half-naked fakir."

Whatever the limits of their application in other situations, Gandhi's methods were certainly successful in eventually winning independence for India in 1947, although he bitterly opposed the Partition of India into two states split along religious lines—predominantly Hindu India and Muslim Pakistan—which led to the displacement of millions of people. Soon after Partition, Gandhi was assassinated by a Hindu nationalist who accused him of appeasing Muslims.

Today's rapidly industrializing India is a far cry from the rural romanticism and asceticism of Gandhi's political ideals. Meanwhile, the ongoing tension with neighbor Pakistan shows that Gandhi's belief in an Indian identity that transcended religion has ultimately been unfulfilled. The caste system, which Gandhi had steadfastly opposed, also maintains a strong hold on Indian society. However, India remains a secular, democratic state, which still aligns with Gandhi's fundamental belief that it is only through peaceful means that a just state can emerge. His example and methods have been taken up by activists around the world, including civil rights leader Martin Luther King Jr., who credited Gandhi as the inspiration for his peaceful resistance to racially biased laws in the US in the 1950s and '60s. ■

Mahatma Gandhi

Mohandas Karamchand Gandhi was born on October 2, 1869, to a prominent Hindu family in Porbandar, part of the Bombay Presidency in British India. Gandhi's father was a senior government official and his mother a devout Jain.

Gandhi was married at the age of just 13. Five years later, his father sent him to London to study law. He was called to the bar in 1891 and set up a law practice in South Africa, defending the civil rights of Indian migrants. While there, Gandhi embarked upon a strict course in *brahmacharya*, or Hindu self-discipline, beginning a life of asceticism. In 1915, he returned to India, where he took a vow of poverty and founded an ashram. Four years later, he became head of the Indian National Congress. He was killed on his way to prayer by a Hindu extremist who blamed him for the Partition of India and the creation of Pakistan.

Key works

1909 *Hind Swaraj*
1929 *The Story of My Experiments with Truth*

POLITICS BEGIN WHERE THE MASSES ARE

VLADIMIR LENIN (1870–1924)

IN CONTEXT

IDEOLOGY
Communism

FOCUS
Mass revolution

BEFORE
1793 During the Reign of Terror following the French Revolution, thousands are executed as "enemies of the revolution."

1830s French political activist Auguste Blanqui teaches that a small band of expert conspirators can execute a revolutionary seizure of power.

1848 Karl Marx and Friedrich Engels publish the *Communist Manifesto*.

AFTER
1921 The Communist Party of China (CPC) is organized as a Leninist vanguard party.

1927 Stalin reverses Lenin's New Economic Policy and collectivizes agriculture.

 We have combined, by a freely adopted decision, for the purpose of fighting the enemy.
Vladimir Lenin

A t the turn of the 20th century, the Russian Empire was a lumbering agrarian colossus that had fallen far behind the industrializing states of western Europe in economic terms. The empire's population comprised many different ethnic groups—including Russians, Ukrainians, Poles, Belorussians, Jews, Finns, and Germans—only 40 percent of whom spoke Russian. The empire was ruled over by an absolutist, authoritarian czar, Nicolas II, and a strict social hierarchy was ruthlessly enforced. There was no free press, no freedom of speech or association, no minority rights, and few political rights. Unsurprisingly, in this atmosphere of repression, revolutionary forces were gaining an ever-stronger foothold, and they would finally be carried to victory in the 1917 October Revolution by a political agitator named Vladimir Lenin.

A law of history
During the 19th century, socialism had developed in Europe as a response to the hardship that characterized the lives of the new industrial working class. Unprotected by social institutions or traditions such as unions, workers were particularly at risk of exploitation by their new employers. In response to their suffering, and believing that class conflict holds within it the dynamics of social change, Karl Marx and Friedrich Engels

proclaimed that an international revolution against capitalism was inevitable. In the *Communist Manifesto* of 1848, they called for an international merger of the proletariat across Europe.

However, Marx and Engels had not foreseen that as workers in the advanced industrialized societies of western Europe became more secure and began to acquire better living standards, they would aspire to become the bourgeoisie (middle class), not revolt against it. Socialists began more and more to work through legal and constitutional channels with the aim of winning the vote for working-class men and thereby achieving change through the democratic process. Socialist opinion became increasingly divided between those who advocated reform through the ballot box and those who sought reform through revolution.

Russian conditions

Russia had come late to industrialization and at the end of the 19th century, its working class had still not won any real concessions from their employers. Unlike the citizens of western Europe, the vast majority of Russia's population had not seen any material benefits from industrialization. In the 1890s, growing numbers of political activists in Russia, including radical young law student Vladimir Lenin, plotted against the »

Vladimir Lenin

Vladimir Ilich Ulyanov, who later adopted the surname Lenin, was born in Simbirsk, Russia, now called Ulyanovsk. He received a classical education and showed a gift for Latin and Greek. In 1887, his brother Aleksandr was executed for the attempted assassination of Czar Alexander III. That year, Lenin enrolled at Kazan University to study law but was expelled for student protests. Exiled to his grandfather's estate, he steeped himself in the works of Karl Marx. He received his law degree and began his real career as a professional revolutionary. He was arrested, jailed, exiled to Siberia, and then traveled through Europe, writing and organizing for the coming revolution. The October Revolution of 1917 effectively made him ruler of all Russia. Lenin survived an assassination attempt in 1918, but never fully regained his health.

Key works

1902 *What Is To Be Done?*
1917 *Imperialism, the Highest Stage of Capitalism*
1917 *The State and Revolution*

To be successful, an **insurrection** must rely on the **actions of the masses**.

↓

To **inspire** the masses into action, a **vanguard party** is needed.

↓

The **aims and interests** of the vanguard party must be **in tune** with those of the masses to carry the masses with them.

↓

Politics begin where the masses are.

Lenin initially attempted to garner support for the revolution from Russian peasants. He concluded that peasants could not form the revolutionary class because they aspired to own land.

increasingly repressive state and its secret police force, and in 1905, a wave of unrest swept the country. This first attempt at a revolution failed to overthrow the czar, but it did win some concessions to democracy. Russian workers continued to endure harsh conditions, however, and revolutionaries continued to plot the total overthrow of the czarist regime.

Throughout his career, Lenin strove to translate Marxist theory into practical politics. Analyzing Russia's position through a Marxist lens, he saw that the country was moving in sudden leaps from feudalism to capitalism. Lenin viewed the peasant economy as another exploitative plank in the capitalist platform—judging that if it were pulled out, the whole capitalist economy would collapse. However, as the peasants aspired to own their own land, Lenin realized they would not be the class to bring about a socialist revolution, one of whose central aims was the eventual ending of private ownership. It was clear to Lenin that the driving force of the revolution would have to be the burgeoning industrial working class.

Vanguard party

In Marxist analysis, the bourgeoisie is the middle class—the social class that owns the means of production (such as the factories)—while the proletariat comprises those

who have no choice but to live off the sale of their own labor. Within the bourgeoisie were educated individuals, such as Lenin himself, who viewed the exploitation of the proletariat by the bourgeoisie as unjust and agitated for change. Such "revolutionary bourgeois" individuals had played a leading role in past revolutions, including the French Revolution of 1789. However, the rapid industrialization of Russia was being financed largely by foreign capital, and this meant that the Russian bourgeoisie was a relatively small class. To make matters trickier still, there were few revolutionaries within their number.

Lenin understood that a revolution required leadership and organization, and he championed Engels' and Marx's idea of a "vanguard party"—a group of "resolute individuals" of clear political understanding, mostly recruited from the working class,

Rich bankers flee as the workers advance under the slogan "Long Live the International Socialist Revolution!," a quote from Lenin emphasizing cross-border class allegiances.

who would spearhead the revolution. They were to inspire the proletariat to become a "class-for-itself," which would then overthrow bourgeois supremacy and establish a democratic "dictatorship of the proletariat." Lenin drew together his vanguard party under the name of the Bolsheviks; this party would ultimately become the Communist Party of the Soviet Union.

International revolution

Like Marx, Lenin believed that a united proletariat would rise in a great revolutionary wave that would transcend borders and national identities, ethnocentrism, and religion, effectively becoming a borderless, classless state in itself. It would be an international expansion of "democracy for the poor" and would occur alongside a forced suppression of the exploiting and oppressing class, who would be excluded from the new democracy. Lenin saw this transitory phase as an essential part of the shift from democracy to communism— the ultimate revolutionary state envisioned by Marx, which would follow the dictatorship of the proletariat. In this ultimate communist state, class would be transcended and private property abolished.

Lenin declared that his political ideas could take hold "not where there are thousands, but where there are millions. That is where serious politics begin." In order to confront the might and force of the heavily armed imperialist state, millions of disaffected workers, alienated by that state, were needed to participate. Only in their united millions, organized by professional revolutionaries, could they hope to destroy a well-armed and well-financed capitalist regime. Under the czars, the working classes and peasants had seen

A rebellious army, sick of the appalling casualties of World War I, played a crucial role in making the 1917 October Revolution a success. The old regime was discredited by the war.

their own interests as dependent upon the interests of the owners of production or the landowner, but Lenin the Marxist urged them to see their rights and welfare as dependent only upon their own social class. The masses had been welded together into a single political body by their suffering, and now this was reinforced by constant rhetoric from Lenin's Bolshevik lieutenants. For Lenin, the power of the masses was the only effective revolutionary power.

When Lenin delivered his political report to the Extraordinary Seventh Congress of the Russian Communist Party on March 6, 1918, a year after the successful 1917 revolution, he provided them with a review of the revolution that was "a truly Marxist substantiation of all our decisions." His Bolshevik party had seized power from the transitional government the preceding October in what was essentially a bloodless *coup d'etat*. They were the first successful communist revolutionaries in the world. Even though Russia was a poor country within the capitalist finance system with a relatively weak proletariat, its bourgeois state was even weaker, and the masses of working-class urban workers had been mobilized to dispossess it, resulting in an "easy victory."

One major factor in the success of the revolution had been Russia's role in World War I. By 1917, the war was causing the Russian people intolerable hardship. Even death squads could not stop troop mutinies and desertions, and the "imperialist" war »

 Victory will belong only to those who have faith in the people, those who are immersed in the life-giving spring of popular creativity.
Vladimir Lenin

This struggle must be organized ... by people who are professionally engaged in revolutionary activity.
Vladimir Lenin

was transformed into civil war between the Bolshevik Red Army and the anti-Bolshevik White Army. Lenin wrote, "In this civil war, the overwhelming majority of the population proved to be on our side, and that is why victory was achieved with such extraordinary ease." Everywhere he saw the fulfillment of Marx's expectation that, as the proletariat learned through harsh experience that there could be no collaboration with the bourgeois state, the "fruit" of mass revolution would "ripen" spontaneously.

In reality, many other factors played a part. As the events of 1917 had played out, the institutions of the old order—the local administration, the army, and the Church—lost their authority. Both urban and rural economies collapsed. Russia's forced withdrawal from World War I and the subsequent civil war took place against a backdrop of severe shortages, which brought about widespread suffering. Lenin had realized that only a dominant and coercive force could hope to create a new order out of this chaos. The Bolshevik party was the vanguard but not the main substance of revolutionary power. Thinking in terms of the Marxian categories of the masses and blocks of workers and peasants, Lenin saw the proletarian democracy of the workers' soviets (councils or groups) as the elementary substance of the new "commune" state. These groups united into one under the cry, "All Power to the Soviets!" In October 1917, the world's first socialist state, the Russian Socialist Federative Soviet Republic, was born.

War Communism

Economically, the revolution was followed by 3 years of War Communism, which saw millions of Russian peasants die of starvation as food produced in the countryside was confiscated and brought to feed Bolshevik armies and cities and to aid in the civil war against the anti-Bolshevik Whites. Conditions were so harsh that Lenin and the Bolsheviks faced uprisings from the same masses on whose support Lenin had based his politics. Historian David Christian writes that War Communism challenged the ideals of Lenin's new Communist party, as "the government claiming to represent the working class now found itself on the verge of being overthrown by that same working class."

While War Communism was the improvised condition that resulted from a revolution, what replaced it at the end of the civil war was a specific policy proposed by Lenin. The New Economic Policy, which Lenin referred to as state capitalism, allowed some small businesses, such as farms, to sell on their surpluses for personal gain. Large industries and banks remained in the hands of the state. The new policy, which was reviled by many Bolsheviks for diluting socialist economics with capitalist elements, succeeded in increasing agricultural production, since farmers were encouraged to produce larger quantities of food through appeal to their own self-interest. The policy was later replaced by Stalin's policy of forced collectivism in the years after Lenin's death, leading to more widespread famines in the 1930s.

During the civil war that followed the revolution, the Bolsheviks fought the antirevolutionary "White Army." Emergency measures were imposed, testing the support of the masses.

In China's Cultural Revolution, young Red Guards formed a vanguard, rooting out anti-revolutionary attitudes. Lenin believed that vanguards were needed to lead a revolution.

Proletarian power

The extent to which Lenin's October Revolution was an authentically socialist revolution depends upon the extent to which "the masses" were actually in accord with and represented by the Bolsheviks. Was the suffering proletariat actually self-liberated "from below," or did Bolshevik leaders ride to power on the Marxist narrative of victory for the suffering masses? How real was this new proletarian power—the power of the masses—which was brought into being and then constantly defined, explained, and eulogized by Lenin?

A contemporary of Lenin, Nikolay Sukhanov, a socialist activist and critic of the Bolshevik Revolution, was skeptical. Sukhanov wrote, "Lenin is an orator of a great power who is capable of simplifying a complicated matter … the one who is pounding, pounding, and pounding people's minds until they lose their will, until he enslaves them."

Labor aristocracy

Many critics have considered that when the Bolsheviks insisted that the dictatorship of the party was synonymous with a true workers' state, they were in reality justifying their dominance over the workers. Lenin excused this dominance through his elitist belief that without the "professional revolutionaries," workers on their own could not rise higher than a "trade union consciousness." By this, he meant that workers would not see beyond

alliances with their immediate colleagues at work to a wider class alliance.

Compounding the problem, in Lenin's eyes, was the fact that the concessions won by the working classes in parts of western Europe had not lifted the working class as a whole. Rather, these concessions had created what Lenin called a "labor aristocracy"—a group of workers who had won significant concessions and as a result had become detached from their true class allegiance. For Lenin, the situation required a "revolutionary socialist consciousness" that could grasp Marxist principles of class unification. This could only be provided by a vanguard from within the working class—and the Bolsheviks formed that vanguard party.

Lenin held that the existence of absolute truth was unconditional, and further that Marxism was truth, which left no room for dissent. This absolutism gave Bolshevism an authoritarian, antidemocratic, and elitist nature that would seem to be at odds with a belief in bottom-up democracy. His vanguard-party revolution has since been replicated across the political spectrum, from the right-wing anti-communist Kuomintang Party in Taiwan to the Communist Party of China. Some intellectuals still describe themselves as "Leninists," including Slovenian philosopher Slavoj Zizek, who admires Lenin's desire to apply Marxist theory in practice and his willingness "to dirty his hands" in order to achieve his aims. Contemporary Leninists see globalization as the continuation of the 19th-century imperialism that Lenin opposed, as capitalist interests turn toward poor countries in search of new labor forces to exploit. Their solution to this problem, like Lenin's a century ago, is an international mass workers' movement. ∎

AN APPEASER IS ONE WHO FEEDS A CROCODILE HOPING IT WILL EAT HIM LAST
WINSTON CHURCHILL (1874–1965)

IN CONTEXT

IDEOLOGY
Conservatism

FOCUS
Nonappeasement

BEFORE
c.350 BCE Statesman and orator Demosthenes criticizes his fellow Athenians for not anticipating Philip of Macedon's imperial goals.

1813 European powers try to settle with Napoleon, but his renewed military campaigns drive a coalition of allies to defeat him at Leipzig.

AFTER
1982 British prime minister Margaret Thatcher refers to Chamberlain when urged to compromise with Argentina during the Falklands War.

2003 US president George Bush and British prime minister Tony Blair invoke the dangers of appeasement in the run-up to the Iraq War.

I n the mid-1930s, the word "appeasement" had not yet taken on the taint of cowardice and ignominy that later events would give it. Conciliatory policy making had become the norm after World War I, as European powers sought to ease what Winston Churchill had called "the fearful hatreds and antagonisms

Churchill denounced the settlement that Chamberlain negotiated with Hitler at Munich in 1938 as "a total, unmitigated defeat."

which exist in Europe." But as the Great Depression took its toll around the world and Adolf Hitler rose to power in Germany, Churchill and a very few others saw that this policy was becoming dangerous.

Defense expenditure in Britain had been constrained by the economic slump. The need to rearm against Hitler came at a time of extreme financial duress for a nation that was still struggling to recover from World War I and deploying most of its military resources in the remote outposts of the British Empire. The idea of confronting Germany again to contain Hitler was dismissed by conservative prime minister Stanley Baldwin and his successor, fellow conservative Neville Chamberlain. Assuaging the dictator's mounting grievances seemed to them the moderate, practical approach.

Churchill's unofficial network of military and government intelligence kept him informed about Nazi aims and movements and the unprepared state of British forces. He warned Parliament about Hitler's intentions in 1933, and continued to raise the alarm in speeches of immense poetic power in the face of what he saw as complacency, only to be mocked as a warmonger and relegated to the back benches of Parliament.

The Munich Agreement

The appeasement mindset in British politics was firmly entrenched, and the British offered no resistance to Hitler's systematic breach of the conditions of the Versailles Treaty they had signed at the end of World War I—including his remilitarization of the Rhineland—or to his legislation against the Jews. Emboldened, Hitler annexed Austria into the Reich in 1938, and in the same year, crudely coerced Chamberlain at Munich to trade Czechoslovakia's Sudetenland for another false promise of peace.

Hitler was bemused by his easy gains. He had planned to "smash" Czechoslovakia with a "shock and awe"-style entry into Prague and instead found her "virtually served up to me on a plate by her friends."

Churchill denounced the Munich Agreement. He contended that to feed the Nazi monster with concessions would simply make it more voracious. Other politicians trusted Hitler, and Churchill stood almost alone—among Conservatives at least—in condemning him. He refused at all times to discuss anything at all with Hitler or with his representatives. Radical but reasoned, this non-negotiable defiance of tyranny, to the death if need be, was the core idea that would bring down the Nazis. ■

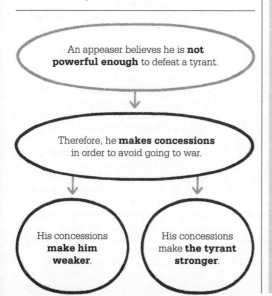

An appeaser believes he is **not powerful enough** to defeat a tyrant.

↓

Therefore, he **makes concessions** in order to avoid going to war.

↓   ↓

His concessions **make him weaker**.

His concessions make **the tyrant stronger**.

Winston Churchill

The son of English lord Randolph Churchill and American heiress Jennie Jerome, Sir Winston Leonard Spencer-Churchill once described himself as "an English-Speaking Union." He was educated at Harrow Public School and Sandhurst Military Academy and then served in India with a cavalry commission. During the 1890s, he distinguished himself as a war correspondent covering the Cuban Revolt against Spain, British campaigns in India and the Sudan, and the Boer War in South Africa. His career in the House of Commons, first as a Liberal and later as a Conservative, spanned 60 years. He took charge of a government of national unity during World War II, and served one more term as prime minister in 1951. Churchill was a prolific writer and received the Nobel Prize for Literature in 1953, largely for his six-part history of World War II.

Key works

1953 *The Second World War*
1958 *A History of the English Speaking Peoples*
1974 *The Complete Speeches*

THE WEALTHY FARMERS MUST BE DEPRIVED OF THE SOURCES OF THEIR EXISTENCE
JOSEPH STALIN (1878–1953)

IN CONTEXT

IDEOLOGY
State socialism

FOCUS
Collectivization

BEFORE
1566 In Russia, Ivan the Terrible's efforts to create a centralized state result in peasants fleeing and a drop in food production.

1793–1794 The Jacobins institute the Reign of Terror in France.

AFTER
1956 Nikita Krushchev reveals that Stalin executed thousands of loyal communists during the purges.

1962 Alexander Solzhenitsyn's *One Day in the Life of Ivan Denisovich*, telling of life in a Russian labor camp, becomes a worldwide bestseller.

1989 Mikhail Gorbachev introduces *glasnost* (openness), saying, "I detest lies."

A fter the Russian Revolution of 1917, Vladimir Lenin's Bolsheviks set about creating a new socialist system through nationalization, taking privately held assets or enterprises into government ownership. Lenin's successor as leader of the Soviet Union, Joseph Stalin, accelerated this process in 1929, and over 5 years, the economy was rapidly industrialized and collectivized by edict from the government.

In the name of modernizing the Soviet Union's agricultural system, Stalin amalgamated farms under state control as "socialist state property." The class of relatively wealthy farmers known as kulaks were compelled to give up their land and join collective farms. Stalin's police confiscated food and took it to the towns, and the peasants retaliated by burning their crops and killing their animals. A disastrous famine ensued, and in the area of Ukraine known as the "breadbasket" because of its rich farmland, 5 million people starved or were shot or deported. By 1934, 7 million kulaks had been "eliminated." Those who survived were now living on state farms run by government officials.

Revolution from above
Stalin reasoned that collectivization was an essential form of class war, forming part of a "revolution from above." This simple conflation gave him the justification he needed to move away from Lenin's policy of using persuasion to organize the peasants into cooperatives. Stalin began by "restricting the tendencies of the kulaks," then moved on to "ousting" them from the countryside, and finally "eliminating" them as an entire class. Lenin had warned that as long as the Soviet Union remained surrounded by capitalist countries, the class struggle would need to continue. Stalin quoted this often as collectivization advanced. He complained that the individual

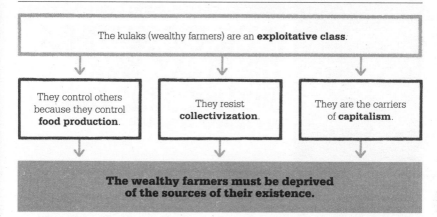

The kulaks (wealthy farmers) are an **exploitative class**.

They control others because they control **food production**.

They resist **collectivization**.

They are the carriers of **capitalism**.

The wealthy farmers must be deprived of the sources of their existence.

peasant economy "generated capitalism," and that as long as it did, capitalism would remain a feature of the Soviet economy.

Stalin framed the mass-murder of millions of individuals as the "liquidation" of a class, to be carried out by "depriving them of the productive sources of existence." However, when the destruction of private farming was complete, he sustained the terror, claiming that the old "kulak mentality" was lingering, and continued to threaten the communist state.

As the terror of Stalin's regime spread, it was not only the kulaks who would suffer persecution. Opponents of Stalin's rule, real and imagined, were killed, including every single surviving member of Lenin's politburo. Lenin's revolution was transformed into Stalin's dictatorship, and the Bolshevik party—which Lenin had seen as a "vanguard party," inspiring the masses—became a hulking, institutionalized state party that performed the role of the instrument of terror in Stalin's regime. Stalin had begun his persecution with the kulaks, but by the middle of the 1930s, few were safe from the state terror machine. ∎

Joseph Stalin

Joseph Stalin was born Ioseb Besarionis dze Jughashvili in the village of Gori, Georgia. He was educated at the local church school and later expelled from Tiflis Theological Seminary, where he had become a Marxist. As a young man, he was a noted poet.

Stalin's political career took off in 1907, when he attended the 5th Congress of the Russian Social Democratic Labor Party in London with Lenin. Active in the political underground, he was exiled to Siberia several times, and in 1913, he adopted the name Stalin from the Russian word *stal* ("steel"). By the revolution of 1917, he had become a leading figure in the Bolshevik party. Stalin's ruthless actions in the subsequent civil war were an early warning of the terrors that would come when he succeeded Lenin as the leader of the Soviet Union. He had a troubled private life, and both his first son and second wife committed suicide.

Key works

1924 *The Principles of Leninism*
1938 *Dialectical and Historical Materialism*

IF THE END JUSTIFIES THE MEANS, WHAT JUSTIFIES THE END?
LEON TROTSKY (1879–1940)

 We must rid ourselves once and for all of the Quaker-Papist babble about the sanctity of human life.
Leon Trotsky

Throughout his career, Russian revolutionary Leon Trotsky always sought to promote what he saw as a truly Marxist position. He worked closely with Vladimir Lenin to translate Karl Marx's theories into practice as the two men led the Bolshevik Revolution of 1917.

According to Marx's theory, the revolution was to be followed by a "dictatorship of the proletariat" as workers took control of the means of production. However, following Lenin's death in 1924, Joseph Stalin's absolutist bureaucracy soon crushed any hope of such a mass movement, imposing a dictatorship of one man instead.

Trotsky had hoped to safeguard the advances he believed had been made in the revolution through a strategy of "permanent revolution," which would be guaranteed by the ongoing support of an international working class. Marx had warned that socialism in one place could not hope to succeed in isolation from the global proletariat, stating that revolution must continue "until all the more or less propertied classes have been driven from their ruling positions ... not only in one country, but in all the leading countries of the world." Lenin had insisted that the socialist revolution in Russia could triumph only if supported by workers' movements in one or several other economically advanced countries. Trotsky's followers have since argued that this failure to achieve a critical

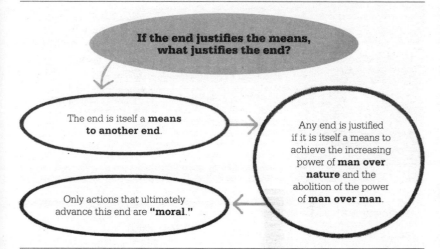

If the end justifies the means, what justifies the end?

The end is itself a **means to another end**.

Only actions that ultimately advance this end are **"moral."**

Any end is justified if it is itself a means to achieve the increasing power of **man over nature** and the abolition of the power of **man over man**.

mass of support internationally was the reason that the Soviet Union fell into Stalin's hands.

Communism under Stalin

Within 4 years of Lenin's death, the inner party democracy and the soviet democratic system—the cornerstone of Bolshevism—had been dismantled within communist parties across the world. Within the Soviet Union itself, Stalin's doctrine of "Socialism in One Country" removed the wider aspiration for an international workers' revolution.

Dissidents were vilified as Trotskyists and expelled from party ranks. When his Left Opposition faction against Stalin failed, Trotsky was expelled from the Communist Party and exiled from the

Stalin, Lenin, and Trotsky were all leading figures in the Bolshevik Revolution. After Lenin died, Stalin took power and Trotsky was a marked man.

Soviet Union. By 1937, Stalin had jailed or killed all of the so-called Trotskyists of the Left Opposition, and Trotsky himself was in Mexico, hiding from assassins.

Against morality

Many on the left reacted to Stalin's excesses by moving to the right and rejecting revolutionary Marxism, taking up what Trotsky described as "moralistic" positions that emphasized universal values. The suggestion was that Bolshevism—the centralist system of Lenin and Trotsky—had allowed the crimes of Stalin.

In *Their Morals and Ours*, Trotsky describes this claim as a reactionary spasm of class conflict disguised as morality. One of the main criticisms leveled at Bolshevism was that Lenin's belief that "the end justifies the means" had led directly to the "amorality" of treachery, brutality, and mass murder. To these critics, morality protected against such atrocities. Trotsky considered that, whether intended or not, this was simply a defense of capitalism, since he believed that capitalism could not exist "through force alone. It needs the cement of morality."

For Trotsky, there is no such thing as morality if it is conceived as a set of eternal values that are not derived from sensory or material evidence. Hence, any behavior that is not motivated by the »

Leon Trotsky

Lev Davidovich Bronshtein was born in 1879 in the small village of Yanovka in what is now Ukraine. Schooled in cosmopolitan Odessa, he was involved in revolutionary activities and took up Marxism after initially opposing it. He was arrested, imprisoned, and exiled to Siberia by the time he was just 18.

In Siberia, he took his prison guard's name, Trotsky, and escaped to London, where he met and worked with Lenin on the revolutionary journal *Iskra*. In 1905, he returned to Russia to support the revolution. Arrested and sent back to Siberia, his bravery earned him popularity. He escaped from Siberia again, joining Lenin in the successful revolution of 1917. He led the Red Army during the Russian Civil War and held other key posts, but after Lenin's death, he was forced out of power by Stalin and into exile. He was assassinated on Stalin's orders by Ramón Mercader in Mexico City in 1940.

Key works

1937 *The Stalin School of Falsification*
1938 *Their Morals and Ours*

existing social conditions or class conflict is illegitimate and inauthentic. Abstract moral concepts that are not based on empirical evidence are simply tools used by ruling-class institutions to suppress the class struggle. The ruling class imposes "moral" obligations on society that its members do not observe themselves and that serve to perpetuate their power.

Trotsky gives the morality of war as an example: "The most 'humane' governments, which in peaceful times 'detest' war, proclaim during war that the highest duty of their armies is the extermination of the greatest possible number of people." The insistence on the prescribed behavioral norms of religion and philosophy was also a tool of class deception. For Trotsky, to expose this deceit was the revolutionary's first duty.

The new aristocracy

Trotsky was eager to show that the centralizing tendencies of Bolshevism were not the "means" whose "end" was Stalinism. Such centralization was necessary to defeat the Bolsheviks' enemies, but its end was always intended to be a decentralized dictatorship of the proletariat, ruling through the system of Soviets. For Trotsky, Stalinism was an "immense bureaucratic reaction" against what he saw as the advances of the 1917 revolution. Stalinism reinstated the worst of absolutist entitlements, "regenerating the fetishism of power" beyond the dreams even of the czars; it had created a "new aristocracy." Trotsky saw the crimes of Stalin as the consequence of the most brutal class struggle of all—that of "the new aristocracy against the masses that raised it to power." He was scathing of self-declared Marxists who linked Bolshevism with Stalinism by stressing the immorality of both. In Trotsky's eyes, he and his followers had opposed Stalin from the beginning, while his critics had only arrived at their position after Stalin's atrocities had come to light.

Critics of Marxism often claim that the idea that "the end justifies the means" is used to justify acts of murder and barbarism, as well as the deception of the masses, purportedly for their own benefit. Trotsky insisted that this was a misunderstanding, stating that "the end justifies the means" simply signifies that there is an acceptable way to do a right thing. For example, if it is permissible to eat fish, then it is right to kill and cook them. The moral justification of any action must be linked to its "end" in this way. Killing a mad dog that is threatening a child is a virtue, but killing a dog gratuitously or perversely for no "end" is a crime.

The ultimate end

So what is the answer to the question, "What may we, and what may we not do"? What end justifies the means needed to achieve it? For Trotsky, the end is justified if it "leads to the increasing power of man over nature and to the abolition of the power of man over man." In other words, the end can itself be seen as a means to this ultimate end. But did Trotsky mean that the liberation of the working classes was an end for which any destructiveness was permissible? He will only consider this question in relation to the class struggle, thinking it a meaningless abstraction to do otherwise. Thus, the only meaningful good is that which unites the revolutionary proletariat, strengthening it as a class for the ongoing struggle.

Trotsky's reasoning has been seen by some notable Marxists as dangerous, counter-revolutionary, and false. Harry Haywood, an African-American Marxist-Leninist who was in the Soviet Union during the 1920s and '30s, believed that "Trotsky was doomed to defeat because his ideas were incorrect and failed to conform to objective conditions, as well as the needs and interests of the Soviet

Slaughter on a grand scale was perpetrated by Trotsky's Red Army in the Russian Civil War, leading critics to compare Bolshevism to Stalin's purges.

> ❝ Root out the counter-revolutionaries without mercy, lock up suspicious characters in concentration camps. Shirkers will be shot, regardless of past service.
> **Leon Trotsky** ❞

people." During the Russian Civil War of 1917–1922, Trotsky had centralized command structures in what was known as "War Communism." This centralizing tendency has been criticized by disillusioned former followers as closed to critical reflection, convinced of the absolute rightness of its own analysis, and allowing no dissent. In addition, such structures necessarily restrict power to a small group of leaders, since they are too demanding of workers' time and effort for a wide-based system of mass participation to develop. Writing in the 1940s, US Marxist Paul Mattick asserted that the Russian Revolution had itself been as totalitarian as Stalinism and that the legacy of Bolshevism, Leninism, and Trotskyism served "as a mere ideology to justify the rise of modified capitalist (state-capitalist) systems … controlled by way of an authoritarian state." ∎

EUROPE HAS BEEN LEFT WITHOUT A MORAL CODE
JOSÉ ORTEGA Y GASSET (1883–1955)

IN CONTEXT

IDEOLOGY
Liberalism

FOCUS
Pro-intellectualism

BEFORE
380 BCE Plato advocates rule by philosopher kings.

1917 In Spain, news of the Russian Revolution instills fear in Primo de Rivera's regime, which consolidates its power by control of the masses.

AFTER
1936–1939 The Spanish Civil War results in the deaths of more than 200,000 people.

1979 French philosopher Pierre Bourdieu examines the ways that power and social positioning have an influence on aesthetics.

2002 US historian John Lukacs publishes *At the End of an Age*, arguing that the modern bourgeois age is coming to an end.

P hilosopher José Ortega y Gasset first rose to prominence during the 1920s, a period of great social unrest in Spain. The monarchy was losing its authority following unrest in Spanish Morocco, and the dictatorial regime of Miguel Primo de Rivera had deepened divisions between left- and right-wing forces. These divisions would eventually lead to civil war in 1936.

World War I had been a period of economic boom in neutral Spain, which supplied both sides during the conflict. As a result, the country had rapidly industrialized, and the swelling masses of the workers were becoming increasingly powerful. Concessions were won, and a strike in Barcelona in 1919 led to Spain becoming the first country to institute an 8-hour day for all workers.

Rise of the masses

As worker power increased, the question of social class was at the center of philosophical and sociological debate in Europe, but Ortega y Gasset challenged the idea that social classes are purely a result of an economic divide. Rather, he distinguished between "mass-man" and "noble-man" on the basis of their allegiance to moral codes based on tradition. In his book *The Revolt of the Masses*, he explained that "to live as one likes is plebeian; the noble man aspires to order and law." Discipline and service bring nobility, he believed. He saw the accession to power of the masses and their increased tendency toward rebellion—through strikes and other forms of social unrest— as highly problematic, calling it one of "the greatest crises that can afflict people, nations, and civilizations."

To Ortega y Gasset, the threat posed by the masses was linked to a wider demoralization in postwar Europe, which had lost its sense of purpose in the world. The decline of imperial power coupled with the devastation of the war had left Europe no longer believing in itself, despite remaining a strong industrial force.

Pseudo-intellectuals

Ortega y Gasset argued that the rise of the masses is accompanied by the decline of the intellectual. This signals the triumph of the pseudo-intellectual—a vulgar man with no interest in traditions or moral codes who sees himself as superior. The pseudo-intellectual represents a new force of history: one without a sense of direction.

For Ortega y Gasset, the masses lack purpose and imagination and limit themselves to demands for a share in the fruits of progress without understanding the classical scientific traditions that made progress possible in the first place. The masses are not interested in the principles of civilization or in the establishment of a real sense of public opinion. As such, he views the masses as highly prone to violence. In his eyes, a Europe without real intellectuals, dominated by disinterested masses, is somewhere that risks losing its place and purpose in the world.

Ortega y Gasset's philosophy remains influential today. His followers stress the links between economic class and culture. ∎

The rise to power in Europe of the **industrial masses** …

↓

… has led to the decline of the **true intellectual** and the rise of the **pseudo-intellectual**.

↓

The pseudo-intellectual has no sense of **tradition, purpose, or morality**.

↓

Europe has been left without a moral code.

José Ortega y Gasset

Ortega y Gasset was born in Madrid to a political family with a deep liberal tradition. His mother's family owned the newspaper *El Imparcial*, while his father edited it. He studied philosophy in Spain and continued his education in Germany at Leipzig, Nuremberg, Cologne, Berlin, and Marburg, where he became deeply influenced by the neo-Kantian tradition.

In 1910, Ortega y Gasset became full professor of metaphysics in Madrid. He later founded the magazine *Revista de Occidente*, which published work by some of the most important figures in philosophy at the time. Elected to Congress in 1931 after the fall of the monarchy and de Rivera's dictatorship, he removed himself from politics after having served for less than a year. He left Spain at the outbreak of the Civil War and traveled to Buenos Aires, Argentina, only to return to Europe in 1942.

Key works

1930 *The Revolt of the Masses*
1937 *Invertebrate Spain*
1969 *Some Lessons in Metaphysics*

SOVEREIGN IS HE WHO DECIDES ON THE EXCEPTION
CARL SCHMITT (1888–1985)

IN CONTEXT

IDEOLOGY
Conservatism

FOCUS
Extrajudicial power

BEFORE
1532 In *The Prince*, Niccolò Machiavelli lays out the principles of sovereignty.

1651 Thomas Hobbes's *Leviathan* uses the concept of the social contract to justify the power of the sovereign.

1934 Adolf Hitler comes to power in Germany.

AFTER
2001 John Mearsheimer uses Schmitt's theories to justify "offensive realism," where states are ever-prepared for war.

2001 The Patriot Act in the US establishes a permanent installment of martial law and emergency powers.

 The exception is more interesting than the rule. The rule proves nothing; the exception proves everything.
Carl Schmitt

arl Schmitt was a German political theorist and lawyer whose work during the early 20th century established him as a leading critic of liberalism and parliamentary democracy. Schmitt saw the "exception" (*Ernstfall*)—unexpected events—as a quintessential characteristic of political life. For this reason, he disagreed with the liberal idea that the law is the best guarantor of individual liberty. While the law is able to provide a framework through which to manage "normal" states of affair, Schmitt argued that it was not designed to deal with "exceptional" circumstances such as *coups d'etat*, revolutions, or war. He saw legal theory as too far removed from legal practice and changing social norms. It was unfit to deal with the unexpected turns of history, many of which could threaten the very existence of the state. A president, he argued, is better able to guard a country's constitution than a court and so should necessarily be above the law. The ruler should be the ultimate lawmaker in exceptional situations.

A constant struggle
Schmitt's criticism of liberalism was directly tied to his unique understanding of "the political" as the constant possibility of struggle between both friends and enemies. He anticipated this struggle at both the international level—with feuding nations—and the domestic level—with feuding individuals. Schmitt disagreed with Thomas Hobbes's vision of nature as being a state of "all against all" and its implication that

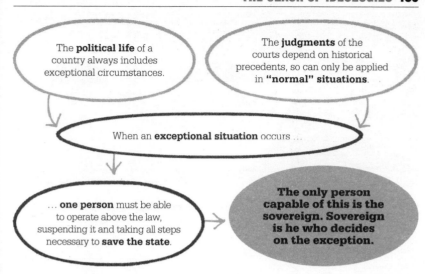

The **political life** of a country always includes exceptional circumstances.

The **judgments** of the courts depend on historical precedents, so can only be applied in **"normal" situations**.

When an **exceptional situation** occurs ...

... **one person** must be able to operate above the law, suspending it and taking all steps necessary to **save the state**.

The only person capable of this is the sovereign. Sovereign is he who decides on the exception.

coexistence is impossible without the rule of law. On the other hand, he argued that liberals had done humanity, and the nation-state in particular, a disservice by promoting the possibility of a perpetually peaceful world. He saw World War I as a consequence of liberalism's failure to recognize the possibility of enmity and blamed liberals for both misunderstanding the true nature of politics and being insincere with regard to the true nature of the political. Under an assumption of perpetual peace and friendliness, he said, states are less likely to be prepared for the exceptional and so risk the lives of their citizens.

Schmitt argued instead that the possibility of enmity always exists alongside the possibility of alliance and neutrality. He envisioned the individual as potentially dangerous; consequently, this provides a constant political danger, with the ever-present possibility of war. Schmitt considered that this constant possibility should be the ultimate guide for the sovereign, who must at all times be prepared for it. The political sphere is necessarily an antagonistic world, not merely an independent domain in which citizens interact, like the realms of civil society or commerce. The law might work »

Carl Schmitt

Born into a devout Catholic family in Plettenberg, Germany, Carl Schmitt later renounced his faith, although elements of his understanding of the divine remained in his work. He studied law and later taught at several universities. In 1933, he joined the Nazi party and was appointed State Councillor for Prussia. However, in 1936, he was denounced by the SS and expelled from the Nazi party.

Schmitt continued to work as a professor in Berlin, but at the end of World War II, he was interned for 2 years for his Nazi connections. In 1946, he returned to Plettenberg, where, shunned by the international community, he continued to study law until his death at 95.

Key works

1922 *Political Theology: Four Chapters on the Concept of Sovereignty*
1928 *The Concept of the Political*
1932 *Legality and Legitimacy*

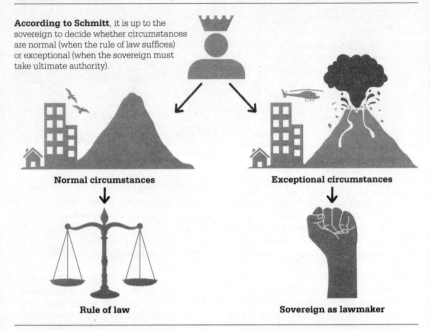

According to Schmitt, it is up to the sovereign to decide whether circumstances are normal (when the rule of law suffices) or exceptional (when the sovereign must take ultimate authority).

Normal circumstances

Rule of law

Exceptional circumstances

Sovereign as lawmaker

adequately through the courts and their associated bureaucracy under normal conditions, but in politics, exceptional conditions—even chaos—can erupt, and the courts are not equipped to make good or rapid judgments under these conditions. Someone must be entitled to suspend the law during exceptional circumstances. Schmitt claimed this was part of the sovereign's role: he or she possesses the ultimate authority to decide when times are "normal" and when they are "exceptional," and as such, can dictate when certain laws are to be applied and when they are not.

By placing life above liberty, Schmitt argued that the legitimacy of the sovereign relies not upon his application of the law, but upon his ability to protect the state and its citizens. Schmitt thought that the true power of a sovereign emerges in exceptional circumstances, when decisions need to be based entirely on new grounds. It is only in these circumstances that the sovereign becomes a true lawmaker, as opposed to a law-preserver, and is thus able to mobilize the population against a designated enemy. Schmitt concluded that

sovereign power, in its full form, requires the exercise of violence, even when not otherwise legitimate under the law.

Defending Hitler

The limits of Schmitt's theory became apparent with his defense of Hitler's policies and rise to power. Schmitt justified "the Night of the Long Knives"—when around 85 of Hitler's political opponents were murdered—as "the highest form of administrative justice." In Schmitt's eyes, Hitler was acting as a true sovereign, taking matters into his own hands under exceptional circumstances that threatened the very existence of the German state. Violence against the left-wing arm of the Nazi party, as well as Jews, was justified in Schmitt's eyes by the supposed threat they posed to the state.

Schmitt's personal support for the Nazi regime strongly suggests that, for him, the survival of the state was more important than the liberty of the individuals within it—and sometimes more important than the lives of the citizens of the state: However, this prioritization of the preservation of the state at all costs fails to take into account the fact that, just like individuals, the state also changes; it is not a monolithic entity whose character is set and forever perfect. It can—and many would say should—be questioned at any point in time.

Contemporary exceptions

Schmitt's inability to see the radical effect of his theory, or that genocide is not an acceptable form of violence under any circumstances, led to his being shunned by the academic and intellectual world. However, in the late 20th century, a revival of interest in his work was led by various authors who saw Schmitt's contribution to legal and political philosophy as significant, despite his shortcomings. Schmitt's understanding of the "political," the "friend–enemy distinction," and the "exceptional" was used by these writers to better understand the conditions under which modern states operate and political leaders make decisions.

US philosopher Leo Strauss built on Schmitt's critique of liberalism, arguing that it tended toward extreme relativism and nihilism by completely disregarding the reality "on the ground"—it focuses not on what is, but on what ought to be. Strauss distinguished between two forms of nihilism: a "brutal" nihilism, as expressed by the Nazi and Marxist regimes, which seeks to destroy all previous traditions, history, and moral standards; and a "gentle" nihilism, as expressed in Western liberal democracies, which establishes a value-free and aimless egalitarianism. For Strauss, both are equally dangerous in that they destroy the possibility for human excellence.

Italian political philosopher Giorgio Agamben argues that Schmitt's state of exception is not a state where the law is suspended—hiding somewhere until it can be reestablished—but rather a state completely devoid of law, in which the

Leading Nazis were put on trial at Nuremberg at the end of World War II. Schmitt was investigated for his role as a propagandist for the regime, but he eventually escaped trial.

sovereign holds ultimate authority over the lives of citizens. Considering the Nazi concentration camps created during World War II, Agamben argues that the prisoners in these camps lost all human qualities and became "bare life"—they were alive but stripped of all human and legal rights. He sees the creation of a state of exception as particularly dangerous, because its effects compound in unpredictable ways. The "temporary" suspension of the law is never really "temporary," because it leads to consequences that cannot be undone upon the restoration of the law.

Schmitt's concept of the exception became particularly pertinent after 9/11, when it was used by conservatives and left-wing political thinkers to justify or denounce antiterrorist measures such as the Patriot Act in the United States. The conservatives used the idea of exceptionality to justify violations of personal liberties such as increased surveillance and longer detention times without trial. Left-wing scholars argued against these very same practices, pointing out the dangers of suspending protections against human rights violations.

The existence of camps such as those at Guantánamo Bay serves to demonstrate the dangers of labeling an event "exceptional" and apportioning it exceptional measures—in particular, the rewriting of rules by the executive without any checks in place. More than 18 years later, the state of exception declared after 9/11 remains more or less in place, with worrying consequences that show no signs of abating. ■

> 66 The state of exception is not a dictatorship ... but a space devoid of law.
> **Giorgio Agamben** 99

COMMUNISM IS AS BAD AS IMPERIALISM
JOMO KENYATTA (1894–1978)

IN CONTEXT

IDEOLOGY
Postcolonialism

FOCUS
Conservative pan-Africanism

BEFORE
1895 The protectorate of British East Africa emerges from British trading interests in East Africa.

1952–1959 Kenya is in a state of emergency during a pro-independence rebellion by the Mau Mau.

1961 In Belgrade in modern-day Serbia, the Non-Aligned Movement is founded for countries wishing to be independent of superpowers.

AFTER
1963 The Organization of African Unity (OAU) is founded to oppose colonialism in Africa.

1968 Britain's last African colonies gain independence.

Jomo Kenyatta was one of the leading figures in Kenya's independence from British colonial rule, becoming its first prime minister and president in the postcolonial era. A political moderate, he pursued a program of gradual change rather than dramatic revolution.

External threats

Kenyatta's ideas melded anticolonialism and anticommunism. He was fiercely opposed to white rule in Africa and promoted the idea of Kenyan independence through the establishment of the Kenyan African National Union. Pursuing a mixed-market economic program, Kenya was opened up to foreign investment and developed a foreign policy that was pro-Western and anticommunist.

Postcolonial nations, Kenyatta believed, were in danger of becoming exploited by external forces in order to consolidate the position of other nations on the world stage. To secure genuine independence, it would not be possible to tolerate the external influence that came hand-in-hand with Soviet communism. In this sense, the threats posed by communism could be as restrictive to Kenyan self-determination as colonial rule. ∎

Leaders of newly independent East African states—Julian Nyerere of Tanganyika, Milton Obote of Uganda, and Kenyatta—met in Nairobi in 1964 to discuss their postcolonial future.

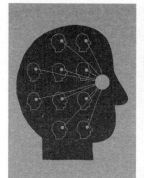

THE STATE MUST BE CONCEIVED OF AS AN "EDUCATOR"
ANTONIO GRAMSCI (1891–1937)

IN CONTEXT

IDEOLOGY
Marxism

FOCUS
Cultural hegemony

BEFORE
1867 Karl Marx completes the first volume of *Capital*, in which he analyzes the capitalist system and the ways in which the masses are exploited by the rich.

1929 José Ortega y Gasset laments the demise of the intellectual as the working class grows in power.

AFTER
1980 Michel Foucault describes the ways in which power is distributed across society in institutions such as schools and the family.

1991 The *Lega Nord* (Northern League) is founded on a platform of greater autonomy for the industrialized north of Italy.

I talian Marxist theorist Antonio Gramsci, while exposing the imbalances between the industrialized north and rural south of Italy, identified that the struggle to tackle the dominance of the ruling classes was a cultural battle as much as a revolutionary one.

 A human mass does not 'distinguish' itself, does not become independent … without organizing itself: and there is no organization without intellectuals.
Antonio Gramsci

Gramsci developed the notion of "cultural hegemony," referring to the ideological and cultural control of the working classes that goes beyond coercion to the development of systems of thought—reinforcing the position of the powerful through consent.

The role of intellectuals
For Gramsci, no government, regardless of how powerful it is, can sustain its control by force alone. Legitimacy and popular consent are also required. By viewing the functions of the state as a means of educating and indoctrinating society into subservience, Gramsci radically altered Marxist thought. He saw that in order to tackle the grip of cultural hegemony on society, education was vital. Gramsci had a particular view of the role of intellectuals in this context. He felt that intellectuals could exist at all levels of society, rather than solely as a traditional elite, and that the development of this capacity among the working class was necessary to the success of any attempt to counter the hegemony of the ruling classes. ∎

POLITICAL POWER GROWS OUT OF THE BARREL OF A GUN

MAO ZEDONG (1893–1976)

IN CONTEXT

IDEOLOGY
Marxism-Leninism

FOCUS
Modernization of China

BEFORE
1912 The Republic of China is established, bringing to an end more than 2,000 years of imperial rule.

1919 The May Fourth Movement politicizes events in China, leading directly to the foundation of the Communist Party of China in 1921.

AFTER
1966–1976 Mao's Cultural Revolution, the suppression of supposedly capitalist, traditional, and cultural elements in China, leads to factional strife and huge loss of life.

1977 Deng Xiaoping implements a program of economic liberalization, leading to rapid growth.

A t the beginning of the 20th century, Chinese students and intellectuals, including the young Mao Zedong, began to learn of the socialist ideologies on the rise in Europe and apply them to China. At the time, Marxism was not as compelling to these young Chinese as Mikhail Bakunin's theory of anarchism and other schools of Utopian socialist thought. Marx had stipulated that a sound capitalist economy was the necessary basis for a socialist revolution, but China was still primarily agrarian and feudal, with no modern industry or urban working class.

Revolutionary inspiration

Before the Russian Revolution in 1917, there was little to encourage disaffected Chinese intellectuals in Marx's conviction that the processes of capitalist production must achieve critical mass before a workers' revolution could succeed. Looking back on the immense changes he had carved out on the Chinese political landscape, Mao would later assert that the Bolshevik uprising struck political thinkers in China like a "thunderbolt." Events in Russia were now a matter of intense interest because of the perceived similarities between the two backward giants. Traveling to Beijing, Mao became the assistant and protégé of the university librarian Li Dazhao, an early Chinese communist who was studying, holding seminars, and writing about the Russian revolutionary movement.

Mao took Marxist and Leninist ideas and adapted them to resolve the problem of a workers' revolution in a land of peasants. Lenin's theory of imperialism envisioned communism spreading through developing countries and gradually surrounding the capitalist West. Mao believed that countries still mired in feudalism would skip the capitalist stage of development and move straight into full socialism. An elite vanguard

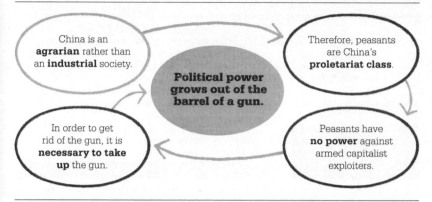

China is an **agrarian** rather than an **industrial** society.

Political power grows out of the barrel of a gun.

Therefore, peasants are China's **proletariat class**.

In order to get rid of the gun, it is **necessary to take up** the gun.

Peasants have **no power** against armed capitalist exploiters.

party with a higher class "consciousness" would instill revolutionary values and a proletarian identity in the peasantry.

Politicization of the people

The excitement generated by the Russian Revolution might have been confined to university discussion groups had it not been for the Western Allies' heedless betrayal of Chinese interests following World War I. More than 140,000 Chinese laborers had been shipped to France to support the war effort of the Triple Entente—Britain, France, and Russia—with the understanding that, among other things, the German protectorate of Shandong on the northeast coast of China would be returned to Chinese hands after the war. Instead, the Allies gave the territory to Japan at the Versailles Peace Conference of 1919.

Students across China protested against their country's "spineless" capitulation.

Rice farmers and other peasants handed over their land to cooperatives in a collectivization program that would form a key part of Mao's drive to reform China's rural economy.

City workers and businessmen in Shanghai joined them, and a coalition of diverse groups united as the May Fourth Movement to force the government to accede to their demands. China's representatives at Versailles refused to sign the peace treaty, but their objections had no effect on the actions of the Allies. The real significance of the May Fourth Movement was that vast numbers of Chinese people began to think about their precarious lives and the vulnerability of their country to threats from the outside world. It was a significant turning point for Chinese political thought, in which Western-style liberal democracy lost much of its appeal and Marxist-Leninist concepts gained traction.

Mao was one of the radical intellectuals who came to the fore at this time and went on to organize peasants and workers in the Communist Party. He would never forget the lesson of Shandong: to negotiate from a position of weakness was to lose. The ultimate power in politics is the power of armed force. Mao would be ruthless both in seeking armed power and in his willingness to use it.

In 1921, Mao attended the First Congress of the Communist Party of China (CPC) in Shanghai, and in 1923, he was elected to the party's Central Committee. He spent the 1920s organizing labor strikes, studying, and developing his ideas. It became clear to him that in China, it would have to be a rural and not an urban proletariat who would carry out the revolution. »

Politics is war without
bloodshed, while war is
politics with bloodshed.
Mao Zedong

Crucible of communism

The CPC shared the ideological outlook of
Marxist-Leninism with the Kuonmintang
(KMT)—China's nationalist and
antimonarchist party founded by Sun Yat-
Sen, with links to Soviet Russia—and both
had the overall aim of national unification.
However, the Communists' popular
movement of peasants and workers was too
radical for the KMT, who turned on their CPC
allies in 1927, crushing them and suppressing
their organizations in the cities. This violent
conflict was the crucible from which the
doctrine of "Maoism" emerged as a guerrilla-
style rural Marxian revolutionary strategy.

In 1934 and 1935, Mao—now the
chairman of the Chinese Soviet Republic, a
small republic declared in the mountainous
region of Jiangxi, southeast China—
cemented his position as foremost among
Chinese communists during "The Long
March." The first of a series of marches,
this 6,000-mile (9,600-km) ordeal, lasting

over a year, was ostensibly undertaken to
repel Japanese invaders, but it also served
as a military retreat by the Communists'
Red Army to evade the Nationalist forces
led by Chiang Kaishek. They crossed 18
mountain ranges and 24 major rivers,
and only one-tenth of the original force
of 80,000 soldiers and workers who set out
from Jiangxi in October 1934 survived the
march to reach Shanghai a year later. Mao's
supremacy was sealed, and he became
leader of the CPC in November 1935.
Following Japan's defeat by the Allies in
World War II, the resumption of civil war
in China, and the eventual surrender of
Nationalist forces, the communist People's
Republic of China was finally established
in 1949, with Mao at the helm.

The Great Helmsman

In 1938, in his concluding remarks to
the Sixth Plenary Session of the Sixth
Central Committee of the CPC, Mao
expounded on his theory of revolution.
He maintained that in a China that was
still semifeudal, the truly revolutionary
class was the peasantry, and only military

Tractors made in China not only increased
output but symbolized Mao's policy of
"maintaining independence and relying
on our own efforts."

struggle could achieve revolution; demonstrations, protests, and strikes would never be enough.

With the peasant-proletariat armed and powerful, Mao—now known as "The Great Helmsman"—did bring about many changes for the good. Among other measures, he banned arranged marriages and promoted the status of women, doubled school attendance, raised literacy, and created universal housing. However, Mao's admiration for Stalin and his infatuation with Marxian language and theories of revolution disguised the many thousands of brutal killings that he and his forces committed on the road to power. There were to be many millions more—some from the violent repression of those deemed opponents of China and some from neglect. In the space of three decades, Mao forced the country to almost complete self-sufficiency, but at an unspeakable cost in human life, comforts, freedoms, and sanity.

The Five-Year Plan, launched in 1953, achieved spectacular increases in output and was followed by the "Great Leap Forward" in 1958. By forcing the Chinese economy to attempt to catch up with the West through mass-labor projects in agriculture, industry, and infrastructure, Mao brought about one of the worst catastrophes the world has ever known. Between 1958 and 1962, at least 45 million Chinese people— mostly peasants—were tortured, overworked, starved, or beaten to death, a fatality rate only slightly smaller than the entire death toll of World War II.

The atrocities of this period were carefully cataloged in the now-reopened Communist Party archives. These records show that the "truly revolutionary class"—Mao's chosen people in the great struggle for social justice—were in fact treated as faceless, expendable objects by Mao and the Party.

In contrast to Marx's conviction that socialism would be an inevitable development from the material and cultural achievements of capitalism, Mao correlated the poverty he saw in China with a moral purity that he believed would lead to a socialist Utopia. In 1966, the Cultural Revolution was introduced with the aim of cleansing China of "bourgeois" influences. Millions were "reeducated" through forced labor, and thousands executed.

Mao in modern China

The politics that for Mao grew "out of the barrel of a gun" turned out to be the totalitarian politics of terror, brutality, fantasy, and deceit. On his death, the CPC declared that his ideas would remain "a guide to action for a long time to come." However, as society evolves and awareness grows of his horrific crimes, Mao's influence on Chinese thought may finally be cast off. ∎

Mao Zedong

The son of a prosperous peasant, Mao Zedong was born in Shaoshan, in Hunan province, central China, in 1893. Mao described his father as a stern disciplinarian who beat his children on any pretext, while his devout Buddhist mother would try to pacify him.

After training as a teacher, Mao traveled to Beijing, where he worked in the university library. He studied Marxism and went on to become a founding member of the Chinese Communist Party in 1921. After years of civil and national wars, the Communists were victorious and, under Mao's leadership, founded the People's Republic of China in 1949.

Mao set out to ruthlessly modernize China with his "Great Leap Forward" mass labor program, and later the Cultural Revolution. Both initiatives failed, resulting in millions of deaths. Mao died on September 9, 1976.

Key works

1937 *On Guerrilla Warfare*
1964 *Little Red Book* or *Quotations from Chairman Mao Zedong*

POSTWAR

1945–PRESENT

Huge industrial and social changes took place in the years that followed the end of World War II. The scale and industrialization of warfare, the decline of the great colonial powers, and the ideological battles between communism and free-market capitalism all had a profound effect on political thought. A world recovering from human tragedy on such a scale urgently needed to be reinterpreted, and new prescriptions for human development and organization were required.

Across western Europe, a new political consensus emerged, and mixed economies of private and public businesses were developed. At the same time, new demands for civil and human rights emerged across the world in the immediate postwar period, and independence movements gathered support in Europe's colonies.

War and the state
There were many questions for political thinkers that plainly stemmed from the experience of global conflict. World War II had seen an unprecedented expansion of military capacity, with a dramatic

impact on the industrial base of the major powers. This new environment provided the platform for a collision of ideas between East and West, and the Korean and Vietnam wars, alongside countless smaller dramas, were in many ways proxies for conflict between the Soviet Union and the United States.

The nuclear bombs that had brought World War II to an end also signaled an era of technological developments in warfare that threatened humanity on a terrifying scale. These developments led many writers to reconsider the ethics of warfare. They explored the moral ramifications of battle, developing the ideas put forward by earlier thinkers such as Thomas Aquinas and Augustine of Hippo.

Other writers, such as Noam Chomsky, explored the configurations of power at play behind the new military-industrial complex. In recent years, the emergence of global terrorism and the subsequent conflicts in Iraq and Afghanistan have thrown these debates into sharp relief.

The period immediately after the war also raised serious questions about the appropriate role of the state. In the postwar period, European democracies established

POLITICS

the foundations of the welfare state, and across Eastern Europe, communism took hold. In response, political thinkers began to consider the implications of these developments, particularly in relation to individual liberty. New understandings of freedom and justice were developed by writers such as Friedrich Hayek, John Rawls, and Robert Nozick, and the position of individuals in relation to the state began to be reconsidered.

Feminism and civil rights

From the 1960s onward, a new, overtly political strand of feminism emerged, inspired by writers such as Simone de Beauvoir, who questioned the position of women in politics and society. Around the same time, the battle for civil rights gathered pace—with the decline of colonialism in Africa and the popular movement against racial discrimination in the United States—driven by thinkers such as Frantz Fanon and inspirational activists such as Nelson Mandela and Martin Luther King Jr. Once more, questions of power, and particularly civil and political rights, formed the main preoccupation of political thinkers.

Global concerns

During the 1970s, concern for the environment grew into a political force, boosted by the ideas about "deep ecology" of Arne Naess and coalescing into the green movement. As issues such as climate change and the end of cheap oil increasingly enter the mainstream, green political thinkers look set to become increasingly influential.

In the Islamic world, politicians and thinkers have struggled to agree on the place of Islam in politics. From visions of an Islamic state to considerations of the role of women in Islam, and through the rise of al-Qaeda to the hope offered by the "Arab Spring," this is a dynamic and contested political arena.

The challenges of a globalized world—with industries, cultures, and communication technologies that transcend national boundaries—bring with them fresh sets of political problems. In particular, the financial crisis that erupted in 2007 has led political thinkers to reconsider their positions, seeking new solutions to the new problems. ∎

THE CHIEF EVIL IS UNLIMITED GOVERNMENT

FRIEDRICH HAYEK (1899–1992)

IN CONTEXT

IDEOLOGY
Neoliberalism

FOCUS
Free-market economics

BEFORE
1840 Pierre-Joseph Proudhon advocates a naturally ordered society without authority, arguing that capital is analogous to authority.

1922 Austrian economist Ludwig von Mises criticizes centrally planned economies.

1936 John Maynard Keynes argues that the key to escaping economic depression is government spending.

AFTER
1962 US economist Milton Friedman argues that competitive capitalism is essential for political freedom.

1975 British politician Margaret Thatcher hails Hayek as her inspiration.

 Economic control is not merely control of a sector of human life which can be separated from the rest; it is the control of the means for all our ends.
Friedrich Hayek

A ustrian-British economist Friedrich Hayek wrote his warning against unlimited government in an appendix called "Why I Am Not a Conservative" in his 1960 work, *The Constitution of Liberty*. In 1975, newly elected British Conservative party leader Margaret Thatcher threw this book on a table at a meeting with her fellow Conservatives, declaring, "This is what we believe."

Thatcher was not the only conservative politician to admire Hayek's ideas, and he has emerged as something of a hero to many politicians on the right. For this reason, it may seem strange that he should have so firmly insisted that he was not a conservative. In fact, such is the apparent ambiguity of his position that many commentators prefer the term "neoliberal" to describe Hayek and others who, like Thatcher and US president Ronald Reagan, championed the idea of unfettered free markets.

Hayek vs. Keynes
The principle of free markets is at the heart of Hayek's insistence that "the chief evil is unlimited government." Hayek first came to public prominence in the 1930s, when he challenged British economist John Maynard Keynes's ideas for dealing with the Great Depression. Keynes argued that the only way to get

out of the downward spiral of unemployment and sluggish spending was with large-scale government intervention and public works. Hayek insisted that this would simply bring inflation, and that periodic "busts" were an inevitable—indeed necessary—part of the business cycle.

Keynes's arguments won over policy makers at the time, but Hayek continued to develop his ideas. He argued that central planning is doomed to failure because the planners can never have all the information required to account for the changing needs of every individual. It is simply a delusion to imagine that planners might have the omniscience to cater to so many disparate needs.

The gap in the planning is data, and this is where free markets come in. Individuals have a knowledge of resources and the need for them that a central planner can never hope to have. Hayek contended that the free market reveals this knowledge perfectly and continually. It does so through the operation of prices, which vary to signal the balance between supply and demand. If prices rise, you know that goods must be in short supply; if they fall, goods must be oversupplied. The market

also gives people an incentive to respond to this knowledge, boosting production of goods in short supply to take advantage of the extra profits on offer. Hayek viewed this price mechanism not as a deliberate human invention, but as an example of order in human society that emerges spontaneously, like language.

Loss of freedom
Over time, Hayek began to feel that the gap between the planned economy and the free market was not simply a matter of bad economics but a fundamental issue of political freedom. Planning economies means controlling people's lives. And so, in 1944, as World War II raged on, he wrote his famous book *The Road to Serfdom* to warn the people of his adopted country, Britain, away from the dangers of socialism.

In *The Road to Serfdom*, Hayek argues that government control of our economic lives amounts to totalitarianism and makes us all serfs. He believed that there was no fundamental difference in outcome between socialist central control of the economy and the fascism of the Nazis, however different the intentions behind the policies. For Hayek, to put any »

According to Hayek, a free market spontaneously matches the availability of resources to the need for them through supply and demand. The knowledge to make these adjustments deliberately is way beyond the possibility of any individual.

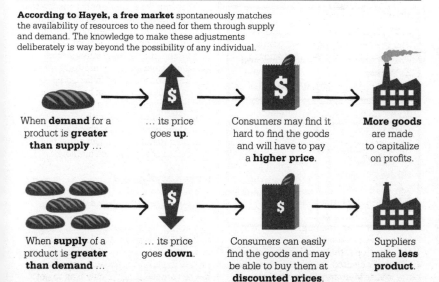

When **demand** for a product is **greater than supply** ... / ... its price goes **up**. / Consumers may find it hard to find the goods and will have to pay a **higher price**. / **More goods** are made to capitalize on profits.

When **supply** of a product is **greater than demand** ... / ... its price goes **down**. / Consumers can easily find the goods and may be able to buy them at **discounted prices**. / Suppliers make **less product**.

economic master plan into action, even one intended to benefit everyone, so many key policy issues must be delegated to unelected technocrats that such a program will be inherently undemocratic. Moreover, a comprehensive economic plan leaves no room for individual choice in any aspect of life.

Government needs limits

It is in *The Constitution of Liberty* that Hayek's arguments about the link between free markets and political freedom are most fully developed. Despite his assertion that free markets must be the prime mechanism to give order to society, he is by no means against government. Government's central role, Hayek asserts, should be to maintain the "rule of law,"

Ronald Reagan and Margaret Thatcher both enthusiastically embraced Hayek's message that government should be shrunk, cutting taxes and state-provided services.

with as little intervention in people's lives as possible. It is a "civil association" that simply provides a framework within which individuals can follow their own projects.

The foundations of law are common rules of conduct that predate government and arise spontaneously. "A judge," he writes, "is in this sense an institution of a spontaneous order." This is where Hayek's claim that he is not a conservative comes in. He argues that conservatives are frightened of democracy and blame the evils of the times on its rise, because they are wary of change. But Hayek has no problem with democracy or change—the problem is a government that is not properly kept under control and limited. He asserts that "nobody is qualified to wield unlimited power"—and that, he implies, includes "the people." Yet, "the powers which modern democracy possesses," he concedes, "would be even more intolerable in the hands of some small elite."

Hayek is critical of laws intended to remedy a particular fault and believes that government use of coercion in society should be kept to a minimum. He is even more critical of the notion of "social justice." The market, he says, is a game in which "there is no point in calling the outcome just or unjust." He concludes from this that "social justice is an empty phrase with no determinable content." For Hayek, any attempt to redistribute wealth—for instance, by raising taxes to pay for the provision of social welfare—is a threat to freedom.

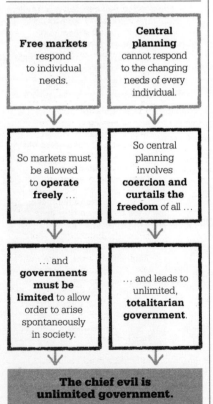

Free markets respond to individual needs.

↓

So markets must be allowed to **operate freely** …

↓

… and **governments must be limited** to allow order to arise spontaneously in society.

↓

Central planning cannot respond to the changing needs of every individual.

↓

So central planning involves **coercion and curtails the freedom** of all …

↓

… and leads to unlimited, **totalitarian government**.

↓

The chief evil is unlimited government.

All that is needed is a basic safety net to provide "protection against acts of desperation by the needy."

For a long time, Hayek's ideas had only a few disciples, and Keynesian economics dominated the policies of Western governments in the postwar years. Many countries established welfare states despite Hayek's warnings against it. But the oil shortage and economic downturn of the 1970s persuaded some to look again at Hayek's ideas, and in 1974, to the surprise of many, he was awarded the Nobel Prize for Economics.

From this point on, Hayek's ideas became the rallying point for those who championed unregulated free markets as the route to economic prosperity and individual liberty. In the 1980s, Reagan and Thatcher pursued policies intended to roll back the welfare state, reducing taxation and cutting regulations. Many of the leaders of the revolutions against communist rule in eastern Europe were also inspired by Hayek's thinking.

Shock policies

Hayek's claim to be a liberal has been criticized by many, including former British Liberal Party leader David Steel, who argued that liberty is possible only with "social justice and an equitable distribution of wealth and power, which in turn require a degree of active government intervention." More damning still from a liberal point of view is the association of Hayek's ideas with what Canadian journalist Naomi Klein describes as the "shock doctrine." In this, people are persuaded to accept, "for their own ultimate good," a range of extreme free-market measures—such as rapid deregulation, the selling of state industries, and high unemployment—by being put in a state of shock, either through economic hardship or brutal government policies.

Hayek's free-market ideology became associated with a number of brutal military dictatorships in South America, such as that of General Augusto Pinochet in Chile—apparently just the kind of totalitarian regime Hayek was arguing against. Hayek was himself personally associated with these regimes, though he always insisted that he was only giving economic advice.

Hayek remains a highly controversial figure, championed by free marketeers and many politicians on the right as a defender of liberty, and despised by many on the left, who feel his ideas lie behind a shift toward hardline capitalism around the world that has brought misery to many and dramatically increased the gap between rich and poor. ∎

Friedrich Hayek

Born in Vienna in 1899, Friedrich August von Hayek entered the University of Vienna just after World War I, when it was one of the three best places in the world to study economics. Though enrolled as a law student, he was fascinated by economics and psychology, and the poverty of postwar Vienna urged him to a socialist solution. Then in 1922, after reading Ludwig von Mises's *Socialism*, a devastating critique of central planning, Hayek enrolled in Mises's economics class. In 1931, he moved to the London School of Economics to lecture on Mises's theory of business cycles and began his sparring with Keynes on the causes of the Depression. In 1947, with Mises, he founded the Mont Pèlerin Society of libertarians. Three years later, he joined the Chicago school of free-market economists, along with Milton Friedman. By his death in 1992, Hayek's ideas had become highly influential.

Key works

1944 *The Road to Serfdom*
1960 *The Constitution of Liberty*

EVERY KNOWN AND ESTABLISHED FACT CAN BE DENIED
HANNAH ARENDT (1906–1975)

IN CONTEXT

IDEOLOGY
Antitotalitarianism

FOCUS
Truth and myth

BEFORE
1882 French historian Ernest Renan claims that national identity depends upon a selective and distorted memory of past events.

1960 Hans-Georg Gadamer publishes *Truth and Method*, focusing on the importance of collective truth creation.

AFTER
1992 British historian Eric Hobsbawn states that "no serious historian can be a committed political nationalist."

1995 British philosopher David Miller argues that myths serve a valuable social integrative function despite being untrue.

1998 Jürgen Habermas criticizes Arendt's stance in *Truth and Justification*.

The German political philosopher Hannah Arendt wrote about the nature of politics at a particularly tumultuous time: she lived through the rise and fall of the Nazi regime, the Vietnam War, student riots in Paris, and the assassinations of US president John F. Kennedy and Martin Luther King Jr. As a Jew living in Germany who later moved to occupied France, and then Chicago, New York, and Berkeley, Arendt experienced these events firsthand. Her political philosophy was informed by these events and their portrayal to the general public.

In her 1967 essay *Truth and Politics*, Arendt is particularly concerned with the way that historical facts often become distorted when politicized—they are used as tools in order to justify particular political decisions. This distortion of historical facts was not new in the political domain, where lies have always played an important part in foreign diplomacy and security. However, what was new about the political lies of the 1960s onward was their significantly wider scope. Arendt notices that they went far beyond simply keeping state secrets to encompassing an entire collective reality in which facts known to everyone are targeted and slowly erased while a different version of historical "reality" is constructed to replace them.

This mass manipulation of facts and opinions, Arendt notes, is no longer restricted to totalitarian regimes—where oppression is pervasive and evident, and people may be on guard against continual propaganda—but increasingly takes place in liberal democracies such as the US, where doctored reports and purposeful misinformation serve to justify violent political interventions, such as the Vietnam War of 1954–1975. In free countries, she claims, unwelcome historical truths are often transmuted into mere opinion, losing

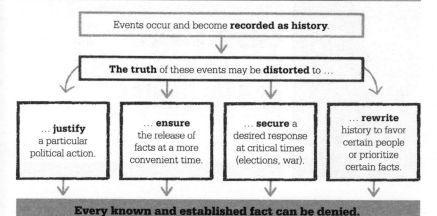

Events occur and become **recorded as history**.

↓

The truth of these events may be **distorted** to …

↓

| … **justify** a particular political action. | … **ensure** the release of facts at a more convenient time. | … **secure** a desired response at critical times (elections, war). | … **rewrite** history to favor certain people or prioritize certain facts. |

↓

Every known and established fact can be denied.

---

their factual status. For example, it is as though the policies of France and the Vatican during World War II "were not a matter of historical record but a matter of opinion."

An alternative reality

The rewriting of contemporary history under the very eyes of those who witnessed it, through the denial or neglect of every known and established fact, leads not only to the creation of a more flattering reality to fit specific political needs, but also to the establishment of an entirely substitute reality that no longer has anything to do with factual truth. This, Arendt argues, is particularly dangerous—the substitute reality that justified mass killings under the Nazi regime is a good example. What is at stake, Arendt says, is "common and factual reality itself."

Contemporary followers of Arendt point to the 2003 invasion of Iraq by the US and its allies as an example of this phenomenon. Arendt's arguments might also be used by Julian Assange, founder of WikiLeaks, to justify the release of secret documents that contradict the official version of events given by governments around the world. ∎

Hannah Arendt

Hannah Arendt was born in Linden, Germany, in 1906, to a family of secular Jews. She grew up in Königsberg and Berlin and studied philosophy at the University of Marburg with philosopher Martin Heidegger, with whom she developed a strong intellectual and romantic relationship, later soured by Heidegger's support for the Nazi party.

Arendt was prohibited from taking up a teaching position at a German university due to her Jewish heritage, and during the Nazi regime, she fled to Paris and later the US, where she became part of a lively intellectual circle. She published many highly influential books and essays and taught at the University of California, Berkeley; the University of Chicago; the New School, Princeton (where she became the first female lecturer); and Yale. She died in 1975 of a heart attack.

Key works

1951 *The Origins of Totalitarianism*
1958 *The Human Condition*
1962 *On Revolution*

WHAT IS A WOMAN?
SIMONE DE BEAUVOIR (1908–1986)

IN CONTEXT

IDEOLOGY
Existentialist feminism

FOCUS
Freedom of choice

BEFORE
1791 Olympe de Gouges writes
the *Declaration of the Rights of
Woman and the Female Citizen*.

1892 Eugénie Potonié-Pierre and
Léonie Rouzade found the Federation
of French Feminist Societies.

1944 Women finally win the right
to vote in France.

AFTER
1963 Betty Friedan publishes
The Feminine Mystique, bringing
many of de Beauvoir's ideas to
a wider audience.

1970 In *The Female Eunuch*,
Australian writer Germaine
Greer examines the limits
placed on women's lives in
consumer societies.

A cross the world, women earn
lower incomes than men, are
frequently deprived of legal
and political rights, and are subject to
various forms of cultural oppression. In this
context, feminist interpretations of political
problems have provided an important

contribution to political theory and inspired
generations of political thinkers.

Throughout the 19th century, the
concept of feminism had been growing
in force, but there were deep conceptual
divides between the various feminist
groups. Some supported the concept of
"equality through difference," accepting
that there are inherent differences between
men and women and that these differences
constitute the strength of their positions in
society. Others held the view that women
should not be treated differently from
men at all and focused first and foremost
on universal suffrage as their main goal,
viewing equal political rights as the key
battle. This battle for rights has since
become known as "first-wave feminism,"
to distinguish it from the "second-wave
feminism" movement that had wider political
aims and gathered pace around the world in
the 1960s. This new movement considered
women's experience of discrimination in
the home and the workplace and the often
subtle manifestations of unconsciously
held prejudices that could not necessarily
be fixed merely through changes in the law.
It took much of its intellectual inspiration
from the work of French philosopher
Simone de Beauvoir.

Transcending feminism
Although she is sometimes described
as the "mother of the modern women's
movement," at the time of writing her
seminal work *The Second Sex* in 1949,
de Beauvoir did not view herself primarily
as a "feminist." She held ambitions to

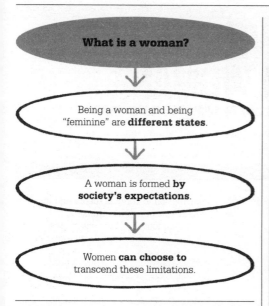

What is a woman?

↓

Being a woman and being "feminine" are **different states**.

↓

A woman is formed **by society's expectations**.

↓

Women **can choose to** transcend these limitations.

Simone de Beauvoir

Simone Lucie-Ernestine-Marie-Bertrand de Beauvoir was born in Paris in 1908. The daughter of a wealthy family, she was educated privately and went on to study philosophy at the Sorbonne. While attending the university, she met Jean-Paul Sartre, who would go on to become her lifelong companion and philosophical counterpart.

De Beauvoir openly declared her atheism when she was a teenager. Her rejection of institutions such as religion later led her to refuse to marry Sartre. Her work was inspired both by her own personal experiences in Paris and by wider political issues such as the international growth of communism. Her interest in the latter led to several books on the subject. She also wrote a number of novels.

After Sartre's death in 1980, de Beauvoir's own health deteriorated. She died 6 years later and was buried in the same grave.

Key works

1943 *She Came to Stay*
1949 *The Second Sex*
1954 *The Mandarins*

transcend this definition, which she felt often became bogged down in its own arguments. Instead, she took a more subjective approach to the concept of difference, combining feminist arguments with her existentialist philosophical outlook. However, de Beauvoir was later to join the second-wave feminist movement and was still active in support of its arguments in the 1970s, examining the wider condition of women in society in a series of novels.

De Beauvoir realized that when she made an effort to define herself, the first phrase that came to her mind was "I am a woman." Her need to examine this involuntary definition—and its deeper meaning—formed the basis of her work. For de Beauvoir, it is important to differentiate between the state of being female and that of being a woman, and her work eventually alights on the definition "a human being in the feminine condition." She rejects the theory of the "eternal feminine"—a mysterious essence of femininity—which can be used to justify inequality. In *The Second Sex*, she points out that the very fact that she is asking the question "What is a woman?" is significant and highlights the inherent "Otherness" of women in society in relation to men. She was one of the first writers to fully define the concept of "sexism" in society: the prejudices and assumptions that are made about women. She also asks whether women are born or whether they are created by society's preconceptions, including educational »

De Beauvoir maintained a long-term relationship with Jean-Paul Sartre, but the two never married. She saw their open relationship as an example of freedom of choice for a woman.

expectations and religious structures, as well as historical precedents. She examines how women are represented in psychoanalysis, history, and biology, and draws on a variety of sources— literary, academic, and anecdotal—to demonstrate the effects on women of these assumptions.

De Beauvoir's approach in answering the question "What is a woman?" is guided by her involvement with existentialism, which is essentially concerned with the discovery of the self through the freedom of personal choice within society. De Beauvoir sees women's freedom in this regard as peculiarly restricted. This philosophical direction was reinforced by her relationship with Jean-Paul Sartre, who she met at the Sorbonne in 1929. He was a leading existentialist thinker, and they were to maintain a long and fruitful intellectual dialogue, as well as a complex and lasting personal relationship.

De Beauvoir's position is also informed by her left-wing political convictions. She describes women's struggles as part of the class struggle and recognizes that her own start in life as a member of the bourgeoisie meant that opportunities were open to her that were not available to women from the lower classes. Ultimately, she wanted such freedom of opportunity for all women— indeed all people—regardless of class. De Beauvoir draws parallels between a woman's physical confinement—in a "kitchen or a boudoir"—and the intellectual boundaries

imposed on her. She suggests that these limitations lead women to accept mediocrity and discourage them from pushing themselves to achieve more. De Beauvoir calls this state "immanence." By this, she means that women are limited by, and to, their own direct experience of the world. She contrasts this position with men's "transcendence," which allows them access to any position in life that they might choose to take, regardless of the limits of their own direct experience. In this, men are "Subjects," who define themselves, while women are "Others," who are defined by men.

De Beauvoir questions why women generally accept this position of "Other," seeking to account for their submissiveness to masculine assumptions. She clearly states that immanence is not a "moral fault" on the part of women. She also acknowledges what she sees as the inherent contradiction facing women: the impossibility of choosing between herself—as a woman—as fundamentally different from a man, and herself as a totally equal member of the human race.

Freedom to choose

Many aspects of *The Second Sex* were highly controversial, including de Beauvoir's frank discussion of lesbianism and her open contempt for marriage, both of which resonated deeply with her own life. She refused to marry Sartre on the principle that she did not want their relationship to be restrained by a masculine institution. For her, marriage lay at the heart of women's subjection to men, binding them in a submissive position in society and isolating them from other members of their sex. She believed that only where women remained autonomous might they be able to rise together against their oppression. She felt that if girls were conditioned to

 He is the Subject, he is the Absolute. She is the Other. **Simone de Beauvoir**

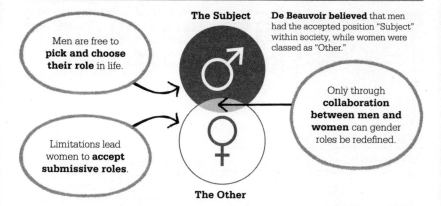

The Subject

Men are free to **pick and choose their role** in life.

De Beauvoir believed that men had the accepted position "Subject" within society, while women were classed as "Other."

Only through **collaboration between men and women** can gender roles be redefined.

Limitations lead women to **accept submissive roles**.

The Other

find "a pal, a friend, a partner," rather than "a demigod," they could enter a relationship on a far more equal footing.

Central to de Beauvoir's thesis is the concept, rooted in existentialism, that women can "choose" to change their position in society: "If woman discovers herself as the inessential, and never turns into the essential, it is because she does not bring about this transformation herself." In other words, only women could liberate themselves—they could not be liberated by men. Taking responsibility for difficult choices was a core idea in de Beauvoir's existentialism. Her own choice of relationship in the 1920s was a difficult one, involving a complete rejection of the values of her own upbringing and a disregard for social norms.

Some of those who read *The Second Sex* believed de Beauvoir was saying that women should become like men—that they should eschew the "femininity" that had been enforced on them, and with it their essential differences from men. However, her main thesis was that collaboration between men and women would eradicate the conflicts inherent in the accepted position of man as Subject and woman as Object. She explored this possibility in her relationship with Sartre and attempted to embody in her own life many of the qualities she championed in her writing.

De Beauvoir has been accused of being against motherhood, in the same way that she was against marriage. In truth, she was not anti-motherhood, but she did feel

that society did not provide women with the choices to allow them to continue to work or to have children out of wedlock. She saw how women might use maternity as a refuge —giving them a clear purpose in life—but end up feeling imprisoned by it. Above all, she stressed the importance of the existence of real choices and of choosing honestly.

Reshaping feminist politics

It is now widely acknowledged that the first translation of *The Second Sex* into English failed to accurately interpret either the language or the concepts of de Beauvoir's writing, leading many outside France to misunderstand her position. De Beauvoir herself declared in the 1980s, having been unaware for 30 years of the shortcomings of the translation, that she wished another one would be made. A revised version of the book was finally published in 2009.

The popularity of *The Second Sex* around the world—despite the shortcomings of the original English translation—led to it becoming a major influence on feminist thinking. De Beauvoir's analysis of women's role in society, and its political consequences for both men and women, struck a chord across the Western world and was the starting point for the radical second-wave feminist movement. In 1963, US author Betty Friedan took up de Beauvoir's argument that women's potential was being wasted in patriarchal societies. This argument was to form the basis for feminist political thought throughout the 1960s and '70s. ■

NO NATURAL OBJECT IS SOLELY A RESOURCE
ARNE NAESS (1912–2009)

IN CONTEXT

IDEOLOGY
Radical environmentalism

APPROACH
Deep ecology

BEFORE
1949 Aldo Leopold's "Land Ethic" essay, calling for a new ethic in conservation, is posthumously published.

1962 Rachel Carson writes *Silent Spring*, a key factor in the birth of the environmental movement.

AFTER
1992 The first Earth Summit is held in Rio, Brazil, signaling an acknowledgment of environmental issues on a global scale.

1998 The "Red/Green" coalition takes power in Germany, the first time an environmental party is elected to national government.

In recent decades, the economic, social, and political challenges of climate change have provided an imperative for the development of new political ideas. Environmentalism as a political project began in earnest in the 1960s, and has now entered the mainstream of political life. As a field of inquiry, the green movement has developed a variety of offshoots and avenues of thought.

The first environmentalists
Environmentalism has well-established roots. In the 19th century, thinkers such as the English critics John Ruskin and William Morris were concerned with the growth of industrialization and its subsequent impact on the natural world. But it was not until after World War I that a scientific understanding of the extent of the damage humans were causing to the environment began to develop. In 1962, American marine biologist Rachel Carson published her book *Silent Spring*, an account of the environmental problems caused by the use of industrial pesticides. Carson's work suggested that the unregulated use of pesticides such as DDT had a dramatic effect on the natural world. Carson also included an account of the effects of pesticides on humans, placing mankind within the ecosystem rather than thinking of man as separate from nature.

Carson's book provided the catalyst for the emergence of the environmental movement in mainstream politics. Arne Naess, a Norwegian philosopher and ecologist, credited *Silent Spring* with providing the inspiration for his work, which focused on the philosophical underpinnings for environmentalism. Naess was a

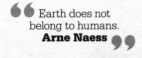

Earth does not belong to humans.
Arne Naess

Mankind forms one part of a **fragile ecosystem**.

↓

Human action is **causing irreparable damage** to the ecosystem.

↓   ↓

Shallow ecology holds that current economic and social structures can be adapted to **solve environmental problems**.	**Deep ecology** holds that profound social and political change is needed to **avert an environmental crisis**.

---

philosopher of some renown at the University of Oslo and was primarily known for his work on language. From the 1970s on, however, he embarked on a period of sustained work on environmental and ecological issues, having resigned from his position at the university in 1969, and devoted himself to this new avenue of thought. Naess became a practical philosopher of environmental ethics, developing new responses to the ecological problems that were being identified. In particular, he proposed new ways of conceiving the position of human beings in relation to nature.

Fundamental to Naess's thought was the notion that the Earth is not simply a resource to be used by humans. Humans should consider themselves as part of a complex, interdependent system rather than consumers of natural goods and should develop compassion for nonhumans. To fail to understand this point was to risk destroying the natural world through narrow-minded, selfish ambition.

Early in his career as an environmentalist, Naess outlined his vision of a framework for ecological thought that would provide solutions to society's problems. He called this framework "Ecosophy T," the T representing Tvergastein, Naess's mountain home. Ecosophy T was based on the idea that people should accept that all living things—whether human, animal, or vegetable—have an equal »

The Industrial Revolution changed people's thinking about the environment. It was seen as a resource to be exploited, an attitude that Naess thought could lead to the destruction of mankind.

> The supporters of shallow ecology think that reforming human relations toward nature can be done within the existing structure of society.
> **Arne Naess**

right to life. By understanding oneself as part of an interconnected whole, the implications of any action on the environment become apparent. Where the consequences of human activity are unknown, inaction is the only ethical option.

Deep ecology

Later in his career, Naess developed the contrasting notions of "shallow" and "deep" ecology to expose the inadequacies of much existing thinking on the subject. For Naess, shallow ecology was the belief that environmental problems could be solved by capitalism, industry, and human-led intervention. This line of thinking holds that the structures of society provide a suitable starting point for the solution of environmental problems and imagines environmental issues in a human-centric way. Shallow ecology was not without value, but Naess believed it had a tendency to focus on superficial solutions to environmental problems. This view of ecology, for Naess, imagined mankind as a superior being within the ecosystem and did not acknowledge the need for wider social reform. The broader social, philosophical, and political roots of these problems were left unsolved—the primary concern was with the narrow interests of humans rather than nature in its entirety.

In contrast, deep ecology says that, without dramatic reform of human behavior, irreparable environmental damage will be brought upon the planet. The fast pace of human progress and social change has tilted the delicate balance of nature, with the result that not only is the natural world being damaged, but mankind—as part of the environment—is ushering itself toward destruction.

Naess proposes that, in order to understand that nature has an intrinsic value quite separate from human beings, a spiritual realization must take place, requiring an understanding of the importance and connection of all life. Human beings must understand that they only inhabit rather than own the Earth, and that only resources that satisfy vital means must be used.

Arne Naess

Arne Naess was born near Oslo, Norway, in 1912. After training in philosophy, he became the youngest ever professor of philosophy at the University of Oslo at the age of 27. He maintained a significant academic career, working particularly in the areas of language and semantics. In 1969, he resigned from his position to devote himself to the study of ethical ecology and the promotion of practical responses to environmental problems. Retreating to write in near solitude, he produced nearly 400 articles and numerous books.

Outside of his work, Naess was passionate about mountaineering. By the age of 19, he had built a considerable reputation as a climber, and he lived for a number of years in a remote mountain cabin in rural Norway, where he wrote most of his later work.

Key works

1973 *The Shallow and the Deep, Long-Range Ecology Movement: A Summary*
1989 *Ecology, Community and Lifestyle: Outline of an Ecosophy*

Resolving environmental issues within current political, economic, and social systems is doomed to failure, according to Naess. What is needed is a new way of looking at the world around us, seeing mankind as a part of the ecological system.

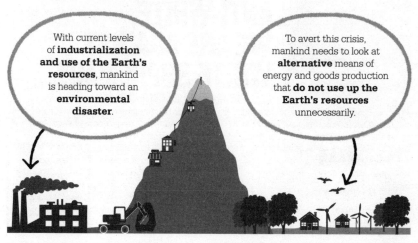

With current levels of **industrialization and use of the Earth's resources**, mankind is heading toward an **environmental disaster**.

To avert this crisis, mankind needs to look at **alternative** means of energy and goods production that **do not use up the Earth's resources** unnecessarily.

Direct action

Naess combined his engagement in environmental thought with a commitment to direct action. He once chained himself to rocks near the Mardalsfossen, a waterfall in a Norwegian fjord, in a successful protest against the proposed site of a dam. For Naess, the realization that accompanied a deep ecological viewpoint must be used to promote a more ethical and responsible approach to nature. He was in favor of reducing consumerism and the standards of material living in developed countries as part of a broad-reaching program of reform. However, Naess disagreed with fundamentalist approaches to environmentalism, believing that humans could use some of the resources provided by nature in order to maintain a stable society.

Naess's influence

Despite his preference for gradual change and his disdain for fundamentalism, Naess's ideas have been adopted by activists with more radical perspectives. Earth First!, an international environmental advocacy group that engages in direct action, has adapted Naess's ideas to support their own understanding of deep ecology. In their version of the philosophy, deep ecology can be used to justify political action that includes civil disobedience and sabotage.

As awareness of environmental issues grows, Naess's ideas are gaining ever-greater resonance at a political level. Environmental issues show no respect for the boundaries of national governments and generate a complex set of questions for theorists and practitioners alike. The green movement has entered the political mainstream, both through formal political parties and advocacy groups such as Greenpeace and Friends of the Earth. Naess's work has an important place in providing a philosophical underpinning to these developments. His ideas have attracted controversy, and criticism has come from many quarters, including the accusation that they are disconnected from the reality of socioeconomic factors and given to a certain mysticism. Despite these criticisms, the political questions raised by the environmental movement—and the place of deep ecological perspectives within them—remain significant and seem sure to grow in importance in the future. ■

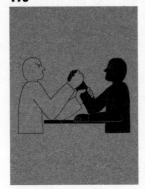

WE ARE NOT ANTI-WHITE, WE ARE AGAINST WHITE SUPREMACY

NELSON MANDELA (1918–2013)

IN CONTEXT

IDEOLOGY
Racial equality

FOCUS
Civil disobedience

BEFORE
1948 The Afrikaaner-dominated National Party is elected to power, marking the start of apartheid in South Africa.

1961 Frantz Fanon writes *The Wretched of the Earth*, outlining the process of armed struggle against an oppressor.

1963 Martin Luther King Jr. delivers his "I Have a Dream" speech in Washington, DC.

AFTER
1993 The Nobel Peace Prize is awarded to Mandela for his work toward reconciliation in South Africa.

1994 In the country's first free and multiracial elections, Mandela is voted the first black president of South Africa.

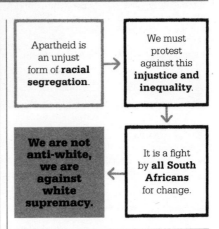

Apartheid is an unjust form of **racial segregation**.

We must protest against this **injustice and inequality**.

It is a fight by **all South Africans** for change.

We are not anti-white, we are against white supremacy.

The fight against apartheid in South Africa was one of the defining political battles of the late 20th century. From 1948, the election of the apartheid National Party spelled the beginning of a period of oppression by the white minority. Nelson Mandela was at the forefront of the resistance, organizing public protests and mobilizing support through his involvement in the African National Congress (ANC) party. This grew in response to the legislation implemented by the new government and, by the 1950s, a popular movement was taking part in the resistance to apartheid, drawing its inspiration from civil rights leaders such as Mahatma Gandhi and Martin Luther King Jr.

For freedom

The strategy pursued by the ANC was intended to make effective government impossible through a mixture of civil disobedience, the mass withdrawal of labor, and public protest. By the mid-1950s, the ANC and other groups within the anti-apartheid movement had articulated their demands in the Freedom Charter. This enshrined the values of democracy, participation, and freedom of movement and expression, which were the mainstays of the protesters' demands. However, it was treated by the government as an act of treason.

From protest to violence

The effect of this dissent on the apartheid regime was gradual but telling. By the 1950s, although the democratic process was still closed to most nonwhites, a number of political parties had begun to promote some form of democratic rights—albeit only partial—for black people in South Africa.

This was significant since, by gaining the support of some of the politically active white minority, the anti-apartheid movement was able to demonstrate that it was not mobilizing along racial lines. This fit Mandela's view of the struggle, which was inclusive in its vision of a new South Africa. He emphasized that the primary motivation for the protest was to combat racial injustice and white supremacy rather than to attack the white minority themselves.

Despite the well-organized and active approach of the ANC, dramatic reform was still not forthcoming, and demands for a full extension of voting rights were not met. Instead, as the intensity of protest escalated, the government's response became ever more violent. This culminated in the Sharpeville Massacre in 1960, when police shot dead 69 people who were protesting against laws that required black people to carry pass books.

However, the struggle against apartheid was not wholly peaceful itself. Like other revolutionary figures, Mandela had come to the conclusion that the only way to combat the apartheid system was through armed struggle. In 1961, Mandela, with other leaders of the ANC, established *Umkhonto we Sizwe*, the armed wing of the ANC, an act which contributed to his later imprisonment. Despite this, his belief in civil protest and the principle of inclusion gained worldwide support, culminating in Mandela's eventual release and the fall of apartheid. ∎

Nelson Mandela

Nelson Rolihlahla Mandela was born in the Transkei, South Africa, in 1918. His father was advisor to the chief of the Tembu tribe. Mandela moved to Johannesburg as a young man and studied law. He joined the African National Congress (ANC) party in 1944 and became involved in active resistance against the apartheid regime's policies in 1948. In 1961, he helped establish the ANC's military wing, *Umkhonto we Sizwe*, partly in response to the Sharpeville Massacre a year earlier. In 1964, he received a sentence of life imprisonment, remaining incarcerated until 1990, and spending 18 years on Robben Island.

On his release from prison, Mandela became the figurehead of the dismantling of apartheid, winning the Nobel Peace Prize in 1993 and becoming president of South Africa in 1994. Since stepping down in 1999, he was involved with a number of causes, including work to tackle the AIDS pandemic.

Key works

1965 *No Easy Walk to Freedom*
1994 *Long Walk to Freedom*

The battle to end apartheid was not an attack on South Africa's white minority, Mandela asserted, it was against injustice and as such was a more inclusive call for change.

JUSTICE IS THE FIRST VIRTUE OF SOCIAL INSTITUTIONS
JOHN RAWLS (1921–2002)

IN CONTEXT

IDEOLOGY
Liberalism

FOCUS
Social justice

BEFORE
1762 Jean-Jacques Rousseau's treatise *The Social Contract* discusses the legitimacy of authority.

1935 American economist Frank Knight's essay *Economic Theory and Nationalism* lays the basis for Rawls's understanding of the deliberative procedure.

AFTER
1974 Robert Nozick publishes a critique of Rawls's *A Theory of Justice* under the title *Anarchy, State, and Utopia.*

1995 Gerald Cohen publishes a Marxist critique of Rawls.

2009 Amartya Sen publishes *The Idea of Justice*, which he dedicates to Rawls.

American philosopher John Rawls's lifelong preoccupation with ideas to do with justice, fairness, and inequality were shaped by his experience of growing up in racially segregated Baltimore and serving in the US Army. Rawls was concerned with identifying a framework of moral principles within which it is possible to make individual moral judgments. For Rawls, these general moral principles could only be justified and agreed upon through the use of commonly accepted procedures for reaching decisions. Such steps are key to the process of democracy—Rawls thought that it was the process of debate and deliberation before an election, rather than the act of voting itself, that gives democracy its true worth.

The inequality of wealth
Rawls attempted to show that principles of justice cannot be based solely on an individual's moral framework. Instead, they are based on the way the individual's sense of morality is expressed and preserved in social institutions, such as the education system, the healthcare system, the tax collection system, and the electoral system. Rawls was particularly concerned with the process by which wealth inequalities translated into different levels of political influence, with the result that the structure of social and political institutions was inherently biased in favor of wealthy individuals and corporations.

Writing at the time of the Vietnam War, which he considered an unjust war, Rawls argued that civil disobedience needs to be understood as the necessary action of a just minority appealing to the conscience of the majority. He argued against the government's policies of conscription, which allowed wealthy students to dodge the draft while poorer students were

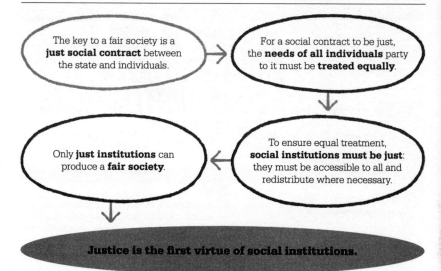

The key to a fair society is a **just social contract** between the state and individuals.

For a social contract to be just, the **needs of all individuals** party to it must be **treated equally**.

To ensure equal treatment, **social institutions must be just**: they must be accessible to all and redistribute where necessary.

Only **just institutions** can produce a **fair society**.

Justice is the first virtue of social institutions.

often taken into the army because of one failed grade. The translation of economic inequalities into discriminatory institutions such as conscription was deeply troubling to him, particularly when those institutions were the very bodies that purported to implement or act on behalf of justice.

Principles of justice

To Rawls, for justice to exist, it has to be considered "fair" according to certain principles of equality. In his theory of justice-as-fairness, Rawls develops two main principles of justice. The first is that everyone has an equal claim to basic liberties. The second is that "social and economic inequalities are to be arranged so that they are both reasonably expected to be to everyone's advantage, and attached to positions and offices open to all." The first principle—the principle of liberty—takes priority over the second principle—the principle of difference. He justifies this by arguing that, as economic conditions improve due to civilization's advancement, questions of liberty become more important. There are few, if any, instances where it is to an individual's or a group's advantage to accept a lesser liberty for the sake of greater material means.

Rawls identifies certain social and economic privileges as "threat advantages." He calls these "de facto political power, or wealth, or native endowments," and they allow certain people to take more than a just share, much as a school bully might take lunch money from other students by virtue of being bigger than them. Inequality—and the advantages based on this inequality—could not lie at the basis of any principle or theory of justice. Because inequalities are part of the reality of any society, Rawls concludes that "the arbitrariness of the world must be corrected for by adjusting the circumstances of the initial contractual situation." By "contractual situation," he means a social contract between individuals—both with each other and with all the institutions of the state, even including the family. However, this social contract involves agreements between individuals on an unequal footing. Because the state has an equal responsibility toward each citizen, justice can only be secured if this inequality is corrected at its root.

For Rawls, social institutions are key to making this correction—by ensuring that all individuals have equal access to them and by developing a redistribution mechanism »

Principles of justice must be based on more than just individual morality, according to Rawls. The entire framework of society must be taken into account when formulating a system of justice.

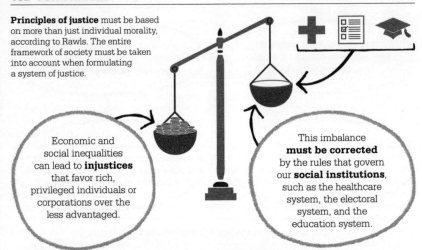

Economic and social inequalities can lead to **injustices** that favor rich, privileged individuals or corporations over the less advantaged.

This imbalance **must be corrected** by the rules that govern our **social institutions**, such as the healthcare system, the electoral system, and the education system.

that makes everyone better off. Rawls considers liberalism and liberal democracies to be the political systems best suited to ensuring that this redistribution is done fairly. He believed that communist systems focus too much on complete equality without considering whether that equality produces the most good for everyone. He thought that a capitalist system with strong social institutions is more likely to secure a fair system of justice. Where capitalism would produce unfair outcomes left on its own, social institutions imbued with a strong sense of justice can correct it.

Multicultural society

Rawls sees a further role for just institutions in binding society together. He believes that one of the most important lessons of modernity is that it is possible to live together under common rules without necessarily sharing a common moral code—as long as all individuals share a moral commitment to the structure of society. If people agree that the structure of society is fair, they will be satisfied despite living among people who might possess significantly different moral codes. This, for Rawls, is the basis of pluralist, multicultural societies, and social institutions are key to ensuring fairness in such complex social systems.

The veil of ignorance

Rawls argues that, initially, the principles underpinning redistribution need to be decided behind what he calls "a veil of ignorance." He imagines a situation in which the structure of an ideal society is being decided, but none of those deciding on that structure knows what their place in the society will be. The "veil of ignorance" means that nobody knows the social position, personal doctrine, or intellectual or physical attributes they themselves will have. They might belong to any gender, sexual orientation, race, or class. In this way, the veil of ignorance ensures that everyone— independent of social position and individual characteristics—is granted justice: those deciding on their circumstances must, after all, be happy to put themselves in their position. Rawls assumed that, from behind the veil of ignorance, the social contract would necessarily be constructed to help the least well-off members of society, since everyone is ultimately afraid of becoming poor and will want to construct social institutions that protect against this.

Rawls accepts that differences in society are likely to persist but argues that a fair principle of justice would offer the greatest benefit to the least advantaged members of society. Other scholars, including Indian theorist Amartya Sen and Canadian Marxist

Gerald Cohen, have questioned Rawls's belief in the potential of a liberal capitalist regime to ensure these principles are adhered to. They also question the benefit of the "veil of ignorance" in modern societies, where inequalities are deeply embedded in social institutions. A veil of ignorance is only of value, many argue, if you are in the position of starting from scratch.

Criticisms of Rawls

Sen believes that Rawls makes a false distinction between political and economic rights. For Sen, inequalities and deprivation are largely a result of the absence of an entitlement to some goods rather than the absence of the goods themselves. He uses the example of the Bengal famine of 1943, which was caused by a rise in food prices brought about by urbanization rather than an actual lack of food. The goods—in this case, food—do not represent an advantage in themselves. Instead, the advantage is defined by the relationship between people and goods—those who could afford food at the higher price versus those who could not.

Sen further argues that the social contract in Rawls's definition is flawed, since it assumes that the contract only occurs at an interpersonal level. He argues that the social contract is instead negotiated through the interests of a number of groups not directly party to the contract, such as foreigners, future generations, and even nature itself.

Intrinsic inequality

Gerald Cohen questions the trust Rawls places in liberalism. Cohen argues that liberalism's obsession with self-interest maximization is not compatible with the egalitarian intentions of the redistributive state policy that Rawls argues for. He sees inequality as intrinsic to capitalism and not simply a result of an unfair state-redistribution system. Capitalism and liberalism, for Cohen, can never provide the "fair" solution that Rawls was looking for.

Despite these criticisms, Rawls's *Theory of Justice* remains one of the most influential contemporary works of political theory and is still the bestselling book published by Harvard University Press. His ideas have spurred a series of debates on the restructuring of the modern welfare system, both in the US and across the world. Many of his former students, including Sen, are at the core of these debates. In recognition of his contribution to social and political theory, Rawls was presented with the National Humanities Medal in 1999 by President Bill Clinton, who stated that his work had helped revive faith in democracy itself. ∎

John Rawls

Rawls was born in Baltimore, the son of prominent lawyer William Lee Rawls and Anna Abell Stump Rawls, president of the Baltimore League of Women Voters. His childhood was marked by the loss of his two brothers to contagious illnesses, which he had passed on to them unknowingly. A shy man with a stutter, Rawls studied philosophy at Princeton University. After completing his BA, he enlisted in the US Army and served in the Pacific, touring the Philippines and occupied Japan. He then returned to Princeton, earning his PhD in 1950 with a thesis on moral principles for individual moral judgments. Rawls spent a year at the University of Oxford, where he established close relations with legal philosopher H. L. A. Hart and political theorist Isaiah Berlin. Over a long career, Rawls trained many leading figures in political philosophy.

Key works

1971 *A Theory of Justice*
1999 *The Law of Peoples*
2001 *Justice as Fairness: A Restatement*

COLONIALISM IS VIOLENCE IN ITS NATURAL STATE
FRANTZ FANON (1925–1961)

IN CONTEXT

IDEOLOGY
Anti-colonialism

FOCUS
Decolonization

BEFORE
1813 Simón Bolívar is called "The Liberator" when Caracas in Venezuela is taken from the Spanish.

1947 Gandhi's nonviolent protests eventually achieve independence for India from British rule.

1954 The Algerian War of Independence against French colonial rule begins.

AFTER
1964 At a meeting of the UN, Che Guevara argues that Latin America has yet to obtain true independence.

1965 Malcolm X speaks of obtaining rights for black people "by any means necessary."

B y the middle of the 20th century, European colonialism was in fast decline. Exhausted by two world wars and challenged by the social changes that accompanied industrialization, the grip of many colonial powers on their territories had loosened.

Grassroots movements demanding independence emerged with growing speed in the postwar era. The UK's hold over Kenya was shaken by the growth of the Kenyan African National Union, while India secured independence in 1947 after a long struggle. In South Africa, the fight against colonial rule was entrenched in the far longer battle against apartheid oppression. Yet questions began to emerge about exactly what form postcolonial nations should take and how best to deal with the legacy of violence and repression left behind by years of colonial rule.

Postcolonial thinking
Frantz Fanon was a French-Algerian thinker whose work deals with the effects of colonialism and the response of oppressed people to the end of European rule. Drawing on the earlier perspectives of Marx and Hegel, Fanon takes an idiosyncratic approach to the analysis of racism and colonialism. His writing is concerned as much with language and culture as with politics and frequently explores the relations between these different areas of inquiry, showing how language and culture are shaped by racism and other prejudices. Perhaps the most influential theorist of decolonization—the process of emancipation from colonial oppression—Fanon has had a major impact on anti-imperialist thinking, and his work inspires activists and politicians to this day.

Fanon examined the impact and legacy of colonialism. His view of colonialism was closely tied up with white domination and linked with a strong egalitarianism, rejecting the human oppression and loss of dignity that colonial rule entails. In part,

What matters is not
to know the world
but to change it.
Frantz Fanon

this reflects Fanon's role as a participant
in the fight against oppression. In his book
A Dying Colonialism, he puts forward an
eyewitness view of the Algerian struggle
for independence from French colonial rule,
detailing the course of the armed conflict
and the way it led to the emergence of
an independent nation. The strategy
and ideology of the armed anticolonial
struggle are presented in their entirety,
and he carries out a detailed analysis of
the tactics used by both sides.

Framework of oppression
Fundamentally, however, Fanon's
contribution was theoretical rather than
practical, exposing the structures of
oppression at work within colonial systems.
He examined the hierarchies of ethnicity
that provided the backbone of colonial
oppression, showing how they ensure not
only a strictly ordered system of privilege,

but also an expression of difference that
is cultural, as well as political. In Algeria—
and in other countries, such as Haiti—a
postcolonial political order was created
with the explicit intention of avoiding
this kind of domination.

Fanon's vision of decolonization has
an ambivalent relationship with violence.
Famously, his work *The Wretched of the
Earth* is introduced by Jean-Paul Sartre
in a preface that emphasizes the position of
violence in the struggle against colonialism.
Sartre presents the piece as a call to arms,
suggesting that the "mad impulse to
murder" is an expression of the "collective
unconsciousness" of the oppressed,
brought about as a direct response to
years of tyranny. As a result of this, it
would be easy to read Fanon's work as
a clarion call to armed revolution.

Colonial racism
However, concentrating on the revolutionary
aspect of Fanon's work does a disservice
to the complexity of his thought. For him,
the violence of colonialism lay on the »

The Mau Mau uprising against colonial rule
in Kenya was violently suppressed by British
forces, causing divisions among the majority
Kikuyu, some of whom fought for the British.

part of the oppressors. Colonialism was indeed violence in its natural state, but a violence that manifested itself in a number of different ways. It might be expressed in brute force, but also within the stereotypes and social divisions associated with the racist worldview that Fanon identified as defining colonial life. The dominance of white culture under colonial rule meant that any forms of identity other than those of white Europeans were viewed negatively. Divisions existed between colonizers and the people they ruled on the basis of the presumed inferiority of their culture.

Fanon believed that violence was part and parcel of colonial rule, and his work is a damning indictment of the violence meted out by colonial powers. He argues that the legitimacy of colonial oppression is supported only by military might, and this violence—as its solitary foundation—is focused on the colonized as a means of ensuring their acquiescence. Oppressed people face a stark choice between accepting a life of subjugation and confronting such persecution.

Any response to colonialism needed to be developed in opposition to the assumptions of colonial rule, but also

 The settler keeps alive in the native an anger which he deprives of an outlet; the native is trapped in the tight links of colonialism.
Frantz Fanon

independently of it, in order to shape new identities and values that were not defined by Europe. Armed struggle and violent revolution might be necessary, but it would be doomed to failure unless a genuine decolonization could take place.

Toward decolonization

The Wretched of the Earth remains Fanon's most significant publication and provides a theoretical framework for the emergence of individuals and nations from the indignity of colonial rule. Exploring in depth the assumptions of cultural superiority identified elsewhere in his work, Fanon develops an understanding of white cultural oppression through a forensic analysis of the way it functioned: forcing the white minority's values onto the whole of society. Nevertheless, he prescribes an inclusive approach to the difficult process of decolonization. Fanon's ideas are based on the dignity and value of all people, irrespective of their race or background. He stresses that all races and classes can potentially be involved in—and benefit from—decolonization. Moreover, for Fanon, any attempt at reform based on negotiations between a privileged elite leading the decolonization process and colonial rulers would simply reproduce the injustices of the previous regime. Such an attempt would be rooted in assumptions of privilege and, more significantly, would fail, because there is a tendency of oppressed people to mimic the behavior and attitudes of the ruling elites. This phenomenon is particularly prevalent in the middle and upper classes, who are able—through their education and relative wealth—to present themselves as culturally similar to the colonialists.

Colonialism involves **repression and loss of dignity**.

⬇

Violence underpins the repression of colonial rule.

⬇

 Colonialism is violence in its natural state.

⬇

 Sometimes it is **necessary to respond** to the violence of colonialism with armed struggle.

By contrast, a genuine transition from colonialism would involve the masses and represent a sustained move toward the creation of a national identity. A successful decolonization movement would develop a national consciousness, generating new approaches to art and literature in order to articulate a culture that was simultaneously in resistance to and separate from the tyranny of colonial power.

Fanon's influence

These ideas about the violence of colonialism and the importance of identity in shaping the future political and social direction of a nation have had a direct impact on the way activists and revolutionary leaders treat the struggle against colonial power. *The Wretched of the Earth* is, in essence, a blueprint for armed revolution. Beyond this, Fanon's role in shaping the understanding of colonialism's workings and effects has left a lasting legacy. His insightful perspectives on the racist underpinnings of colonialism—in particular, his theories concerning the conditions for a successful decolonization—have been hugely influential in the study of poverty and the phenomenon of globalization. ∎

Frantz Fanon

Frantz Fanon was born in Martinique in 1925 to a comfortably well-off family. After fighting for the Free French Army during World War II, he studied medicine and psychiatry in Lyon. Here, he encountered the racist attitudes that were to inspire much of his early work.

On completing his studies, he moved to Algeria to work as a psychiatrist and became a leading activist and spokesman for the revolution. He trained nurses for the National Liberation Front and published his accounts of the revolution in sympathetic journals. Fanon worked to support the rebels until he was expelled from the country. He was appointed ambassador to Ghana by the provisional government toward the end of the struggle, but fell ill soon afterward. Fanon died of leukemia in 1961 at the age of just 35, managing to complete *The Wretched of the Earth* shortly before his death.

Key works

1952 *Black Skin, White Masks*
1959 *A Dying Colonialism*
1961 *The Wretched of the Earth*

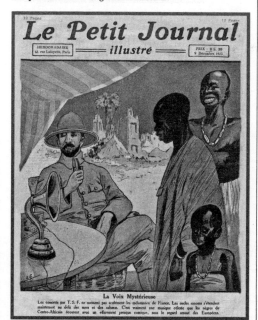

In France, colonizers were portrayed as civilized Europeans bringing order to savage natives. Such racist attitudes were used to justify the use of oppression and violence.

WE NEED TO "CUT OFF THE KING'S HEAD"

MICHEL FOUCAULT (1926–1984)

IN CONTEXT

IDEOLOGY
Structuralism

FOCUS
Power

BEFORE
1532 Machiavelli publishes *The Prince*, which analyzes the cynical use of power by individuals and the state.

1651 Thomas Hobbes completes his magnum opus, *Leviathan*, a comment on the role of the sovereign and man's corrupt state of nature.

AFTER
1990s Green theorists use Foucault's ideas to explain how ecological policies can be developed by governments alongside experts.

2009 Australian academic Elaine Jeffreys uses Foucault's theories to analyze power structures in China, emphasizing the rational nature of Chinese society.

The **nature** of society has **changed**.

↓

Power no longer resides only **within the state** or with one single **authority figure**.

↓

Power also exists in **"micro-sites"** across society, such as schools, workplaces, and families.

↓

The power of the state can **no longer be separated** from power in society.

↓

To understand the workings of power, we need to "cut off the King's head" in political theory.

P olitical thought has long been concerned with how best to define and locate the source of power in society. Many of the most significant political works have imagined a powerful state as the center of legitimate political authority. Machiavelli, in *The Prince*, viewed the crude expression of power as justified in the interests of government. Hobbes, in *Leviathan*, saw a powerful monarch as the antidote to the corrupt spirit of mankind. These and other thinkers set the template for a lot of modern political scholarship, and the analysis of state power has remained the dominant form of political analysis.

For French philosopher Michel Foucault, power—rather than being centered on the state—was diffused across a great many "micro-sites" throughout society. Foucault criticized mainstream political philosophy for its reliance on notions of formal authority and its insistence on analyzing an entity called "the state." For Foucault, the state was simply the expression of the structures and configuration of power in society rather than a single entity that exerts dominance over individuals. This view of the state as a "practice" rather than a "thing in itself" meant that a true understanding of the structure and distribution of power in society could only be reached through a broader analysis.

Foucault's analysis concerned the nature of sovereignty. He wanted to get away from what he considered to be a mistaken idea—that political theory should involve understanding the power wielded by an individual sovereign who passes laws and punishes those who break them. Foucault believed that the nature of government changed between the 16th century—when the problems of politics related to how a sovereign monarch could obtain and maintain power—and the present day, when the power of the state cannot be disconnected from any other form of power in society. He suggested that political theorists needed to "cut off the King's head" and develop an approach to understanding power that reflected this change.

Governmentality

Foucault developed these thoughts in lectures at the Collège de France in Paris, where he proposed the concept of "governmentality." He viewed government as an art involving a range of techniques of control and discipline. These might take place in a variety of contexts, such as within the family, at school, or in the workplace. By broadening his understanding of power away from the hierarchical structures of sovereignty, Foucault highlighted different kinds of power in society, such as the collection of statistics and knowledge. He elaborated on this analysis of power in his works, looking at areas such as language, punishment, and sexuality. ∎

The school classroom is a "micro-site" of political power, according to Foucault. Micro-sites exercise this power within society, away from the traditional structures of government.

Michel Foucault

Foucault was born in Poitiers, France, to a wealthy family. Academically gifted, he soon established a reputation as a philosopher. In 1969, he became the first Head of the Philosophy Department at the newly created University of Paris VIII, itself created in response to the 1968 student unrest in France. He gained notoriety by embracing student activism, even engaging in running battles with police. In 1970, he was elected to the prestigious Collège de France as professor of the History of Systems of Thought, a position he held until his death.

Foucault engaged in activism in his later career, which was spent mainly in the US. He published widely throughout his life and became a major figure in a variety of fields across philosophy and the social sciences. He died of an AIDS-related illness in 1984.

Key works

1963 *The Birth of the Clinic*
1969 *The Archaeology of Knowledge*
1975 *Discipline and Punish*
1976–1984 *The History of Sexuality*

LIBERATORS DO NOT EXIST. THE PEOPLE LIBERATE THEMSELVES
CHE GUEVARA (1928–1967)

IN CONTEXT

IDEOLOGY
Revolutionary socialism

FOCUS
Guerrilla warfare

BEFORE
1762 Jean-Jacques Rousseau opens *The Social Contract* with "Man is born free, yet everywhere he is in chains."

1848 Political theorists Karl Marx and Friedrich Engels publish the *Communist Manifesto*.

1917 Revolutions in Russia depose the czar and his family and establish a communist Bolshevik government.

AFTER
1967 French political philosopher Régis Debray formalizes the tactics of guerrilla warfare as "focalism."

1979 The Somoza dictatorship in Nicaragua is overthrown through the use of guerrilla warfare tactics.

Because of his participation in revolutions in Cuba, Congo-Kinshasa, and Bolivia, Guevara is popularly seen as a "man of action" rather than a political theorist, but his adoption of guerrilla tactics was a major contribution to the development of revolutionary socialism. Having seen firsthand the oppression and poverty throughout South America under dictatorships backed by the US, he believed the salvation of the continent could only come about through anticapitalist revolution, as advocated by Karl Marx.

However, Guevara's practical interpretation of revolution was more political and militant than Marx's economic analysis, which was intended to be used against the capitalist states of Europe. The tyrannical regimes of South America made European states seem relatively benign, and Guevara realized that the only way to achieve their overthrow was through armed struggle. Rather than waiting for the arrival of conditions that would allow for a successful revolution, Guevara believed that these conditions could be created through a strategy of guerrilla warfare, which would inspire the people to rebellion.

Power to the people
In his *Reminiscences of the Cuban Revolutionary War* and *Guerrilla Warfare*, Guevara explains how the success of the 1956 Cuban Revolution was dependent on the mobilization of a popular front. Rather than seeing the revolution in terms of a liberator bringing freedom to the people, he saw it as a grassroots movement to topple an oppressive regime, with the people liberating themselves. The starting point for this kind of revolution, he believed, was not in industrialized towns and cities, but in rural areas where small groups of armed rebels could have maximum effect against a regime's forces. This insurrection

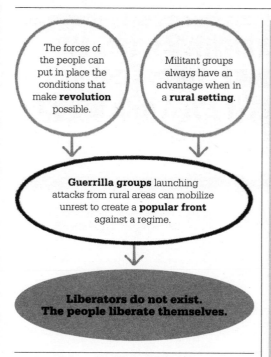

The forces of the people can put in place the conditions that make **revolution** possible.

Militant groups always have an advantage when in a **rural setting**.

Guerrilla groups launching attacks from rural areas can mobilize unrest to create a **popular front** against a regime.

Liberators do not exist. The people liberate themselves.

Che Guevara

Ernesto Guevara, better known by the nickname Che ("friend"), was born in Rosario, Argentina. He studied medicine at the University of Buenos Aires but took time out to make two motorcycle journeys around Latin America. The poverty, disease, and appalling working conditions he saw on his travels helped consolidate his political views.

After graduating in 1953, Guevara made a further trip across Latin America, when he witnessed the overthrow of the democratic Guatemalan government by US-backed forces. In Mexico in 1954, he was introduced to Fidel Castro, with whom he led the rebels during the successful Cuban Revolution. In 1965, he left Cuba to aid guerrillas in Congo-Kinshasa, and the next year he fought in Bolivia. He was captured by CIA-backed troops on October 8, 1967, and, against the wishes of the US government, was executed the next day.

Key works

1952 *The Motorcycle Diaries*
1961 *Guerrilla Warfare*
1963 *Reminiscences of the Cuban Revolutionary War*

would then provide a focus for discontent, and support for the rebellion would develop into a popular front, providing the impetus necessary for a full-scale revolution.

After his success in Cuba, Guevara expressed his support for the armed struggles in China, Vietnam, and Algeria and later fought in the unsuccessful revolutions in Congo-Kinshasa and Bolivia. Guevara's guerrilla warfare was key to his *foco* ("focus") theory of revolution, and his ideas later inspired many other movements to adopt the tactics, including South Africa's ANC in their fight against apartheid and Islamist movements such as the Taliban in Afghanistan.

Guevara was also recognized as an able statesman. While a minister in the Cuban socialist government, he helped establish Cuba as a leading player among international socialist states and instituted policies in industry, education, and finance that he believed would continue the liberation of the Cuban people by eradicating the egotism and greed associated with capitalist society. He left a legacy of writings, including his personal diaries, that continue to influence socialist thinking today. ■

EVERYBODY HAS TO MAKE SURE THAT THE RICH FOLK ARE HAPPY
NOAM CHOMSKY (1928–)

IN CONTEXT

IDEOLOGY
Libertarian socialism

FOCUS
Power and control

BEFORE
1850s Karl Marx argues that one societal class holds complete political and economic power.

1920s German sociologist Max Weber claims that bureaucrats form elites that manage societies.

1956 In *The Power Elite*, US sociologist Charles W. Mills claims that important policies come from big business, the military, and a few politicians.

AFTER
1985 Czech playwright Václav Havel publishes his essay "The Power of the Powerless."

1986 British sociologist Michael Mann claims that societies are made up of overlapping power networks.

O ne question that continues to fascinate political thinkers and politicians is: Where is power concentrated in society? Many different types of people and social institutions are involved in shaping human progress and organization, and over time, a dense network of power relations has established itself across the globe. However, does this mean that power is diffused throughout society, or has it instead become concentrated in the hands of a few privileged individuals who make up an elite?

US linguist and political philosopher Noam Chomsky's view is that in most countries, a wealthy minority controls the key social and political institutions, such as the mass media and the financial system, ensuring that the functioning of modern society favors a powerful elite. In turn, this means that dissent and meaningful change are nearly impossible, because the dominant institutional structures in society—from newspapers to banks—focus on maintaining their positions to their mutual benefit. Not only are social elites advantaged by their wealth and position, but they are also at the pinnacle of a society that is structured to favor them still further.

Any attempt at widespread reform would, in Chomsky's view, result in one of two outcomes: a military coup, which would restore power to the hands of private individuals; or (more likely) the drying up of investment capital, which would have serious consequences for the economy. The latter outcome ensures that all members of society, no matter how humble, have a stake in supporting the privileged position of the very wealthy. Everybody has to make sure that the rich folk are happy to ensure the health of the economy.

Dominant institutions in society, such as the media and banks, are controlled by a **wealthy minority**.

This minority runs the institutions in a way that **favors its interests**.

Any **attempts at reform** lead to a drying up of investment, which **ruins the economy**.

To keep the economy healthy, everyone—even the poor—must **support** a system that is run in the **interests of the rich**.

Everybody has to make sure that the rich folk are happy.

Keeping profits up

This concentration of power is structural rather than a conspiracy carried out by a small number of individuals. The economic interests of large corporations, the government, and investors ensure that public decisions are made by groups whose interdependence means that radical change is not possible. Instead, a mutually supporting network of institutions work to ensure the maintenance of a stable economic system, which is said to be beneficial to all. However, Chomsky notes that many of the "benefits" of this system are "good for profits, not for people, which means that it's good for the economy in the technical sense." Chomsky also considers the wealthiest countries of the world to be elites that threaten the security and resources of smaller, less-developed nations. However, he points out that while the principles of imperial domination have changed little, the capacity to implement them has declined as power becomes more broadly distributed in a diversifying world. ∎

Noam Chomsky

Avram Noam Chomsky was born in Philadelphia. After graduate study at the University of Pennsylvania and a period as a Junior Fellow at Harvard University, he began work at MIT, where he has remained for more than 50 years. During this time, he has forged a career that has been notable both for its significant contribution in the field of linguistics and a willingness to engage with questions of broad political significance. Chomsky published an article criticizing fascism at the age of 12 and has been a political activist ever since, concerning himself particularly with questions of power and the global influence of the US. Often controversial, his work has had a significant influence in a wide range of fields, and he has won many prestigious awards. He has authored over 100 books and has lectured widely around the world.

Key works

1978 *Human Rights and American Foreign Policy*
1988 *Manufacturing Consent*
1992 *Deterring Democracy*

NOTHING IN THE WORLD IS MORE DANGEROUS THAN SINCERE IGNORANCE

MARTIN LUTHER KING JR. (1929–1968)

IN CONTEXT

IDEOLOGY
Social justice

APPROACH
Civil disobedience

BEFORE
1876–1965 The Jim Crow laws are implemented, legalizing a series of discriminatory practices in the southern states of the US.

1954 *Brown* v. *Board of Education*, a case adjudicated by the Supreme Court, mandates the desegregation of public schools on the grounds that segregation is unconstitutional.

AFTER
1964–1968 In the US, a series of laws are passed banning discriminatory practices and restoring voting rights.

1973 US ground forces are withdrawn from Vietnam amid waves of antiwar protest on the home front.

Discrimination is the result of **fervently held beliefs**.

⬇

However wrong, these beliefs lead people to **commit barbaric** acts.

⬇

Nothing in the world is more dangerous than sincere ignorance.

⬇

A **change in attitudes** is needed to tackle discrimination.

B y the 1960s, the battle for civil rights in the United States was reaching its final stages. Since the reconstruction following the Civil War a century earlier, the Southern states of the US had been pursuing a policy of disenfranchisement and segregation of black Americans through overt, legal means. This was codified in the so-called "Jim Crow" laws—a set of local and regional statutes that effectively stripped the black population of many basic rights. The struggle to win civil rights for black people had been ongoing since the end of the Civil War, but in the mid-1950s, it had developed into a broad movement based on mass protest and civil disobedience.

Struggle against ignorance
At the forefront of the movement was Dr. Martin Luther King Jr., a civil rights activist who worked with the National Association for the Advancement of Colored People

Freedom is never voluntarily
given by the oppressor;
it must be demanded
by the oppressed.
Martin Luther King Jr.

(NAACP). Inspired by the success of civil rights leaders elsewhere, and in particular by the nonviolent protests against British rule in India led by Mahatma Gandhi, King became perhaps the most significant figure to emerge from the struggle. In 1957, with other religious leaders, King had established the Southern Christian Leadership Conference (SCLC), a coalition of black churches that broadened the reach of the organizations involved in the movement. For the first time, this had generated momentum on a national scale.

Like many others in the civil rights movement, King characterized the struggle as one of enlightenment against ignorance. The long-standing beliefs of racial superiority and entitlement that dominated the government of the Southern states of the US had given rise to a political system that excluded black people and many other minorities. King felt that this position was fervently believed in by those in power and that this "sincere ignorance" was at the root of the problems

of inequality. Therefore, any attempt to deal with the problem solely through political means would be doomed to failure. Direct action would be needed to reform politics and win equality of participation and access in democratic life. At the same time, the movement for civil rights would also have to tackle the underlying attitudes of the majority toward minorities in order to achieve lasting change.

Nonviolent protest

In contrast to other leaders within the civil rights movement, such as Malcolm X and Stokely Carmichael, King was committed to nonviolence as one of the fundamental principles of the struggle for equality. The utmost moral strength was required to adhere to nonviolence in the face of extreme provocation, but Gandhi had shown what was possible. Gandhi believed that the moral purpose of the protesters would be eroded, and public sympathy lost, if resistance became violent. As a result, King took great pains to ensure that his involvement in the civil rights movement did not promote violence, going so far as to cancel speeches and protests when he felt that they might result in violent action on the part of the activists. At the same time, King pursued a fearless confrontation of intimidation and violence when it was visited on civil rights activists. He frequently led demonstrations from the front, was injured more than once, and was jailed on numerous occasions. »

Nine black students challenged the segregation at Little Rock's whites-only Central High School in 1957. They were refused entry, and federal troops were sent in to ensure their safety.

Images of the brutality of the police toward civil rights activists became one of the most effective means of garnering nationwide support for the cause.

King's adherence to nonviolence also inspired his opposition to the Vietnam War. In 1967, he delivered his celebrated "Beyond Vietnam" speech, which spoke out against the ethics of conflict in Vietnam, branding it as American adventurism and taking issue with the resources lavished upon the military. In part, King felt that the war was morally corrupt since it consumed vast amounts of the federal budget, which could otherwise be spent on relieving the problems of poverty. Instead, as he saw it, the war was in fact compounding the suffering of poor people in Vietnam.

The difference of opinion between those advocating nonviolence and those prepared to use violence in the struggle for civil rights is a major area of debate in the discussion of civil disobedience to this day. In his "Letter from Birmingham Jail," King articulated his strategy for confronting the ignorance of racism in the US, stating that "nonviolent direct action seeks to create such a crisis and foster such a tension that a community, which has constantly refused to negotiate, is forced to confront the issue." However, critics within the movement felt that the pace of change was too slow and that there was a moral imperative to respond to violence and intimidation in kind.

Against all inequality
King's vision for the civil rights movement developed as the 1960s progressed, and he broadened his focus to include inequality more generally, proposing to tackle economic, as well as racial, injustice. In 1968, he began

Nonviolent civil disobedience took many forms during the fight for civil rights, such as refusing to sit in the "colored" section at the back of public buses.

the "Poor People's Campaign," focusing on income, housing, and poverty and demanding that the federal government invest heavily in dealing with the problems of poverty. Specifically, the campaign promoted a minimum income guarantee, an expansion in social housing, and a commitment on the part of the state to full employment. The campaign was intended from the outset to unite all racial groups, focusing on the common problems of poverty and hardship. However, King died before it began and, despite a widely publicized march and series of protests, the movement did not match the success of the campaigns for civil rights. The link between racism and poverty had long been a theme of the civil rights movement and formed a part of much of the activism in which King was involved. The 1963 "March on Washington for Jobs and Freedom" had the fight against racism at its core but also demanded the extension of economic rights. King's stand against the Vietnam War had explicitly criticized US involvement in the conflict as distracting attention and financial support from the battle against poverty. Beyond these specific campaigns, a commitment to an extension of social welfare was a consistent theme throughout much of the activism King had pursued with the SCLC.

King believed that solving the problems of poverty meant tackling another facet of the ignorance he had identified in the fight

 Discrimination is a hellhound that gnaws at Negroes in every waking moment of their lives to remind them that the lie of their inferiority is accepted as truth.
Martin Luther King Jr.

for racial equality. In his final book, *Where Do We Go From Here: Chaos or Community?*, he argued for the need for change in attitudes toward poor people. Part of the problem of poverty, he felt, lay in stereotyping the poor as idle. He suggested that prevailing attitudes had meant that "economic status was considered the measure of the individual's abilities and talents" and that "the absence of worldly goods indicated a want of industrious habits and moral fiber." In order to tackle poverty, this underlying attitude needed to be challenged.

King's legacy

King remains one of the most influential civil rights leaders of the modern era. His oratory is timeless and has passed into the modern vernacular, and his work has inspired the activists who followed him in the US and worldwide. Perhaps the most concrete measure of his influence, however, is in the reform of civil rights that occurred as a result of the movement he helped lead. The Voting Rights Act introduced in 1965 and the Civil Rights Act of 1968 signaled the end of the Jim Crow laws and removed overt discrimination from the Southern states. The last great injustice he tackled, however—the problem of poverty—remains unsolved. ∎

King knew he was a target for assassination, but this did not stop him from leading the civil rights movement from the front. The Civil Rights Act was passed just days after his death.

Martin Luther King Jr.

Born in Atlanta, Georgia, Martin Luther King Jr. was educated at Boston University. By 1954, he had become a pastor and a senior figure within the National Association for the Advancement of Colored People (NAACP). In this capacity, he became a leader in the civil rights movement, organizing protests across the South, including the 1955 boycott of the Montgomery bus system. In 1963, he was arrested during a protest in Birmingham, Alabama, and jailed for more than 2 weeks.

On his release, King led the March on Washington and delivered his iconic "I Have a Dream" speech. He was awarded the Nobel Peace Prize in 1964 and led the popular pressure for the repeal of the Jim Crow laws. King was assassinated in Memphis, Tennessee, in March 1968, while on a visit in support of striking sanitation workers.

Key works

1963 *Why We Can't Wait*
1963 *Letter from Birmingham Jail*
1967 *Where Do We Go From Here: Chaos or Community?*

NO STATE MORE EXTENSIVE THAN THE MINIMAL STATE CAN BE JUSTIFIED

ROBERT NOZICK (1938–2002)

IN CONTEXT

IDEOLOGY
Liberalism

FOCUS
Libertarian rights

BEFORE
1689 John Locke writes two treatises on government outlining a social contract.

1944 In *The Road to Serfdom*, Friedrich Hayek condemns government control through central planning.

1971 John Rawls's book *A Theory of Justice* argues for the state to correct inequalities in society.

AFTER
1983 Michael Walzer looks at how society distributes "social goods" such as education and work in *Spheres of Justice*.

1995 Canadian theorist Gerald Cohen publishes a Marxist critique of Rawls and Nozick titled *Self-ownership, Freedom, and Equality*.

The state should provide **basic rights**, such as protecting its people against force.

⬇

If it becomes involved in any other activities, it **begins to infringe** on people's rights.

⬇

No state more extensive than the minimal state can be justified.

The position of individual rights in an era of strong states and extensive public institutions has proved a fertile ground for political theory. Prominent in the debate has been philosopher Robert Nozick, whose work was in part a response to the ideas of John Locke and John Rawls.

Locke, writing his *Second Treatise on Government* in 1689, provided the foundations of the theory of the modern state by suggesting that people held individual rights but that some form of state was needed to enforce them. From this came the notion of the social contract outlined by Jean-Jacques Rousseau, whereby individuals give up some of their freedom in order to have protection from the state.

Rawls's influential 1971 book *A Theory of Justice* built on this idea by proposing a variant of the social contract, which he believed reconciled it with the ideas of liberty and equality that were explored in Locke's work. Rawls suggests a framework that allows individuals to collectively agree on an idea of justice that is based on fairness and equality rather than personal self-interest, laying a foundation for social democracy. Nozick drew on Locke and Kant to argue that there were dangers in the forms of cooperation that lay in Rawls's argument. He revived the idea of libertarianism, which holds that the reach of the state should be as limited as possible.

The result of Nozick's argument was the notion that any form of state other than the minimal was incompatible with individual rights, and therefore unjustifiable. Where the state became involved in any activity other than the most basic—"protection against force, theft, fraud, enforcement of contracts, and so on"—then it would infringe the rights that Rawls sought to preserve.

Anarchy, State, and Utopia

Nozick's most vivid description of this view was in his book *Anarchy, State, and Utopia*, which argued for a minimal state and provided a series of direct responses to the claims made by Rawls. The book was developed from a course taught by Nozick at Harvard with the political theorist Michael Walzer, which took the form of a debate between the

 Individuals have rights and there are things no person or group may do to them.
Robert Nozick

two. Later, Walzer became one of the most significant critics of the arguments made in the book.

Perhaps the most famous conclusion reached in *Anarchy, State, and Utopia* was the idea that taxation, as employed by modern states to redistribute income and fund public agencies, was morally indefensible. In Nozick's view, it amounts to a form of forced labor, where a proportion of a person's work compulsorily benefits others. Indeed, Nozick went as far as to imagine this as a form of slavery, where every member of society had some claim of ownership to an individual's labor.

Anarchy, State, and Utopia proved hugely influential and helped define the modern boundaries of the debate between libertarian thought and liberalism. Often read alongside *A Theory of Justice*, it ranks as one of the most important works of political philosophy in the modern era. ∎

Robert Nozick

Born in New York in 1938, Robert Nozick was the son of a Jewish entrepreneur. He pursued an academic career, training at Columbia, Oxford, and Princeton universities.

Initially drawn to the ideas of the Left, his reading of Friedrich Hayek, Ayn Rand, and other free-market thinkers during his graduate studies moved his standpoint toward libertarianism. His career was spent mostly at Harvard, where he established himself as one of the leading figures in libertarian thought. Famously, he is said to have only ever taught the same course twice.

Nozick's most significant work of political theory was his first, *Anarchy, State, and Utopia*, though he wrote on a variety of subjects throughout his career and did not restrict himself to political philosophy. In later life, he rejected extreme libertarianism and suggested limits on inheritances.

Key works

1974 *Anarchy, State, and Utopia*
1981 *Philosophical Explanations*
1993 *The Nature of Rationality*

INDEX

Numbers in **bold** refer
to a person's main entry.

A

B

C

R

S